EARLY CHILDHOOD EDUCATION SERIES
Sharon Ryan, Editor

Don't Leave the Story in the Book: Using Literature to Guide Inquiry in Early Childhood Classrooms
MARY HYNES-BERRY

Starting with Their Strengths:
Using the Project Approach in
Early Childhood Special Education
DEBORAH C. LICKEY & DENISE J. POWERS

The Play's the Thing:
Teachers' Roles in Children's Play, 2nd Ed.
ELIZABETH JONES & GRETCHEN REYNOLDS

Twelve Best Practices for Early Childhood Education:
Integrating Reggio and Other Inspired Approaches
ANN LEWIN-BENHAM

Big Science for Growing Minds: Constructivist
Classrooms for Young Thinkers
JACQUELINE GRENNON BROOKS

What If All the Kids Are White? Anti-Bias Multicultural
Education with Young Children and Families, 2nd Ed.
LOUISE DERMAN-SPARKS & PATRICIA G. RAMSEY

Seen and Heard:
Children's Rights in Early Childhood Education
ELLEN LYNN HALL & JENNIFER KOFKIN RUDKIN

Young Investigators: The Project Approach in the
Early Years, 2nd Ed.
JUDY HARRIS HELM & LILIAN G. KATZ

Supporting Boys' Learning: Strategies for Teacher
Practice, PreK–Grade 3
BARBARA SPRUNG, MERLE FROSCHL, & NANCY GROPPER

Young English Language Learners: Current Research and
Emerging Directions for Practice and Policy
EUGENE E. GARCÍA & ELLEN C. FREDE, EDS.

Connecting Emergent Curriculum and Standards in the
Early Childhood Classroom: Strengthening Content and
Teacher Practice
SYDNEY L. SCHWARTZ & SHERRY M. COPELAND

Infants and Toddlers at Work: Using Reggio-Inspired
Materials to Support Brain Development
ANN LEWIN-BENHAM

The View from the Little Chair in the Corner: Improving
Teacher Practice and Early Childhood Learning (Wisdom
from an Experienced Classroom Observer)
CINDY RZASA BESS

Culture and Child Development in Early Childhood
Programs: Practices for Quality Education and Care
CAROLLEE HOWES

The Early Intervention Guidebook for Families and
Professionals: Partnering for Success
BONNIE KEILTY

The Story in the Picture:
Inquiry and Artmaking with Young Children
CHRISTINE MULCAHEY

Educating and Caring for Very Young Children:
The Infant/Toddler Curriculum, 2nd Ed.
DORIS BERGEN, REBECCA REID, & LOUIS TORELLI

Beginning School: U.S. Policies in International Perspective
RICHARD M. CLIFFORD & GISELE M. CRAWFORD, EDS.

Emergent Curriculum in the Primary Classroom:
Interpreting the Reggio Emilia Approach in Schools
CAROL ANNE WIEN, ED.

Enthusiastic and Engaged Learners: Approaches to
Learning in the Early Childhood Classroom
MARILOU HYSON

Powerful Children: Understanding How to Teach and
Learn Using the Reggio Approach
ANN LEWIN-BENHAM

The Early Care and Education Teaching Workforce at
the Fulcrum: An Agenda for Reform
SHARON LYNN KAGAN, KRISTIE KAUERZ, &
KATE TARRANT

Windows on Learning:
Documenting Young Children's Work, 2nd Ed.
JUDY HARRIS HELM, SALLEE BENEKE, & KATHY STEINHEIMER

Ready or Not: Leadership Choices in Early Care
and Education
STACIE G. GOFFIN & VALORA WASHINGTON

Supervision in Early Childhood Education:
A Developmental Perspective, 3rd Ed.
JOSEPH J. CARUSO WITH M. TEMPLE FAWCETT

Guiding Children's Behavior:
Developmental Discipline in the Classroom
EILEEN S. FLICKER & JANET ANDRON HOFFMAN

The War Play Dilemma: What Every Parent and Teacher
Needs to Know, 2nd Ed.
DIANE E. LEVIN & NANCY CARLSSON-PAIGE

Possible Schools: The Reggio Approach to
Urban Education
ANN LEWIN-BENHAM

Everyday Goodbyes: Starting School and Early Care—
A Guide to the Separation Process
NANCY BALABAN

Playing to Get Smart
ELIZABETH JONES & RENATTA M. COOPER

How to Work with Standards in the Early
Childhood Classroom
CAROL SEEFELDT

(continued)

Early Childhood Education Series titles, continued

In the Spirit of the Studio: Learning from the Atelier of Reggio Emilia
LELLA GANDINI, LYNN T. HILL, LOUISE BOYD CADWELL, & CHARLES SCHWALL, EDS.

Understanding Assessment and Evaluation in Early Childhood Education, 2nd Ed.
DOMINIC F. GULLO

Negotiating Standards in the Primary Classroom
CAROL ANNE WIEN

Teaching and Learning in a Diverse World, 3rd Ed.
PATRICIA G. RAMSEY

The Emotional Development of Young Children, 2nd Ed.
MARILOU HYSON

Effective Partnering for School Change
JIE-QI CHEN & PATRICIA HORSCH WITH KAREN DeMOSS & SUZANNE L. WAGNER

Let's Be Friends
KRISTEN MARY KEMPLE

Young Children Continue to Reinvent Arithmetic– 2nd Grade, 2nd Ed.
CONSTANCE KAMII

Major Trends and Issues in Early Childhood Education: Challenges, Controversies, and Insights, 2nd Ed.
JOAN PACKER ISENBERG & MARY RENCK JALONGO, EDS.

The Power of Projects: Meeting Contemporary Challenges in Early Childhood Classrooms– Strategies and Solutions
JUDY HARRIS HELM & SALLEE BENEKE, EDS.

Bringing Learning to Life: The Reggio Approach to Early Childhood Education
LOUISE BOYD CADWELL

The Colors of Learning: Integrating the Visual Arts into the Early Childhood Curriculum
ROSEMARY ALTHOUSE, MARGARET H. JOHNSON, & SHARON T. MITCHELL

A Matter of Trust
CAROLLEE HOWES & SHARON RITCHIE

Widening the Circle
SAMUEL L. ODOM, ED.

Children with Special Needs
MARJORIE J. KOSTELNIK, ESTHER ETSUKO ONAGA, BARBARA ROHDE, & ALICE PHIPPS WHIREN

Developing Constructivist Early Childhood Curriculum
RHETA DEVRIES, BETTY ZAN, CAROLYN HILDEBRANDT, REBECCA EDMIASTON, & CHRISTINA SALES

Outdoor Play
JANE PERRY

Embracing Identities in Early Childhood Education
SUSAN GRIESHABER & GAILE S. CANNELLA, EDS.

Bambini: The Italian Approach to Infant/Toddler Care
LELLA GANDINI & CAROLYN POPE EDWARDS, EDS.

Serious Players in the Primary Classroom, 2nd Ed.
SELMA WASSERMANN

Telling a Different Story
CATHERINE WILSON

Young Children Reinvent Arithmetic, 2nd Ed.
CONSTANCE KAMII

Managing Quality in Young Children's Programs
MARY L. CULKIN, ED.

The Early Childhood Curriculum, 3rd Ed.
CAROL SEEFELDT, ED.

Leadership in Early Childhood, 2nd Ed.
JILLIAN RODD

Inside a Head Start Center
DEBORAH CEGLOWSKI

Bringing Reggio Emilia Home
LOUISE BOYD CADWELL

Master Players
GRETCHEN REYNOLDS & ELIZABETH JONES

Understanding Young Children's Behavior
JILLIAN RODD

Understanding Quantitative and Qualitative Research in Early Childhood Education
WILLIAM L. GOODWIN & LAURA D. GOODWIN

Diversity in the Classroom, 2nd Ed.
FRANCES E. KENDALL

Developmentally Appropriate Practice in "Real Life"
CAROL ANNE WIEN

Experimenting with the World
HARRIET K. CUFFARO

Quality in Family Child Care and Relative Care
SUSAN KONTOS, CAROLLEE HOWES, MARYBETH SHINN, & ELLEN GALINSKY

Using the Supportive Play Model
MARGARET K. SHERIDAN, GILBERT M. FOLEY, & SARA H. RADLINSKI

The Full-Day Kindergarten, 2nd Ed.
DORIS PRONIN FROMBERG

Assessment Methods for Infants and Toddlers
DORIS BERGEN

Young Children Continue to Reinvent Arithmetic–3rd Grade: Implications of Piaget's Theory
CONSTANCE KAMII WITH SALLY JONES LIVINGSTON

Moral Classrooms, Moral Children
RHETA DEVRIES & BETTY ZAN

Diversity and Developmentally Appropriate Practices
BRUCE L. MALLORY & REBECCA S. NEW, EDS.

Changing Teaching, Changing Schools
FRANCES O'CONNELL RUST

Physical Knowledge in Preschool Education
CONSTANCE KAMII & RHETA DEVRIES

Ways of Assessing Children and Curriculum
CELIA GENISHI, ED.

Scenes from Day Care
ELIZABETH BALLIETT PLATT

Making Friends in School
PATRICIA G. RAMSEY

The Whole Language Kindergarten
SHIRLEY RAINES & ROBERT CANADY

Multiple Worlds of Child Writers
ANNE HAAS DYSON

The Good Preschool Teacher
WILLIAM AYERS

The Piaget Handbook for Teachers and Parents
ROSEMARY PETERSON & VICTORIA FELTON-COLLINS

Visions of Childhood
JOHN CLEVERLEY & D. C. PHILLIPS

Ideas Influencing Early Childhood Education
EVELYN WEBER

The Joy of Movement in Early Childhood
SANDRA R. CURTIS

Don't Leave the Story in the Book

Using Literature to Guide Inquiry in Early Childhood Classrooms

Mary Hynes-Berry

FOREWORD BY JIE-QI CHEN

Teachers College, Columbia University
New York and London

Published by Teachers College Press, 1234 Amsterdam Avenue, New York, NY 10027

The following images in Figure 5.1 are gratefully acknowledged:

Figure 5.1a: From GOLDILOCKS AND THE THREE BEARS by Jim Aylesworth, illustrated by Barbara McClintock. Text copyright © 2003 by Jim Aylesworth. Illustration copyright © 2003 by Barbara McClintock. Reprinted by permission of Scholastic Inc.

Figure 5.1b: From GOLDILOCKS AND THE THREE BEARS by Caralyn Buehner, illustrated by Mark Buehner, text © 2007 by Caralyn Buehner, illustrations © 2007 by Mark Buehner. Used by permission of Penguin Young Readers Group, A Member of Penguin Group (USA) Inc., 345 Hudson Street, New York, NY 10014. All rights reserved.

Figure 5.1c: From GOLDILOCKS AND THE THREE BEARS by Candice Ransom, illustrated by Laura J. Bryant.Used with permission from Carson-Dellosa Publishing 0769638155, *Goldilocks and the Three Bears.*

Library of Congress Cataloging-in-Publication Data

Hynes-Berry, Mary.
Don't leave the story in the book : using literature to guide inquiry in early childhood class-rooms / Mary Hynes-Berry ; foreword by Jie-Qi Chen.
    p. cm.—(Early childhood education series)
Includes bibliographical references and index.
ISBN 978-0-8077-5287-6 (pbk.)—ISBN 978-0-8077-5288-3 (hardcover)
1. Literature—Study and teaching (Early childhood) 2. Children—Books and reading. 3. Storytelling. 4. Inquiry-based learning. I. Title.
    LB1139.5.L58H96 2011
    372.64'044—dc23
                                                                            2011031852
ISBN 978-0-8077-5287-6 (paper)
ISBN 978-0-8077-5288-3 (hardcover)

Printed on acid-free paper

Manufactured in the United States of America

19 18 17 16 15 14 13   7 6 5 4 3 2

Contents

Foreword *by Jie-Qi Chen*   vii

Acknowledgments   ix

Introduction: The Work of a Lifetime   1

PART I: PRAXIS AND PRACTICES

1. How Are Learning Communities Like *Stone Soup*?
   Exploring a Praxis   11

2. What Can We Learn from the *Three Little Pigs?*
   The Three Es of Quality Intellectual Work   20

3. Can Cinderella's Slipper Be Gold Instead of Glass?
   The Role of Questions in Quality Intellectual Work   39

4. How Can We Play with *Abiyoyo?*
   The SIP of Play and Quality Intellectual Work   59

5. What Makes a Good *Goldilocks?*
   Assessing the Quality of Picture Books   80

PART II: DISCIPLINED INQUIRES

6. How Long Is *Tikki Tikki Tembo?*
   What's the Problem with Naked Numbers?   103

7. How Did the Sun and Moon Come to be in the Sky?
   Playing with the Amazing Facts of Science   120

8. How Do You Get from Patches to a Patchwork Quilt?
    Reading an Object to Spark Inquiry Across the Curriculum   136

9. Who's the Strongest? What Makes Stories
    Such Effective Tools for Quality Intellectual Work   153

Appendix: The Essential ABCs   168

Notes   170

Bibliography of Children's Literature   179

References   185

Index   194

About the Author   204

Foreword

I attended a dinner party at Mary's house a couple of years ago. After dinner, I suggested that everyone around the table tell a personal story. "Which one did you like the most?" I asked my son afterwards. "Mary's! She's the best storyteller! Her stories just draw me in." My son independently confirmed a commonly known fact: Mary, who has lived with and through storytelling for more than 30 years, is one of the best storytellers in town. When she tells a story, everyone, young and old, gets a special treat. She draws you in so completely that the story stays with you long after it is done. In this book, Mary tells a series of stories that contribute richness and depth to our understanding of quality intellectual work in early childhood classrooms.

When educators talk about quality intellectual work in classrooms, they often use buzzwords like "teaching for understanding," "disciplined inquiry," "constructive learning," "critical thinking skills," and "habits of the mind," to name a few. Many scholarly works on our bookshelves focus on these important issues in teaching and learning. This volume opens a new window for us and we see these issues from a different perspective—the perspective of stories and children's books.

Books and stories are among the most powerful tools available for teaching and learning in early childhood classrooms. They cover a range of topics and issues at the heart of children's concern, such as sharing, perspective-taking, and mischievous behavior. They help children develop important concepts and skills in school related content areas such as early literacy, mathematics, science, and social studies. They present multiple points of views on solving difficult tasks and encourage critical thinking when encountering dilemmas. They free children to go beyond the here and now, expanding their imagination and exploring many possibilities.

The power of books and stories comes from their connection to children's experiences, struggles, and dreams. With this connection, good stories capture children's attention and bring positive emotions to the learning process. Beginning by touching children's feelings, stories then reach to children's curious minds. Touching hearts and minds, stories impact the whole child's learning in a natural, meaningful, and lasting way.

Books and stories do not automatically produce quality intellectual work in the classroom. Intellectual quality depends also on adults—committed and intentional teachers and parents who activate the potential of stories. To help teachers build on what they know about stories, Mary describes practices for using books that are grounded in well-defined principles of teaching and learning: focusing on children's reactions, thoughts, and questions rather than attending only to what happens in the story; helping children construct the story's meaning for themselves rather than limiting them to a single interpretation; and asking children different kinds of questions to elicit different kinds of answers. Readers will find Mary's guidance accessible and applicable. Each praxis is illustrated and supported with stories that have emerged through Mary's time with young children and their teachers.

The praxes presented in this book have been tested for efficacy by the author, her colleagues, and the many teachers and children that Mary has worked with in classrooms. In today's educational environment, where learning and teaching priorities are heavily affected by focusing on discrete skills for accountability purposes, these praxes deliver an especially urgent message, calling for educators to respect young children, value their ways of knowing, listen to their ways of understanding, and remain mindful that children have the potential to produce quality intellectual work.

Closing Mary's book, I thought about a Chinese poem by Du Fu, the Sage of Poetry who lived early in the eighth century during the Tang Dynasty. The poem goes like this: "Good rain knows the season, when spring is here, sneaks into the night wind, nurtures plants silently." Good books and stories are like good rain: influencing the hearts and minds of children with a gentle touch but also a lasting impact. This book in your hands is also like good rain, nurturing the reader with its rich stories and useful strategies that lead to discoveries of the beauty and power of using literature to produce quality intellectual work when you let stories out.

Jie-Qi Chen
Erikson Institute

Acknowledgments

There is no question that this book would be impossible were it not for the decades of delightful conversations and playing with ideas and stories with a host of wonderful people. I couldn't possibly name everyone, but the following friends/professional colleagues have inspired and supported me for decades (in alphabetical order since there is no way to rank how profoundly I have benefited from their friendship and insights): Jie-Qi Chen, Ann Connaughton Felker, Sue Gottschall, Joan Grimbert, Dan and Lois Holm, Liz Hurtig, Rebeca Itzkowich, Donna Johnson, Rick Laurent, Marlene McKenzie, Gil McNamee, Basia Miller, Eleanor Nicholson, Pam Whalley, and Mary-O Yeager.

I am deeply grateful to the hundreds of children who have given me the pleasure of telling stories with and to them, beginning eons ago with my youngest brothers: Michael, TMore, Tim, and Chris Hynes; moving on to my four favorite sons: Geb, Sebastien, Nico, and Daniel Berry, as well as their splendid Hynes cousins; and most recently to my darling grands: the Broccoli-Headed girls, Mireille, Savannah, Ava, Tyra, Simone, and Saskia Berry. I learned so much from telling stories on a regular schedule to the gifted listeners at the Ancona School as well as in the Chicago Public Schools: Marconi, Murray Language Academy, Jackie Robinson, Revere Elementary, and James Ward.

Separate thanks to members of the different learning communities I have been involved with professionally:

- Ancona School, Chicago. Since we moved to Chicago in 1972, so much of my thinking has grown out of exploring the teaching/learning dynamic with such wonderful colleagues as Rona Brown, Carol Burch-Brown, Ellen Cole, Eliza Davey, Molly Day, David Dunning, Gwen Ford, Anne Goudvis, Charlotte Johnson, Annika Levy, Hannah McLaren, Jan Migaki, Bea Mitchell, Eleanor Nicholson, Pam Pifer, Mickey Sommerman, Pam Whalley, Bonnie Wishne, Mary-O Yeager, and John Zurbrig.
- Valuable associates from Hug-a-Book and other projects abound, above all, Sue Gottschall, Gwen Hilary, Liz Hurtig, Mary Lee

Greenfield, Lisa Ferguson, Rebeca Itzkowich, and Donna Johnson; also the Stone Soup literacy leaders: Judy Avila, Mary Bartgen, Renee Henner, Peggy Johnson, Mireya Mata-Donnelly, Ontario Wilkins, and all the other great teachers and staff at Marconi, James Ward, and Irma Ruiz Schools; Jean Clements and Dorothy Kirschner in PIIP (Parent Infant Intervention Project); Gil McNamee and participants at Le Claire Courts; as well as the many Chicago Public Schools professionals who have inspired me, including Diane Asberry, Chiquita Augusto, Steve Gilbert, Heather Pogue, Julie Snyder, Veronica Thompson, Aretha Turner-Jones, and Ginny Vaske.

- I owe a special debt to Sandra Belton, who got me started as a freelance writer and has taught me much about the difficult gifts learning and life can deal us, and Marty Hopkins, who persuaded me to take on the Britannica math project.

- CAN TV has made a significant contribution to giving ordinary people in Chicago a voice thanks to the vision of Barbara Popovic and Greg Boozell, among many others. Making over 50 episodes of a storytelling show, *Fantasies and Fairytales,* allowed me to explore how the power of stories told with minimal props can translate from live to video performance—I couldn't have done it without my stalwart homeboy crew—Nico and Daniel Berry.

I have many good friends and colleagues at the Erikson Institute who have done much to enrich my thinking.

- Mega-thanks to Debby Mantia for sharing a passion for books and stories, but also through her role as Director for Professional Development, for getting me into the *StoryBus;* thanks also to Lou Banks and the Dolores Kohl Foundation for keeping the program.

- *Erikson Early Math* project team, including Jie-Qi Chen, our principal investigator; Jennifer McCray, the program director; and the other team members: Jeannine Brownwell, Lisa Ginet, Rebeca Itzkowich, Donna Johnson, and Cody Meirick. Thanks as well to our principal funders: the CME Foundation, the McCormack Foundation, and the U.S. Department of Education Investing in Innovation Fund (i3).

- Other faculty and staff who have done much to support and encourage me over the years include: Chip Donahue, Jane Fleming, Patty Horsch, Chris Maxwell, Marvell Pomeroy, Dan Scheinfeld, Chris Simons, and Sharon Syc. Too many to list are the remarkable Erikson students I've had, both as part of the Columbia College/Erikson and the Erikson MST program. I can't even begin to acknowledge how much I have learned from teaching you.

I greatly appreciate all the support in starting and carrying through this project that Marie Ellen Lacarda of Teacher's College Press has provided. Thanks to Frances Rust for her encouragement and a special thanks to Colleen Sims, whose eagle eye, sharp pencil, and keen understanding have saved the manuscript from many gifts of error.

Last but hardly least, I am grateful to my family. I owe so much to the amazing learning community I experienced from birth, thanks to my parents Emerson and Arleen McCarty Hynes, and my siblings Denis, Patrick, Hilary, Brigid, Peter, Michael, TMore, Timothy John, and Christopher, along with their choosers and their progeny. I can't imagine life without the joy of my four sons, their lovely choosers, and beautiful daughters. So too, what would I do without the legion of relatives and friends in Minnesota. All count among my first and still best friends, always willing to be supportive as well as critical when necessary. In addition to my parents, other important mentors who fed my love for story include Joe O'Connell, Nancy Brown, Eugene Vinaver, and my first teacher, Sister Leonida, OSF.

And then there's my lifemate all these years, Gordon "GoGo" Berry. His lifetime of seriously playing with physics meant we had opportunities to live in France, Sweden, and Great Britain (his home country). I got to appreciate firsthand what it means to be a second language learner and to see how story transcend cultures. Maybe just as important, the way he and I have gradually worked out how science and literature are really different ways of playing has been authentic high-quality intellectual work, complete with all the bumps and peaks good learning always includes.

The Work of a Lifetime

Essentially, this book is the work of a lifetime. The ideas and strategies discussed here were set in my childhood and have been evolving ever since. From the first, I experienced teaching and learning as a dynamic—and one that functions best in a community. I am the third in a family of 10 children; the elementary school I went to was a two-room schoolhouse, with about 40 students in each class. Cooperation, as well as teaching and learning from others, was a necessity, not a theory—nor, for that matter, an option.

I grew up with stories as a primary way to understand the world. Our parents told us stories and read to us; every day after lunch, our teacher read from a chapter book. I was a voracious reader; my siblings and I were so grateful for the Stearns County Bookmobile that provided a steady stream of classic chapter books, mysteries, biographies, historical fiction, and more for us to read, share, and work into our play.

I became a storyteller almost as soon as I became a reader. I read and told stories to my little brothers and cousins; the stories I told, I made up on the spur of the moment, weaving in elements of fairy tales and odd facts.

At about 8, I was thrilled to learn from an older cousin who was an English major in college that I could spend the rest of my life reading and talking about stories. I immediately resolved that would be what I would do, and essentially that is what I have done. I was drawn to medieval literature. My dissertation explored the narrative structures of Arthurian legends, looking at how the style and details of character, setting, and point of view could shift the meaning, even when the plot was the same.

Unfortunately, however interesting I found this field, the reality was that medievalists ranked high among the hopelessly overeducated. As a further complication, our family was growing: On the plus side, I had another set of little boys to whom I could tell stories. Then I became active at Ancona, the Montessori-based school our sons attended. I set up and ran a part-time resource room/library. It seemed natural to extend my activities into oral storytelling in the preprimary and primary classrooms.

I was much more intentional about selecting and preparing the story than I had been with my family listeners in the 15-plus years that I went into 10–15 classrooms on a weekly basis. I consulted with the teachers about what was currently happening in the curriculum. I then researched legends, myths, and folk and fairy tales from around the world and chose ones to tell that complemented the themes and issues they identified.

My fascination with how the precise way a story was told could affect the meaning took on new force. I became familiar with a folklore classification tool called the Stith-Thompson Index (MacDonald, 1982, 1999). It provides a Dewey-Decimal-like system to classify world folk tales, myths, and legends according to related elements such as character, motif, or plot. I told story cycles: At the start of each year, I might tell 5 or 6 weeks of stories about "beginnings"—myths about the creation of the earth, or astronomical bodies such as the sun and moon, or the coming of fire. I did other series looking at variations of a powerful tale type such as *Cinderella*. Sometime during the year, I would take 6 to 8 weeks to recount an epic. Among those that I told were the *Iliad* and the *Odyssey*; the *Ramayana* from India; *Beowulf*; the *Song of Roland*; *Sundiata*, the African epic warrior; *Gilgamesh*; and the Irish hero tales of Finn McCool.

I would often use one story with the preprimary and another with the primary, based on what was developmentally appropriate. In keeping with oral storytelling tradition, no matter how often I told a story there were always variations in each telling, in response to the wonderfully individual character of each group of listeners. At the end, I would remind the children that if they liked the story, it was now theirs—they could tell it to themselves or others in their own words, in their own way.

WHAT DOES IT MEAN FOR STORYTELLING TO BE TRANSPARENT?

I became aware that I was deliberately downplaying the storytelling as a performance. I didn't use props and, given my severe musical impairment, didn't dare sing except as a villain. In effect, I wanted my telling to be *transparent*—to let the story do the wonderful work of engaging the listeners in meaning-making. I did prime the pump, however. As I settled myself in, I would say something about what brought me to tell this particular story; I might suggest an open-ended question to think about as they listened. With the younger children, I had a toy dragon that I brought along, claiming he had suggested I retell to the children a story that had helped him with a question or problem. With the older children, I used a globe to show how the story had traveled over time and distance yet could still speak to us. After the telling, we had a brief conversation about the story, perhaps comparing it to others in the sequence. Other times, I proposed a project the teachers and I had talked about, relating the story to something currently under study.

Without thinking about it, my academic background asserted itself. Though I didn't know the term at the time, I was doing what is now known as "teacher action research." After each session I would go home, make notes, and reflect on the kind of conversations that the same story sparked in different classrooms. I also kept track of which stories engaged the children most deeply and which they begged for again and again.

Over time, I realized that while I was a good storyteller, the real reason children literally hung onto my words was that I only told *good* stories—tales that had stood the test of time because they said something essential about the mysteries that surround and confound us humans.

WHAT MADE PROJECTS LIKE THE STONE SOUP NETWORK SO IMPORTANT?

In time, I extended my storytelling into several early childhood and family literacy programs. First of all, Sue Gottschall and the Hug-a-Book Foundation opened up new ways to explore with children and teachers all that happens when you take the story out of a book; all the years I have been associated with Hug-a-Book have been enriching.

Then I spent 6 particularly fruitful years with the Stone Soup Network Project, funded by the Annenberg Foundation. I was very involved in designing and directing, as well as implementing, a project that created classroom libraries in 60 inner-city classrooms in three Chicago schools. Our objective was not just to fill empty bookshelves with high-quality children's literature that celebrated diversity; the real mission was to create *a culture of literacy* in the schools so that children and their families would see reading and writing as a meaningful, engaging activity and would develop the habits of mind of lifelong readers and writers. The program involved ongoing professional development with staff of the schools, as well as regular on-site consulting and modeling teaching strategies, using authentic literature across the curriculum.

As the Network's program director, I wrote weekly field notes, similar to those I had always done at Ancona, collected data, reported to the funders, and developed handouts and idea books that would reinforce the strategies and beliefs about literacy we were promoting. To strengthen the network community, we did a weekly newsletter, and coordinated literacy events that brought students, their families, and teachers together on a regular basis within and between schools. Thanks to Chicago's Public Access TV, the call-in show *Hotline 21* allowed our Stone Soup Network to have the children in our schools speak for themselves about the stories they loved.

One of the delights of the project was the way it allowed me to return to the same classrooms again and again, telling stories, listening to what children heard, and modeling teaching/learning strategies that would link to the curricular goals. While I had seldom brought in a book in my years at Ancona, I now purposefully chose stories that could be found in the classroom libraries we were building. I told the story in my own words, as I had always done, and I continued to begin with a framing question or point of information about why I chose the story. At the end, I'd show the book, and the teacher and I would suggest an extension: more often than not, one that would have the children create a classroom book, exhibit, or performance. Our data provided overwhelming evidence that books that were introduced as read-alouds or through storytelling and then extended into lessons became the most popular books in the classroom libraries. I cannot count how many children approached me as I came into the school or classroom to ask about a story told months and even years before. They even remembered details.

Once again, the issue is not my skill as a storyteller. The fact is, good stories stay in children's minds and hearts; the tales tell them something they need to know. The social-emotional truths of great stories can be so compelling that the listener asks more and more questions. And that makes them among the most powerful tools we have for learning.

I began to appreciate the importance of this social-emotional force when I agreed to work with my mother, Sister Arleen Hynes, on a handbook for the field of biblio-poetry therapy, a creative arts therapy of which she was a pioneer. *Biblio-poetry Therapy: The Interactive Process* (1984, 2011) came out in 1984 with Westview Press and has been in print ever since. Discussions over the years with gifted practitioners of this creative arts therapy has added a rich dimension to my thinking about the power and importance of talking through texts in all forms.

HOW CAN SCIENCE AND MATH COME OUT OF STORIES?

It might seem a reach to go from creative arts therapy to science and math, but in fact, my eclectic experience was proving the opposite. The children had all kinds of things they wanted to discuss about the stories they loved the most. In addition to—or maybe it is more accurate to say at the same time as—they wondered about important social-emotional truths of a story, they were curious about the facts, the logistics, or plot details: *Are heroes ever afraid or confused? Were there really giants? Why does the story say it's a beanstalk that grows?*

Questions like that about the beanstalk made sense in a different way after I directed a project involving an early math program for Encyclopedia Britannica Educational Corporation in the early 1990s. Between that and living with a "pure scientist" (my husband is an atomic physicist), I began doing workshops and presentations on using books to promote mathematical and scientific literacy along with literacy in the traditional sense.

In the mid-1990s, I also began teaching as an adjunct at Erikson Institute in Chicago in a graduate program in child development. In the last decade I have concentrated my professional life around teaching methods courses, including those focused on mathematics and science, for the Teacher Education Department at Erikson, supervising students and several important professional development (PD) projects including the following:

- As part of the New Schools Project, under the direction of Patty Horsch, I worked with the Jackie Robinson and Revere Schools on improving school climate using classroom structures and instructional strategies to increase student achievement. The rich discussions our Erikson team had for the 4 years I was involved have been invaluable in helping me clarify my thinking about learning.
- Designing the curriculum and implementing workshops for the StoryBus project extended what we did at Hug-a-Book, particularly in terms of playing seriously with stories.
- Finally, it is a real joy to be actively thinking about foundational mathematics as a member of the Erikson Early Mathematics project. As a team we have developed yearlong PD sessions that have deepened the understanding of foundational mathematics and the most effective ways to teach it for 300 Chicago Public School preschool and kindergarten teachers.

WHAT KIND OF MEANING COMES OUT OF TEACHING AND LEARNING?

The point of recounting the meandering path of my professional life is to show that this book truly is the work of a lifetime. However, my experience is in no way unique. It reflects what has been happening since human life began; one way or another story plays a central role in the human impulse to find meaning in our existence. At the same time, the fundamental understanding of what it means to learn and what it means to teach is one that I share across the ages with the many who have always understood that learning and teaching are inseparable; you cannot teach well if you are not still a learner.

Thus this book is a statement of *praxis:* while it outlines a series of pedagogical practices, every strategy reflects deeply held, core philosophical beliefs about the nature of teaching and learning including the following:

- *Teaching and learning are dynamic*—effective teachers are lifelong learners whose major objective is to develop and foster the lifelong habits of mind that will motivate their students to continue learning long after they have left the classroom.
- *Teaching for understanding,* not for achievement, should drive what happens in classrooms at all levels. Without solid foundational knowledge and authentic reasons for remembering what we've learned, lessons are quickly forgotten.
- *Quality intellectual work* is the desired outcome of the teaching/learning dynamic. This term is defined in Chapter 2 as "evidence that the learners are actively involved in constructing understanding through a disciplined inquiry that has meaning beyond the classroom."
- *Learning communities* are the most effective way for classrooms to function, where inquiries are sparked and sustained by input from learners as well as from teachers—who themselves are learning.

Finally, the 30-plus years I have spent as an oral storyteller, working directly with children as well as with inservice and preservice teachers, underlies my passionate belief: Digging deeply into a rich story so that we go from literal comprehension to discovering and exploring the subtexts that connect the story to self, to other texts, and to the world of ideas is more efficacious than casting a wide net of examples. Thus each chapter begins with a case study about how a particular story or text was used in an early childhood classroom in ways that exemplify the teaching/learning issue that is the focus. The case study is revisited throughout the chapter to help readers construct their own understanding of the key points. While the focus is on early childhood classrooms, both the underlying beliefs and the strategies in this praxis extend across all ages and stages of learning and teaching.

HOW IS THE BOOK ORGANIZED?

This book falls into two parts: The five chapters of Part I are concerned with exploring the philosophical beliefs that inform the kind of practice I am endorsing. For the most part, the teaching/learning examples involve literacy, including many practices associated with the approach known as *Balanced Literacy*.

Chapter 1 uses the *Stone Soup* story as a metaphor for the way that teachers and learners need authentic experiences of doing quality intellectual work in classrooms. The case studies for each chapter are examples of *parallel processing* in which inservice and preservice teachers are introduced to pedagogical practices and strategies through experiences that involve them as adult novice learners.

Chapter 2 uses the classic tale of the *Three Little Pigs* to look at what is meant by quality intellectual work. The definition calls for actively involving the learner in constructing understanding by emphasis on the 3 E's of Engage, Explore, Evaluate, rather than the 3 R's of rote instruction.

Chapter 3 introduces a Chinese version of *Cinderella* as it examines the nature of inquiry and the crucial role of conversation in the teaching/learning dynamic. It looks at how problem-solving can engage the whole classroom community in discussing open-ended questions that move back and forth from lower-order to higher-order thinking.

Chapter 4 builds on a dramatization activity with the story *Abiyoyo* to dig more deeply into the nature of play and the crucial role it has in motivating inquiry and problem solving. This chapter includes descriptions of interactive teaching/learning strategies focused on literacy.

Chapter 5 brings the first part of the book to a close by looking at several versions of *Goldilocks* to establish criteria for judging the quality of both literary and informational juvenile literature that are such important tools for promoting quality intellectual work.

Part II of the book looks at how the foundational principles associated with quality intellectual work enter into teaching for understanding in the disciplines of mathematics, science, and social studies. While the primary examples are drawn from early childhood classrooms (pre-K to 3), there is good evidence that the guided inquiry approach used in all of these areas works well at all levels and is related to what "real" professionals do.

Chapter 6 uses a measurement activity that grew out of the story *Tikki Tikki Tembo*. The chapter examines the importance of focusing on mathematics and mathematizing. Instead of drilling the "naked numbers" of arithmetic and counting, the emphasis should be on problem-solving the story behind the many mathematical problem situations that can be found all around us.

Chapter 7 begins with a pourquoi legend about why the sun and moon are in the sky. It explores the central role of guided inquiry in teaching/learning science; it looks at strategies that structure learning in a way that supports national standards for teaching science as a problem-solving process.

Chapter 8 explores how several picture books about quilts were at the heart of integrated curriculum projects that embedded social studies into the full array of disciplines. The chapter looks at the importance of intentional design, so that the teaching/learning dynamic is responsive to the needs, interests, and abilities of the specific classroom community.

Chapter 9 uses the parable of *Who Is the Strongest?* to look at the importance of recognizing the developmental trajectory of early childhood as well as the individual profile of intelligences that everyone brings to learning.

Part I

PRAXIS AND PRACTICES

CHAPTER 1

How Are Learning Communities Like *Stone Soup*?

Exploring a Praxis

CASE IN POINT

For many years I have told my own version of *Stone Soup*. I go back to the Scandinavian tale called "Nail Soup" that I remember from an old reader in my childhood.[1] Whether I'm telling it to children or as part of a community Thanksgiving food drive, I place the story anywhere that one might find refugees fleeing from whatever civil terror was current—Bosnia, the Sudan, Iran, Afghanistan, the Tex-Mex border, or any inner-city neighborhood.

I tell of a sudden devastating storm and weary, frightened, mutually suspicious families or individuals who seek shelter in the same old barn. Only an old lame soldier feels free to offer everyone a share of his marvelous soup, made from a stone dropped in a pot of boiling water. It doesn't really matter if the teller calls it a nail instead of a stone because what happens next depends on interactions rather than an object. As the old soldier chats on about how much better it might taste if he had a bit of this or that, individuals dig into their closely guarded bags and add potatoes, carrots, onions, beans, even a few old soup bones, and finally, a crowning taste of salt. In the end, the story says, there was enough soup for everyone. The next day, as the once-isolated clumps of refugees move on together, now willing to trust and support each other, they wonder about that old man and his nail or stone—was it magic?

More often than not, in the discussion afterward we conclude that cooperation and sharing are indeed a kind of magic—better than a magic wand or three wishes because it is always at our command.

WHAT IS THE STONE IN THE SOUP FOR LEARNING COMMUNITIES?

The kind of magic found in *Stone Soup* is complex, requiring the interaction of three components: the stone, the old soldier, and the community—take one away and all you have is a cold stone and a group of isolated individuals. The same complexity is true of the work done by all who see stories as highly effective tools for learning. For the magic to work, the three necessary components are a rich story, a teacher/facilitator who invites interactions, and the learners/listeners who contribute further questions and insights that come together in a way that nourishes everyone's understanding.

Many years ago, a 5-year-old was sure that the stone itself was magic; I asked him to help the rest of us understand how the magic worked— was it an "abracadabra" kind of thing or a transforming power? "No," he said, "it's like that little brown thing Mama puts in soup that has all the flavors in it and you just boil them out. But it's magic so you can make them be whatever you like for your favorite kind."

In many ways the child's perception of the story/stone as kind of bouillon cube capable of changing flavors according to individual tastes is a very apt image. It speaks to the importance of using a story/stone that is rich—that is loaded with all kinds of worthwhile ingredients. It also suggests the importance of being intentional about the way the old soldier/teacher/facilitator invites comments and questions. In later chapters I explore more closely strategies that keep questions open, yet guide and focus the inquiry the learning community engages in.

Still, the image of a bouillon cube doesn't really work, when we think of the story/text as a *catalyst*. In chemistry, a *catalyst* is something that brings about a change, but that does not change itself. In the same way, the story or text itself remains the same, just as the old soldier claims to use the same stone or nail again and again to make soup. It is the reaction, or processing, that changes each time; in other words, it is the interaction between facilitator and the learning community. As I can attest, in the dozens of times that I have told *Stone Soup*, each time the conversation afterward was unique, resulting in different nuances in the understandings that emerged and the questions that lingered.

Nonetheless, there is a common element to all the discussions, reflecting the nature of the story itself. This too is consistent with the nature of a catalyst. Something that is an effective catalyst for certain reactions does nothing when combined with other components. Thus, while the story of *Stone Soup* is wonderful for exploring the power of sharing or cooperation, it is not a very good catalyst for discussing anger. In later chapters we will be looking at crucial instructional decisions that go into choosing stories that can be a catalyst for the goals we have for a particular inquiry into one discipline, or across several.

How Can Texts Act as a Catalyst in Biblio-Poetry Therapy?

I had become aware of the complexity of seeing the story/stone as a catalyst when I worked with my mother to coauthor a book on *biblio-poetry therapy,* the therapeutic use of poems or extracts from literature.[2] She and I teased out the differences between using a poem in a literature class, such as I might teach, and the therapeutic sessions she conducted in a mental hospital. We saw that it was not enough to "prescribe" a text that someone would go off to read and thus gain insight into the issues troubling them. The effectiveness comes from the way the poem or story acts as a catalyst for self-understanding through a skillfully guided discussion.

Like other creative arts therapies, biblio-poetry therapy is strengths-oriented. Sessions do not begin with the patients' problems; they begin instead with their responses to a rich text that can trigger a recognition—that is, the images of a poem connect to something in the participant's life. As the carefully facilitated discussion goes on, participants dig deeper into their own responses and juxtapose them with those of other participants. The goal is not a single "right answer" for everyone, but an enriched understanding that each constructs. It is the interactive process involving the facilitator and the group that brings out the insight and meaning that can be healing (Hynes & Hynes-Berry, 1984/ 2011).

We discussed the difference between her work with mental health patients and personal growth groups and the storytelling I had been doing for a decade at that point. I was definitely not doing therapy. However, there was no question that part of the magic of the stories I told was that they had a strong biblio-therapeutic element. In the chapter on play, I will go deeper into this distinction as well as into the importance of maintaining boundaries. However, my field notes show that the stories that captured the children most profoundly were those that allowed them to think more clearly about who they were, what they were feeling, whether they were lovable/competent/powerful, or how they might deal with problems in a way that developed those qualities.

How Do Texts Act as a Catalyst in the Teaching/Learning Dynamic?

The importance of a catalyst also came up in the early 1990s, when Sue Gottschall asked me to join in formulating a proposal to the Annenberg Foundation Schools Initiative.³ We got the funding for what we called the Stone Soup Network; as the third annual report indicates, we felt the metaphor of *Stone Soup* was a perfect image for what we were doing.

> In the more than three years of existence, we have come to understand how aptly we named our Network. The Stone Soup story is about the rewards of cooperation and the importance of a catalyst. The external partner, Hug-a-Book, is like the old soldier in the story—he knows that while no one alone has much to eat, the potential of having more than enough for everyone is there—if the individuals can drop the barriers of isolation and fear and work together. His strategy works but he is the first to recognize that the richness of the mixture—the cooking up of a real culture of literacy—comes not from him but from what has happened in minds, hearts, and classrooms of the participating schools. (Stone Soup Network, 1999)

All that I have said about the workings of a catalyst only reinforces the profound message of the *Stone Soup* story. The greatest nourishment comes from acting as a community. The catalyst is important, but it is equally vital that someone acts in the role of the old soldier to facilitate the collection of individuals in an interaction that will bring them together to collectively construct meaning and understanding—something that is the social-emotional and cognitive equivalent to the best soup ever.

As I go into more detail about the way learning develops through the interplay of stories and guided interactions, it is important to clarify that I am not talking about isolated strategies or a curriculum. My concern is much more fundamental: it concerns a *praxis*—a term that means the strategie*s* used in one's practice work because they are grounded in well-defined beliefs about the nature of teaching and learning. In effect, this praxis calls for expanding the Stone Soup Network's mission to create a culture of literacy to a general mission to create a *culture of inquiry* in early childhood classrooms. Thus the overarching goal is to engage classroom learning communities in quality intellectual work; that is, to promote education in its root sense as "the condition of drawing or leading out" learning.⁴

It asks teachers to see themselves as *members* of their classroom community, playing the role of the old soldier in *Stone Soup*. At the same time, teachers need the support that comes from belonging to another level of community—a *professional community of practice*⁵—whose members actively support one another in continuously developing and improving their ability to orchestrate learning in a way that reflects their beliefs.

WHAT'S THE STORY ABOUT
PEDAGOGICAL CONTENT KNOWLEDGE?

Perhaps the most fundamental core belief of the praxis we are discussing is that teaching and learning are profoundly interconnected. Lifelong learners are always their own teachers—when they are very young as well as when they are very old—but at all stages and ages, one's ever-expanding understanding owes much to the guidance of a coach/facilitator and to fellow learners, as well as to the texts and concepts being explored.

By the same token, in the course of guiding learners, good teachers are always learning more themselves. For them—as for all lifelong learners—digging deeper and being highly intentional are habits of mind. This praxis inspires them to be constantly working to

- Understand better what kinds of specific knowledge (information/facts and concepts) are relevant to the inquiry and are appropriate for the development stage and interests of a particular group of learners
- Clarify their own conceptual understanding of the foundational "big ideas" that underlie a specific inquiry; you cannot teach for understanding if you do not have a good understanding of what you are teaching
- Explore strategies and structure lessons and activities that are most likely to be effective in helping this particular group of learners carry out quality intellectual work

Schulman (1987) coined the term *pedagogical content knowledge* (PCK) to describe the complex interaction of these three elements: content knowledge, teaching strategies, and the students' needs.[6] Those concerned with teacher education in many disciplines, though especially in science and mathematics, have found his framework particularly helpful in addressing the serious implications for learning and teaching, for reasons such as the following:

- Especially in early childhood settings, teachers find it difficult to teach for understanding or to guide rich inquiries because of their own limited content knowledge. Particularly for areas such as math and science, teachers may bring negative attitudes that lead them to rely heavily on direct instruction, referencing teacher guides rather than setting goals based on formative as-

sessment of the needs and interests of the children in their class-room, including developmental considerations.
* Between teachers' own uncertainty about content and the over-whelming emphasis on achievement as measured by high-stakes testing, many classrooms do not function as learning communi-ties. Too often, the norm is highly teacher-directed classrooms, where there is limited concern to engage, motivate, or empower the children. Classroom management strategies are also hierar-chical, with an emphasis on extrinsic discipline rather than in-trinsic self-regulation.

According to Chen and Chang (2006), the PCK approach calls for preser-vice and inservice training that addresses the *whole teacher* in that same way that early childhood educators recognize the importance of teaching the whole child.

HOW DOES PARALLEL PROCESSING PROMOTE PCK?

Addressing the whole teacher means the praxis that informs early child-hood classrooms should also inform preservice and inservice teacher de-velopment. Both should promote teaching and learning as a dynamic that honors the Confucian dictum:

* If I teach by telling, you are likely to forget.
* If I teach by showing, you may remember.
* If I teach by engaging you in exploring and evaluating, you will learn for yourself, for a lifetime.

What Is Parallel Processing?

Ever since I first began doing workshops and presentations, it has seemed natural to me to begin with a story and an extending activity. This approach, which is used by other colleagues at Erikson, can be described as *parallel processing*. Teachers are introduced to a strategy or concept in a way that parallels the pedagogical content knowledge they need to sup-port their classroom learning communities. The power of this strategy is that the adult learners are engaged by the story and use it to problem-solve. In effect, they not only have a model of how to use a story to engage young learners in problem solving, they know in their hearts, as well as their minds, how a story can draw one in to explore and to learn.

Why Start with a Story?

The story might be done as an oral storytelling; yet often it is strategic to use a picture book and to literally involve the group in a reader's theater presentation. In any case, beginning with a story and an extending activity creates a dynamic that is very different from that of the full frontal demonstration or lectures. At best, the "sage on the stage" scatters pedagogic pearls that the audience may (or may not) scramble to pick up; but there is no question about who *owns* the knowledge. At worst, the line between lecturing and scolding gets very thin when the presentation focuses on a catalog of what ought or ought not to be going on in classrooms. In contrast, hearing a good story is always a pleasure. At the same time, it is a *story*—it's about someone else dealing with a problem in a context distanced enough to free the group from feeling defensive or scrutinized. Usually all listeners get drawn into making sense of the story for themselves. Even if the group expects the tale to turn the focus back to them and their teaching, it can be enjoyable to predict how the characters or the problem situation might relate to that session's topic.

The group is given a learning task that is set at a high level of complexity. The intention is not to model how teachers might use this specific task in their classrooms, nor to have them pretend or simulate the responses children might give. Rather this is a purposeful and authentic problem situation that is meant to engage adults in experiencing the cognitive dissonance of a novice learner. In other words, they are being asked to construct their own understanding of something that parallels the kind of understanding they will be guiding their students toward.

For example, we have asked adults to make sense of an English shepherd's counting system in order to help them understand how a young child can easily confuse arbitrary number names and numerals with the numerosity or quantity represented by a number (Hynes-Berry & Itzkowich, 2009). In the debriefing that follows, the group analyzes how their assumptions and misconceptions, as well as their personal level of mathematical understanding, might have played a part in frustrations and breakthroughs that they experienced in completing the task. They also discuss the role group functioning played in their learning. Then they look for parallels and connections between their experiences and the strategies they might use to help young children move through the landscape of learning, from confusion to misconception to understanding. The ways that parallel processing has been used to introduce preservice and inservice teachers to all the strategies and practices discussed in this book include the following:

- A professional development session on higher-order thinking begins with the adult group members doing a reader's theater of a classic tale like *Goldilocks* or *Cinderella* and then going on to brainstorm questions and problems they have from an adult perspective.
  * The debriefing begins by reviewing how open or how closed their questions were; they go on to analyze how these questions led the group into moving up and down the inquiry ladder.
  * As they dig deeper into the connection between the kinds of questions that are asked and the kind of thinking and learning that results, participants work with partners to plan how to get the children in their classrooms asking and answering more open-ended questions.
- To emphasize the strong impact the classroom climate can have on a classroom, a teacher study group session opens with a read-aloud of a picture book in which the social-emotional dimension plays a central part in the book's problem situation; a few of the texts I've used this way include Pete Seeger's *Abiyoyo*, John Burningham's *Edwardo, the Horrriblest Boy in the Whole Wide World*, Alice Schertle's *Down the Road*, David Shannon's *David Goes to School*, and a chapter from *Mr. and Me* by K. W. Willis.
  * The discussion focuses on the adult characters' responses to a child's mistakes and misbehavior; drawing evidence from the words in the text and the body language and facial expressions in the illustrations, the group considers in what ways the responses may or may not have been productive in helping the child recognize or change the behavior.
  * The group moves quickly to examining their own beliefs about the relationship between classroom climate and classroom management problems; they also explore how their school and classroom rules function and whether punishment or positive discipline is more effective. Many indicate they are going to use the book in question to open up a discussion of these issues with their students.

What Is the Parallel Between the Problem Solving Done by Learners and by Teachers?

Parallel processing also takes place in the planning and implementation phases of the teaching/learning dynamic. An effective guided inquiry calls for teachers and learners alike to be problem solvers. However, the problem situation each confronts is parallel to but quite distinct from that of the other.

- The teacher's first task is to set an authentic, open-ended problem or inquiry in a way that makes it likely the learners will be able to solve it successfully.
- In the implementation stage, while the learners are exploring possible solutions, the teacher is engaged in assessing what concepts or challenges might be roadblocks for individual learners and seeking ways to scaffold and facilitate each child to experience competence as a problem solver.

At the end of the day, classroom learning communities and communities of practice function in the same way. Something or someone acts as a catalyst that engages a group of learners in a meaningful inquiry. As the problem-solving process plays out, everyone is learning something and everyone is learning from others. Everyone is eager to go further, to dig deeper, or to go on to a new inquiry.

TRY AND APPLY

1. Describe a teaching/learning experience you have had that parallels the making of stone soup in the story–that is, a time when something or someone acted as a catalyst for a dynamic interaction that resulted in rich learning. The outcome does not need to be academic; it could be that some kind of social-emotional understanding emerged or it could be that you developed increased proficiency or skill in a sports or other activity.
2. Write a reflection on which of the following discipline(s) you feel your own PCK is strongest or weakest: reading for meaning, writing, mathematics, science, social studies. Talk about what factors might account for this, including how competent you feel in that subject area, your own school experiences, personal life influences such as family members or the environment in which you grew up, and so on.

CHAPTER 2

What Can We Learn from the *Three Little Pigs?*

The Three Es of Quality Intellectual Work

Heidi's 24 first graders were in an English-speaking classroom in a school that is 97% Hispanic. They had spent several weeks discussing and doing literacy activities that explored how the traditional story of the *Three Little Pigs* compared and contrasted with versions such as Jon Sczieka's *The True Story of the Three Little Pigs* or Susan Lowell's *The Three Little Javelinas*. Given how enthusiastic the children were, Heidi decided to use the *Three Little Pigs* to introduce them to the scientific method—beginning with a problem situation, developing a hypothesis, designing an experiment to test it, and finally, analyzing the results.

Heidi discussed the third little pig's house with the children and what it means to construct something that is "strong" and can withstand a powerful wind like those generated by hurricanes, tornados, wind storms, or a big bad wolf. She brought in a wide variety of found materials including popsicle sticks, twigs, different kinds of cardboard, plastic, and paper as well as various tapes and glue.

Working in groups of two or three, she had the children talk together to hypothesize about which materials were most likely to make a strong house. After recording their decisions on a report form that included hypothesis, experiment, results, and evaluation, each group had several days to use their chosen materials to make a house.

By Friday the groups were eager to see how "wolf-proof" their constructions were. "We're doing a scientific experiment," they proudly explained to a visitor admiring the display of finished houses. "We did the hippo-thing and now we're going to test it," one added.

In a classroom meeting the children decided on a fair test—each house would be huffed and puffed at by two children who were not involved in making it; the number of blows would be limited to the children's age—seven.

Many huffs, puffs, and cheers later, all of the structures passed the test. The children now worked cooperatively to finish the reports for a display that was exhibited in the hall for other classrooms and their families to review.

The children were ready to go on doing more with the *Three Little Pigs*, but Heidi suggested they now take a look at another big bad wolf, like the one in *Little Red Riding Hood*, a tale for which she also had several versions.

WHAT CONSTITUTES QUALITY LEARNING?

Heidi's wonderful activity was one of many developed in the 60 pre-K to fifth-grade classrooms that were involved in the Stone Soup literacy initiative. The teachers had selected 20 high-quality books for use in their classroom. This particular year, we asked the teachers to include at least 10 of the folk and fairy tales that we all know children love to read again and again; Heidi was one of many to chose several variants of one tale. Facilitators were in the schools once a week, working with the teachers to explore and share ways these stories could be extended across the curriculum.

The thought and planning meant that what happened in Heidi's classroom went far beyond a cute idea picked up at a make-and-take workshop. It is representative of how taking a rich text out of the book and moving it into the hearts and minds of children can have a significant impact on the quality of the learning/teaching experience.

Death to Delight: What Best Motivates Learning?

Our discussion of quality reflects some basic understanding about what it means to learn. Brain functioning obeys a biological imperative: all learning is a response to a *need to know*. However, the needs that trigger the impulse to learn cover a wide spectrum.

At one extreme, the need is urgent—once the fight-or-flight instinct is triggered, we make a decision based on what we already know or have learned about which choice offers the best chance for survival. Our concern is immediate and spending too much time on metaphysics or conceptual frameworks might kill us.

At other times, the need to know grows out of cultural and social considerations; then we may well be driven to develop "big ideas" as well as to acquire specific knowledge and skills that will help us function successfully as a member of our family, community, and larger units of society and culture. So, too, the need to know may have social-emotional roots—we may be seeking approval, success, or power. We learn what we need in order to get along and get ahead.

At the far other end of the spectrum from life-or-death exigency, the human need to know springs from pure and simple *delight*; what one personally wants and needs to know ranges from the simple to the sublime:

- It pleases the 5-year-old to be able to accurately identify 50 different dinosaurs and to know the preferred diet of each.
- It is a cause for great personal satisfaction for some to know that they are magnificent shoppers, well skilled at finding the absolutely best deal on absolutely anything.
- It stirs the very soul of yet others to meditate with increasing profundity on eternal mysteries.

We should not underestimate the role delight plays in learning. Quite simply, delight gives learning its staying power. We tend to quickly forget what we have learned only under duress; all the names and dates crammed for a test are gone almost as soon as the bubble sheet is turned in or the blue book is closed. On the other hand, it's been over 40 years since I learned "ontogeny recapitulates phylogeny" in my high school biology class and every so often I find myself saying the phrase out loud—what fun for the tongue all those syllables are! I smirk to think I can still tease out the conceptual meaning so many years later, though I have had very little need to think about or apply the concept.

By the same token, I take even more delight in knowledge that is useful and meaningful to me in my personal and professional life. Certain lines of poetry help me get up and get through days that are sure to be emotionally draining. Having a detailed awareness of early language development gives me confidence that I can competently observe and evaluate a child a caregiver has concerns about.

What Are the Delights of Intellectual Curiosity?

Clearly, the term *delight* is not being used here lightly—it is not a fuzzy or ephemeral sensation; it is meant to connote the sense of intrinsically meaningful satisfaction that lifelong learners experience when they discover or understand yet another thing. Another name for the delight in learning that has become a habit of mind is *intellectual curiosity*.

This quality of delight in learning spills over and through the full spectrum of needs one might have to know something. At the same time, having a *habit of curiosity* about the whats, whys, and wherefores of both the mundane and the exotic, or, we might say, a *disposition toward inquiry,* means that learning is seen as having an intrinsic benefit—it is something worth doing. Even better, intellectual curiosity has a "velcro" effect on knowledge—we are much more inclined to retain what is learned when it has personal value. So when exigency strikes, crucial knowledge that has been sprinkled with delight is retrieved much more quickly than something learned just because we had to.

In her discussion about the disposition to learn, Lillian Katz (2010) goes even further: She suggests that the disposition to intellectual curiosity is inborn—and that we fail our responsibilities as educators when we fail to nurture that disposition.

WHO OWNS THE LEARNING?

In fact, the remarkable advances in brain research in recent years confirm Katz's conclusion. While the need to know goes back to survival instincts in the most primitive part of the brain, delight triggers more complex chemical reactions that involve more sophisticated brain functioning. Positive emotions release chemicals known as endorphins and dopamines—both of which stimulate the prefrontal area of the brain where cognitive functions are located. When learners feel positive toward the learning process, they see finding out something new or understanding something better as a *benefit*—all those endorphins and dopamines make them feel good. This positive disposition makes it easier to learn and can motivate learners to persist when they run into difficulty. So, too, the sense of ownership that comes when knowledge, skills, and understandings are seen as personally meaningful and useful means this kind of knowledge tends to move more quickly into long-term memory and to be retained and referenced again and again

However, a negative disposition has just as powerful consequences. When a learning situation triggers negative feelings such as fear, anxiety, boredom, or dislike, the chemical cortisol activates the brain areas that focus on emotion in the limbic area of the brain; the stronger the negative emotions, the harder it is for the prefrontal cortex or the cognitive center of the brain to function. The more experiences one has finding learning stressful, the less able one is to get past the negative emotions. While adults can override their emotional response and focus on learning, children are still developing their control of what is called the *executive function*—the ability to consciously control their responses (Sousa, 2006, 2009; Washburn, 2010).

In effect, it all comes down to the question, *Who owns the learning?* As advocates of positive discipline such as Alfie Kohn (1999, 2000, 2006) and Gartrell (2003) have persuasively argued, intrinsic rewards have more staying power than extrinsic behaviorist incentives. Kohn argues that gold stars, grades, and behavior charts divert children from focusing on problem solving and from deepening understanding of a particular topic or concept. Instead of delighting in knowing more about why dinosaurs are real and dragons are fantasy creatures, they are preoccupied with gaining a sweet treat or a sticker that has little connection with what is being learned. Once the reward is won, the fact or skill that was mastered tends to quickly slip out of short-term memory or be buried deep in our long-term memory.

By the same token, negative consequences such as punishments or adult disapproval for poor performance or behavior do little to inspire learning or develop self-regulation (Sousa, 2009; Kohn, 1999). There is good evidence that a negative learning environment is likely to trigger strong negative responses to school and lead to classroom management problems (Bowen, 2007).[1]

WHAT'S THE RELATIONSHIP BETWEEN COMPETENCE, CONFIDENCE, AND QUALITY INTELLECTUAL WORK?

Why Is Feeling Competent Important for Learning?

Another way to put all this is to say that successful learners are characterized by confidence and competence—they not only have a need to know, *they believe themselves capable of learning*. In the early 1970s, Bandura began studying evidence of a strong correlation between this belief, which he called *self-efficacy*, and levels of achievement, academic and otherwise (for self-efficacy, see Bandura, 1997). More recently, Dweck (2007) has done important work on the role *mindset* plays in learning. Her research shows that the learners who believe that their intelligence is fixed do considerably less well than those who believe that their own efforts play an important role in how successful they are. Lifelong learners are those who believe the work they have done to acquire knowledge and skills means they should be able to apply what they already know to new problem situations and feel reasonable confidence that they will be successful in resolving them.

While much of the research about these theories reflects work with older learners, there is a good body of research that establishes that the importance of feeling competent begins at birth. Infants and toddlers who are ignored or neglected lose incentive to even try; they face a terrible risk of never catching up with those who are stimulated and responded to positively (Bowen, 2006; Hughes, Luo, Kwok, & Loyd, 2008; Pianta, La Paro, & Hamre, 2007).

However, the first decade of the twenty-first century has given rise to a threat to early childhood classrooms in general; the push to test children earlier and earlier in order to measure and predict later student achievement is seriously developmentally inappropriate. But what is more problematic is that the emphasis on testing—and on teaching to tests—is highly counterproductive.

As my farming relatives can attest, repeatedly measuring a pig's weight does nothing to turn it into a prize-winning sow. Serious harm is being done as the pressure to achieve, using one-size-fits-all standards, is creating high levels of stress for children and teachers alike. Even worse, brain research suggests that the negative climate that results is more likely than not to sour children's disposition toward schooling earlier and earlier—and the earlier a disposition is set, the harder it is to change (Williams et al., 2008; Zins et al., 2004).

The complicated tension between standardized achievement and authentic learning has a long history in the United States and elsewhere, as Diane Ravitch (2000, 2010) has chronicled.[2] One problem is that it is much more complex to measure student success in terms of the capacity to make meaning and to use and apply knowledge than it is to score standardized achievement tests.

Even so, there also has always been a strong tradition for making schools a place that promotes problem solving and learning. For more than a decade I have been assessing classrooms on these terms, drawing on a framework developed by Newman, Lopez, and Bryk (1998). In a study commissioned by the Annenberg Schools Challenge Grant project, this research team looked at what they called *authentic intellectual work*. In my work, I prefer the term *quality* over *authentic* to emphasize that decisions about where a particular activity might fall on the scale from high quality to lacking quality are based on objective criteria.

What Is Quality Intellectual Work?

Newman's research team argued the best way to assess authentic learning was to look at whether students were being given the tools to take on the kind of complex intellectual work they would be asked to perform as competent adults: "The ways in which these adults work with knowledge differ from ways that students usually work with knowledge in school. These differences suggest criteria for intellectual quality that honor basic knowledge and skills, but also extend beyond them" (Newman, Lopez, & Bryk, 1998, p. 12). Their team gathered and analyzed data involving teacher assignments and student work samples.

Building on earlier work by Newman (1996),[3] the report defined authentic intellectual work as having three essential features:

- Construction of knowledge
- Thorough use of disciplined inquiry
- To produce discourse, products, or performances that have value beyond school.

To unpack these features, let's go back to the first graders and their *Three Little Pigs* experiment and consider each factor.

How Is Knowledge Constructed?

After a read-aloud of the *Three Little Pigs*, many teachers will ask, "Which of the three little pigs' houses was strongest?" This is a closed question, with only one right answer—an answer that is so transparent that it is hard to imagine how one might get it wrong. It does nothing to promote new learning.

But now consider the query that Heidi chose to pose: "What does it mean for a house to be strong enough not be blown away?" This open-ended question and the wide-ranging discussion it triggered got a group of inner-city ELL first graders to think for themselves by:

- Creating a scaffold so they could make connections between the story and a question they cared about: What does it mean to be strong?
- Offering them an authentic opportunity to problem-solve as they clarified their thinking and posed more questions.
- Affirming that they were competent and confident learners; the children could see that while the teacher was facilitating the discussion, she was equally engaged in the problem-solving process.

In effect, as the children busily worked at constructing their strong houses, they were *constructing their own understanding* both of what it means to be strong as well as what it means to think through and test one's answers. They were satisfying the first condition for authentic/quality intellectual work.

As the phrase *construction of knowledge* makes transparent, the concept of authentic intellectual work reflects the constructivist philosophy of education that says learning is not a passive act, with knowledge funneled into—or inflicted upon—the student's mind. The learner must be an active agent in constructing his or her understanding. Furthermore, precisely because the learner is actively involved, the process of making meaning is *more efficacious*—that is, it has more staying power and more potential for leading to further understanding than rote learning; in biochemical terms, the endorphins and dopamines keep the negative effects of cortisol at bay.

Constructivism comes from the seminal thinking of Vygotsky and Piaget in the first third of the twentieth century and was nurtured and expanded in the last third by cognition theorists such as Bruner (1992), Katz (2010), Katz and Thomas (2003), and Duckworth (2006), among others. It sees learning as a process that is *essentially creative*—not in the sense that the knowledge or understanding we come to is something totally unique and that no one ever thought or understood before. Rather, it is creative in that we have come to make sense of something that we did not understand before; we have made some kind of step toward satisfying our need to know. As Piaget (1970) so lucidly declared, "Each time one prematurely teaches a child something he could have discovered for himself, that child is kept from inventing it and consequently from understanding it completely" (p. 715).

In the next chapter I look further at how constructivism understands learning in a way that differs in essential ways from that held by behaviorists, who argue that humans and rats in a maze can be trained, or conditioned by rewards, to find their way to the right answer or the way out.

What Is a Disciplined Inquiry?

The question about what makes a strong house was very *intentional*, as we say these days. As she planned the lesson, Heidi factored in a number of considerations.

Her first graders were fascinated with the *Three Little Pigs* and she could see many ways to keep doing literacy activities. However, she needed to prove that her classroom was addressing the state science standards. In our Stone Soup Partnership meetings and consultations, we discussed how difficult it was to meet such demands, given that only 40 minutes a week were available for science and social studies. We advocated integrating these areas into the literacy block as not only a strategic but also an appropriate way to meet the demands. After all, we noted, the definition of literacy calls for reading and writing for a variety of purposes, including gaining information.

At the same time, developmentally, first graders are still very concrete in their thinking. Even though the "scientific method" was included in the state science standards, young children can only make sense of the general principles underlying a good science experiment if they are given step-by-step guidance through an activity that interests them.

This intentional teacher also took the developmental needs of the children into consideration as she selected the materials. She purposefully used recycled materials but chose things such as light cardboard, popsicle sticks, pipe cleaners and scraps of plastic or wood that had attributes that made it easy to see how they could be used to build a house.

As good teachers do, she thought through what kinds of questions and prompts she might use when she circulated as the children worked in small groups. She avoided quick statements of approval as well as suggestions for trying something else. Instead, in a neutral but interested tone of voice, she asked them to explain their reasons for selecting materials or for developing a plan; she made it clear that changing the plan was a part of the process; she also provided a template that would make it easy for them to record what they were doing in a way that reinforced their understanding of the process. While she used terms like *hypothesis*, her first concern was that the children understood what it meant, even if they mangled the pronunciation into the "hippo-thing." Furthermore, children who were still in earlier stages of acquiring English could talk through their ideas in their home language of Spanish.

The careful intentional structuring of this activity reflects the standards Newman (1996) established. They argue that a disciplined inquiry must do three things:

1. Build on a prior knowledge base that is specific to the discipline or field under discussion. Those who work with 6- and 7-year-olds know this age is easily sidetracked by the general question of what it means to be strong. Specifying that the structures had to withstand the forces of wind kept the inquiry directed toward issues of science.

2. Strive for in-depth understanding rather than superficial understanding. Even though they are concrete thinkers, children are able to fairly quickly generalize an answer to a question such as "What makes brick stronger than straw or wood?" However, they are also able to think a little more deeply when asked a question that pushes them. Shown a picture of the usual haphazard sticks-and-stones house and a log cabin, children might have quite a bit to say when asked, "Is it possible to construct a wooden house in a way that is just as strong or possibly stronger than a brick one?" In other words, if we don't facilitate ways for children to ask more questions and to use what they already know to try out answers, both intellectual curiosity and intellectual work get short-circuited.

3. Express findings through elaborated communication. Whatever the Victorians might have desired, young learners are both seen and heard. But there are significant differences among a chaotic classroom, one in which everyone is compliantly silent unless called upon, and one in which children are actively engaged in negotiating and clarifying their thinking. When children are engaged in the kind of elaborated communication defined by Newman et al. (1998, pp. 14–16), they might need reminders to use inside voices as they work out their understanding. Often enough authentic/quality learning can be a bit messy; even so, having to clarify, expand, or reconstruct understanding can be highly engaging. Learning takes on a life that is much more engaging than passively spitting back right answers.

Moreover, communication about what has been learned is by no means just verbal: It involves what children do, sense, and feel—as all the drawing, building, and blowing, along with the discussion and writing, in Heidi's classroom indicates.

What Are Discourses, Products, or Performances That Have Meaning Beyond the Classroom?

Children who are engaged in a project such as building a strong house may appreciate but don't need a grade or a gold star to tell them that they have done quality intellectual work. However, in early childhood classrooms, it is worthwhile to have the discourses, products, or performances take place in the familiar context of the classroom as a display, classroom book, or a performance to which other classrooms or parents are invited. The intrinsic rewards of having gained meaningful knowledge and of feeling competent are multiplied by a public celebration. However, if the outcome is to have meaning beyond the classroom, these events or products should be inclusive and not limited to the "best." When children know that their work is going to "go public" they tend to be much more strongly motivated to go through the drudgery of revising and reworking. Their motivation is even stronger if they are given a rubric beforehand that helps them know what "good work" looks like and if they have a voice in deciding what will go on display.[4]

For the children in Heidi's classroom, the intrinsic rewards of feeling confidence and competence were readily apparent as children pulled other students, parents, and siblings over to explain what made them pick the materials they did and to speculate on why their design passed the blowing test. Even better, family members' involvement and comments showed that everyone was going away with new ideas and further questions to explore.

HOW DO THE THREE Es PROMOTE
QUALITY INTELLECTUAL WORK?

How Do the Three E's Compare with the Three R's?

The teaching/learning dynamic that informs constructivism calls for a fairly radically shift away from traditional ideas about schooling. In the late nineteenth and well into the twentieth century, the thrust of public education was to promote the 3 Rs—Reading, 'Riting, and 'Rithmetic. This understanding was so entrenched that few noticed the irony that one can only get to 3 Rs by misspelling two of them. But irony was not really part of the curriculum. Rather the concern was to produce workers who had mastered skills and could quickly give back the overarching "Rs" –*R*ote answers, delivered *R*apidly.

- Reading instruction emphasized decoding and vocabulary activities—woe to the phonics-challenged dyslexics.
- 'Riting had more to do with penmanship, grammar, and spelling than composition—woe again to dyslexics, and also those with fine motor skills problems, and all whose home language was not standard English.
- 'Rithmetic in elementary school focused exclusively on very quick performance of number operations, with a superficial nod to naming shapes as geometry—woe to all the "mathphobes"— especially the girls (who grow up to be the majority of early childhood and elementary teachers).

By the late twentieth century, as technology began to dominate the workplace, there were strong indicators that education had to move beyond the 3 Rs—and that the more socially oriented curricula of the mid-twentieth century also left many children behind.[5] By the late 1980s it was equally clear that most children entering kindergarten would end up in jobs that hadn't yet been dreamed of—that remains true, as does the fact that it is highly likely individuals will change professions two or three times in the course of their work lives. Unquestionably, the three Rs have been transformed:

- *Reading and 'Riting* have been folded into *Literacy*: While the phonics war still rages, there is general agreement that the definition of literacy calls for "reading and writing for a variety of purposes, including information and pleasure." That definition implies, at the very least, that being literate calls for *meaning-making*, beyond the more mechanical aspects of decoding or spelling. In fact, literacy has been generalized across the curriculum, so that there is talk of math literacy, science literacy, social studies literacy and even music or arts literacy.[6]
- At the same time, *'Rithmetic* has virtually turned into a dinosaur of academic vocabulary. When the National Council of Teachers of Mathematics (NCTM) issue their frameworks, they speak of "Number Sense and Number Operations" as one of five basic strands of *mathematics*.
- Current thinking about rote memorization and drill and kill points out that it is certainly advantageous to be able to automatically retrieve information. However, the greatest advantage comes when things are known "by heart"—that is, with meaning attached to them.[7]

The change in terminology is a reflection of new directions in beliefs about what it means to learn and teach. In her highly applauded recent book, Galinsky (2010) identifies seven essential skills that children need to master if they are to be successful adult learners, including focus and self-control, perspective taking, communicating, making connections, critical thinking, and taking on challenges and engaged learning. Notice that these skills are *habits of mind*, rather than snippets of content knowledge or mastery of rote skills. Instead of emphasizing *products*, schools need to be sure children are able to process and problem-solve—or there will be no place for them in the twenty-first-century world of work.

While content varies from one academic discipline to another, the teaching/learning dynamic holds true across the curriculum and beyond: The toddler exploring his world is engaged in discovering meaning just as much as an octogenarian fascinated by the most recent theories about the origin of life.

What Does It Mean to Engage, Explore, and Evaluate?

If we want to assure that the toddler will become the curious octogenarian, however, we need to shift the emphasis from content to process and replace the 3 Rs with the 3 Es of *Engage, Explore and Evaluate* across the disciplines.[8] Quality intellectual work follows a dynamic cycle:

- Begins with Engagement—all learning begins with a need to know—for pragmatics or for pleasure. As brain research shows, the more positively learners are disposed, the more quickly activity moves to the "thinking" parts of the brain in the prefrontal cortex. The lower or more external the engagement, the less likely the learner is to process the learning because of the dampening effects of negative emotions (Immordino-Yang, 2007, 2008; Sousa, 2009).
- Moves to Exploration—the learner begins to systematically explore the question that engaged his or her interest. Effective learning uses a disciplined inquiry, that is, the exploration builds on understandings and procedures appropriate to the topic. Good teachers structure the exploration, providing a scaffold for the learners.
- Progresses to Evaluation—we take a careful look at what our exploration uncovered—does it fit what we wanted to know? Was it good enough or should we try to get an even better understanding/answer? Does it raise another question—leading us back through the 3 Es cycle?

What Makes Error a Productive Fourth E?

In marked contrast to the 3 Rs, which carry a subtext of right and rote answers, the 3 Es recognize the important role *Error* plays in the teaching/learning dynamic. On one hand, engagement often begins with *cognitive dissonance*, that is, the realization that we are faced with something we know absolutely nothing about, or that something we took for granted is not true, or that solving a problem is much more complicated than we assumed. On the other hand, as Dweck's research confirms (2007), all working investigators know that the greatest discoveries are the result of struggling to reconcile a host of mistakes and missteps

For the scientists I know, pinpointing precisely how and where they went wrong is often the most satisfying stage of their research. In an illuminating article on problem solving, Martinez (1998) points out, "Errors are part of the process of problem solving, which implies that both teachers and learners need to be more tolerant of them. *If no mistakes are made, then almost certainly no problem solving is taking place*" (p. 609).

In other words, Martinez's discussion suggests that the way that children were comfortable using trial and error as they explored how to make a strong house is a good indicator that they were engaged in quality intellectual work that had meaning beyond the classroom.

At the same time, celebrating the role of error links *Evaluation* to the third condition for quality intellectual work, namely, doing the work for purposes that go beyond the classroom. Effective evaluation is not something *done to the learner* as a pop quiz or final exam. Rather, it is something that a *constructive learner does* naturally. The learner/worker is the one who must decide if the need to know has been satisfied.

How Are Projects and Guided Inquiry Related to Learning Communities?

Admittedly, the process of implementing activities that use the 3 E's to involve learners in quality intellectual work is demanding. It certainly tends to be messier than direct instruction and worksheets. However, those who use this approach find it is much more interesting to plan as well as to implement.

It is also more likely to result in greater learning, as Philip Schlechty (2002) shows in his discussion of the WOW factor ("Working on the Work"): the more teachers work to provide students with activities that call for quality intellectual work, the more likely it is that students will not only work harder, but also that their academic performance will improve.

Katz and others (Helm & Katz, 2001; Katz, 1998) who advocate so strongly for the project approach in early childhood classrooms make a similar argument for the importance of designing and implementing quality intellectual work.[9] We have already alluded to how much of the work on guided inquiry in science agrees.

What Learning Communities Were Involved in the *Three Little Pigs* Project?

The discussion of parallel processing in Chapter 1 pointed to the efficacy and power of having classrooms work as learning communities.[10] It is noteworthy that the quality of the work done in the *Three Little Pigs* project owes much to the interlocking learning communities involved. On one hand, the way that children were able to share ideas, engage in error analysis, and achieve success by working with others makes it clear the classroom was functioning as a learning community. At the same time, Heidi and others were very appreciative of the way that the Stone Soup Network had established a community of practice. The extended discussions and sharing between their colleagues at their own school site as well as those in other network schools supported and expanded their understanding and increased their ability to design rich lessons embedded in high-quality children's literature.

WHAT DOES QUALITY INTELLECTUAL WORK LOOK LIKE IN PRE-K TO GRADE 3 CLASSROOMS?

A good teacher who promotes quality intellectual work, like the third pig, takes Schectly's WOW factor seriously. The task the teacher sets grows out of the text to pose a compelling problem that learners can become deeply engaged in solving and that will result in their constructing understanding.

A less skilled teacher finds something appealing in the text and comes up with an idea that is "cute" but doesn't call for rich thinking or learning. Finally, like the slapdash house of straw, at the bottom end of the scale, there is only a "cosmetic" attempt to make a connection between the text and the activity; at the same time the learner is given a closed question that has very little meaning or purpose beyond supplying data for giving a grade. Table 2.1 compares how "cute ideas" and "big ideas" look in the classroom.

HOW DOES PRACTICE BECOME PRAXIS?

The engaged first graders in Heidi's classroom were focused on building their strong houses, oblivious to how their activities might reflect academic theories and research. By the same token, Heidi herself did not consciously undertake to construct an activity that could be analyzed in terms of how it reflected the philosophies of Piaget and Vygotsky nor was she ticking off how well her lesson met the standards for quality intellectual work set by Newman[11] or Schlecty.

That is to say, when Heidi and other effective teachers come up with a wonderful way to go from a great book to an activity that calls for quality intellectual work, they don't do so as the result of theoretical readings. It is much more likely that these good teachers are themselves lifelong learners and lovers of stories.

They are doing in their way what Aesop, Homer, the nameless *griots*, Hassidic rabbis, and village spinners of folk tales have done from the beginning of time. Intrigued by the fascinating problem of how to teach in a way that would help this particular group understand something, their instinct is to use a tool that would first act as a hook *(Engage)* and then offer compelling material to study *(Explore)* and finally leave it to the learner

TABLE 2.1. "Cute Idea" Activities versus "Big Idea" Quality Intellectual Work

"Cute Idea" Activities	"Big Idea" Quality Intellectual Work
Project or activity is done as a one-shot deal with	Project or activity is carefully structured with
• Loose or no connection to other curricular plans	• Specific connection to other classroom learning
• No explicit introduction or framing of the activity/project with explicit learning goals in mind	• Introduction (anticipatory set) to activity that explicitly connects to learning goals and builds *engagement*
• Facilitation during the activity on logistics, not on processing	• Facilitation that encourages children's processing and group skills as well as logistics
• Limited or no reflection or extension of the activity to further learning/thinking	• Explicit discussion and or some kind of "going public" that helps children deepen their thinking/understanding and reflect on what they have learned
The project or activity may be	The project or activity offers an opportunity for children to
• *Highly teacher-directed:* Teacher may provide explicit directions or do a great deal of prep and intervention so that the finished projects all "look nice" in the eyes of the adults	• *Explore* a specific concept/understanding as a "disciplined inquiry" but they are given latitude to come up with their own representations/solutions
• *Child-directed:* Children are allowed to "be creative/play around/ do what they like" with little or no structuring of the activity other than provision of materials	• Evaluate or debrief as a group and for themselves what they have learned, and what they see meaningful about their work

to find the meaning that satisfies the individual need to know *(Evaluate)*.

1. How have you personally experienced quality intellectual work?

Think back to something you learned about or learned how to do because you had a "need to know" and discuss how these learnings met the criteria for quality intellectual work.

- Think first in terms of a hobby, sport, or some other voluntary activity/interest.
- Now think of something that you have learned in a school setting that you still remember.

Which of these two kinds of learning was easier for you to identify? What does that suggest to you about your learning? About the kind of learning you want to have happen in your classroom?

2. How can you use a classic tale to engage students in quality intellectual work?

Review the following list of classroom activities based on the *Three Little Pigs*. Use them as an inspiration to come up with an idea of your own or choose one that seems especially appealing to you. Identify who you might like to try this out with—if you are not working directly with children, specify a particular age/grade level. What are some ways you can see you would need to tailor, adjust, or expand on this idea to assure that it would be a "big idea"/quality intellectual work activity, not just a "cute idea"?

Note that some of the projects had the children working from 1 to 3 weeks; others were done in a day or two. Several could be used from pre-K through primary or even middle school; some are clearly most appropriate for a given developmental level.[12]

- *Are wolves really big and bad?* Two kindergarten teachers paired up to develop a science unit comparing wolves in nature with those of wolves in stories; each implemented the unit somewhat differently, both in that initial year and in other years when they did it with different groups of children. Another teacher used the real animal/story animal idea to look at pigs. Yet another had third graders brainstorm storybook animal villains and sweeties and investigate the facts behind their reputations.

- *If you use bricks to make a strong house, what do you use to make bricks?* A primary classroom explored this question after the teacher came across a copy of the informational book *From Mud to House* (Knight, 1998). *The Three Little Pigs* versions they used included *The Three Little Javelinas* (Lowell, 1992), in which the third pig's house was made of adobe, and *Pig, Pigger, Piggest* (Walton, 2003), which features mud constructions. The classroom library also featured books on construction. A different classroom had a grandfather who was a bricklayer come in and talk about his craft. The activity culminated in children practicing their bricklaying skills using sugar cubes, wooden blocks, and miniature bricks.

- *How can pictures change the story?* Third graders used Whately's *Wait No Paint* (2005) and Wiesner's *The Three Pigs* (2001) to investigate the decisions an illustrator of a story makes and how those decisions can change the tone and feel of a story. Each of several small groups looked at one version of the *Three Little Pigs* and reported on the style of the illustrations and how they added to the characterization of the wolf and the three pigs.

- How does *Little, Littler, Littlest* compare to *Big, Bigger, Biggest?* Classrooms that have *Pig, Pigger, Piggest* in their libraries inevitably use it in a language arts lesson on comparative and superlative cases. Many follow up with a writing assignment to write a brief story that uses many comparative and superlatives, using Walton's text as a model. In one classroom, the first drafts were so enjoyable that the students voted to collect them in a classroom book they titled *Story, Storier, Storiest,* although some voted for *Silly, Sillier, Silliest.* A kindergarten class went in a quite different direction and used the book for a mathematics lesson. As a group they made a model chart that featured a house in the center and then drew others to show progression in size from a bigger to the biggest house, and on the other side to a littler and littlest house. Children then did an individual representation of how one object can be seen as going from littlest to biggest.

- How do we want to tell this story? Many kindergarten and primary grade classrooms got the children eagerly looking at the different versions they had read and then making decisions about how they wanted to tell the story. Pre-K and kindergarten classrooms tended to do simple dramatizations, narrative pantomimes, or dictated stories. Elementary classes worked in small groups or as a whole to produce a classroom book, while a few did the story as a comic book; in other classrooms, the work concentrated on producing a written script or just a plan for acting out or doing a puppet show. In all cases, terms like setting, plot, and characters took on meaning as the students grappled with questions such as the following:

* *Which versions changed the setting?* What details were different, such as what each house was built out of or which dangerous creature threatened the pigs? If the young authors decided to alter the setting, what decisions would they make about such details?

* *What plot variations occur often?* Examples are having the wolf eat the first two pigs instead of having them escape or adding incidents before the wolf goes down the chimney, such as when the third pig goes to get apples earlier than the wolf. What will this telling do about these plot elements?

* *How much personality do the characters have?* Some versions don't give the characters much personality or even names; others give each character a clear persona. What will this telling do about names and personalities?

* *What elements made some versions funny?* Some versions were funny and others were very traditional. What kind of details would the young authors use if they decided to make their version funny?

* *The Big Bad Wolf on Trial.* The year that Heidi's children worked on their strong houses, another school in the network involved the whole school community in putting Mr. A. Wolf on trial. The project began with a fifth-grade class studying the judicial system; a seventh grader was the judge, while parents and faculty acted as prosecuting and defending lawyers. All the students from second to sixth grade and two classes from other network schools attended the trial, at which A. Wolf was accused of "pigicide" and felony destruction of property. Prosecution witnesses included Little Red Riding Hood. After careful deliberation, the wolf was found innocent by the jury of 5th graders. He was saved when the defense attorney had the wolf demonstrate his asthma inhaler, establishing that he was in no shape to blow a house down.

CHAPTER 3

Can Cinderella's Slipper Be Gold Instead Of Glass?

The Role of Questions in Quality Intellectual Work

Jenny, a newly certified third-grade teacher, had been advised she needed to work on using questions and conversations. She agreed to have me come in to do a storytelling, followed by a discussion; still, she was skeptical that anything could change the way her inner-city students were always more than ready to talk to one another but only mumbled a word or two when asked about school work, including read-alouds.

Since it was around the Chinese New Year, I decided to tell *Yeh-Shen*. Like so many of its story cousins, the Chinese version of *Cinderella* features an abused child, whose loving mother has died, and whose father unwisely marries a cruel woman with her own daughters.[1] Yeh-Shen finds refuge in a magic fish and later a tree who replaces Disney's fairy godmother. Thanks to its magic, the girl is able to go to an important festival, dressed in magnificent clothes, including golden slippers. Afraid of discovery as the evening ends, the beautiful girl runs off, frantic to return her finery. In this case, Yeh-Shen loses one golden slipper as she dashes along the twisted, rocky mountain path, but doesn't recognize the loss until too late. Eventually, of course, the lost slipper leads to her discovery and marriage to the local prince.

When I asked for questions and comments, several made observations about similarities with Disney's *Cinderella*. Then Antoine, who had a reputation as a troublemaker, challenged me, "You said this was a Cinderella story. So how come you said she had a golden slipper? Cinderella has a glass slipper."

He listened skeptically as I explained how this was a kind of "story cousin" to the Cinderella we knew best and that some details were different. I pointed out that gold was precious and in China they may have thought gold slippers made the clothes seem very special.

There were other questions as the discussion ranged back and forth. I could see that Antoine was carrying on sidebar conversation with the child next to him, but I didn't comment since they were being quiet. Just as we were winding up, he raised his hand to announce, "I know why you said this Cinderella didn't have a glass slipper." He reminded us that in this story the girl was running along a rocky mountain path; that meant, if the slipper had come off, it would have broken on the rocks and there would be no slipper left for the prince to match. Since she just kept running, the slipper couldn't have been made of glass; it made more sense for it to be gold. The child he had consulted with chimed in, "Yeah, and her foot would have been all bloody!" I joined the rest of the class in marveling at what a good explanation he'd come up with.

When I discussed the session with Jenny later, she admitted she had used my visit to take care of some paperwork; still, she had noticed all the discussion; she'd been surprised by Antoine's participation, confiding, "He hardly ever answers. Sometimes I call on him deliberately to see if he's been paying attention; I'm lucky to get a 'yes' or 'no'!"

As she hustled the children off to lunch, I left a little frustrated myself. Jenny hadn't registered what made the discussion take off; she certainly hadn't seen that it was Antoine's *own question* that got him talking. In fact, Antoine is one of the most striking examples of what I have seen happen again and again: All it takes to get a good discussion going is to start by asking what questions and comments the children have. Almost always, that gives me a better understanding of how the story is being processed—and I get new insights. Though I have told this story dozens of times, I had never thought or been asked about Antoine's point. I got another insight into why it's worth returning again and again and again to a good story—each new encounter can lead to a new or deeper understanding.

HOW DO THE QUESTIONS WE ASK INFLUENCE THE ANSWERS WE GET?

Jenny's focus on paperwork and logistics, rather than with what or how her students were learning, is typical of the teacher-training factory she had attended. She had been conditioned to focus on managing a textbook-driven curriculum, where assessment is equated with standardized test scores. No one had asked her to consider how focusing on achievement overrides paying attention to evidence that the children are actually learning. She thought reciting equaled understanding; she had no idea that disposition was an important factor in learning.

What Kind of Questions Can Be Asked?

When Jenny was asked to work on her questions and conversations, she clearly didn't understand that there are quite *different kinds of questions*—and that each type sets different expectations about what a "good answer" will look like.

Open-and-shut closed questions call for a yes or no or can be answered with a single word or phrase. Unfortunately, the majority of questions asked in traditional classrooms and on many standardized tests fall into this category. After reading or telling *Yeh-Shen*, one asks: "What was Yeh-Shen's slipper made out of? "The only acceptable answer is "gold." Saying "glass" means the child was not paying attention to the way this story was different from the Disney *Cinderella*.

"Unlocked" closed questions and leading questions call for an answer that gives some explanation or support. However, while responses may be expressed quite differently, they should all reflect a correct answer that can be traced back to the text. "Describe something cruel the stepmother did to Yeh-Shen" could be answered by expanding on any one of three or four incidents from the story. Answering "Why did Yeh-Shen get chosen as the bride instead of her stepsisters?" calls for inference or deeper thinking but responses should indicate that Yeh-Shen (like other Cinderellas from around the world) was good-hearted, while the stepsisters were mean and selfish.

Open questions call for evaluation and synthesizing—that is, for constructing a network of connections that lead to a new understanding.

More than one response is possible, but all must include explanations or support. Antoine's question—"You said this was a *Cinderella* story. So how come you said she had a golden slipper?"—is a striking example of how children's questions often are open—they are also authentic in that they express something that the questioner really wants to know.[2]

Is "Getting It Right" the Same as "Making Sense"?

Questions are crucial tools for teachers. Furthermore, the type that gets used most often tells us much about the core beliefs about teaching and learning in a classroom.

1. *Teaching for achievement/mastery*: This approach emphasizes *direct instruction;* it depends on closed and leading questions to assess whether the students know the "right" answers; that is, have they mastered the basic skills and information they have been fed? This perspective tends to privilege rote learning and reinforce what Dweck (2007) calls a *fixed mindset*.
2. *Teaching for understanding/learning*: Open-ended questions are used to trigger inquiry. In classrooms that emphasize process over final product, the concern is to develop the learners' deeper understanding of specific information as well as connections between that information and the conceptual frameworks and "big ideas" of a discipline.

What Problems Might Be Created by Teaching Reading with a Focus on Right Answers?

The way that Jenny registered the fact that for once Antoine had something to say but failed to understand how or why that had happened is consistent with the teaching-for-mastery training she received. Another incident involving Antoine and Jenny suggests the problems that come when the learner's instinct to make meaning is suppressed.

Several weeks before the *Yeh-Shen* storytelling, I had stopped by Jenny's classroom for a consultation during prep time. Antoine should have been in gym. Instead, he was sprawled across the desk, laboriously copying a letter that announced to his family that once again he had been "bad."

Jenny pointed to Antoine as a primary example of what she found discouraging. "This is the third time he's had to write the letter and I don't see any change. I don't know what to do with him. It's hopeless!"

Antoine seemed glum rather than hostile when Jenny agreed to let me talk with him. He readily admitted that he hadn't been doing his work.

When asked to read aloud the letter he was copying, Antoine stumbled through all the multisyllable words (*responsibility, disruption, misbehaving*). It was painfully clear that he was decoding but not making any sense of what he was reading or writing down.

When asked if he could tell me in his own words what the letter meant, Antoine looked blank until Jenny commanded, "Tell her why you are being punished!" Again he freely confessed that he had been playing around instead of doing a vocabulary comprehension activity called Stars. When asked if he thought playing around was being bad, he shrugged.

"I wonder if the Stars activity was hard for you?" I commented casually.

"Yeah, sort of," he muttered.

"Is there anything in reading that you are good at?" I wondered aloud.

Antoine brightened a bit and said, "I can sound out real good!"

He demonstrated with a few familiar words from the word wall. However, when I pointed to *opinion* he very slowly called out "up . . . in . . . yon." Despite the laborious and accurate decoding, he was unable to blend the syllables or recognize the word, even when I did the blending—though he did know what an *opinion* was once I said the word.

Jenny had to go pick up the rest of class. As I walked out with her, she shook her head. "You can see how poor Antoine's skills are—and no matter what I try, he plays around, instead of getting his work done—I've pretty much given up on him. I'm just going to concentrate on those kids who do want to learn."

Jenny clearly did not see Antoine's consistently inattentive behavior as a signal that he was as deeply frustrated as she was. The impasse between them comes down to her implicit belief that there was a fixed path to reading, and if you didn't or couldn't follow it, you didn't want to learn.

She was reflecting the *basic skills approach* that sees alphabet knowledge, phonics, and other decoding skills as building blocks that must be firmly cemented in place; once these skills have been drilled and mastered, readers can advance to establishing literal comprehension by giving correct answers about elements of a narrative such as sequence, identity of characters, and setting, or by providing vocabulary definitions. As children approach "fluency" in the mechanics of reading, the number of questions that call for inference increase, though the majority of them are phrased as closed or leading questions. It is always the teacher who "owns" both the questions and the answers.

In this approach, only accomplished readers are permitted to indulge in the intriguing kind of meaning-making that happens with leading or open-ended questions—conversations that are about genuine meaning making. By second or third grade, a typically performing child will have at least some regular opportunities to explore themes, motivation, or imagery or to make personal connections.

Poor readers like Antoine continue to be subjected to a disparate array of skill-based drills, sometimes all the way through elementary and even high school. This flies in the face of evidence from brain research that indicates many individuals are neurologically wired in ways that cripple their ability to learn to read using an isolated skills approach. They are never allowed to use the significant problem-solving skills that tend to accompany what Davis and Braun (2010) call the *Gift of Dyslexia* (see also Hart & Risley, 2003; Miller & Almon, 2009).

It is hardly surprising that Antoine regularly preferred the immediate gratification of joking with a friend to the humiliation of struggling with a task that has no interest and at which he's very likely to fail. As indicated in Chapter 2, his reaction comes down to biochemical forces. The repeated messages from Jenny leave Antoine feeling under attack and incompetent, setting off negative feelings fired by cortisol; his "fooling around" can be seen as an attempt to get at least a small taste of the pleasure-giving dopamines and endorphins (Sousa, 2009, Washburn, 2010).

Over time, the constant reinforcement of negative feelings associated with school means the disposition to learning is eroded. Children are battered into accepting Dweck's fixed mindset that labels them as "bad," beginning with being "bad at schoolwork." The tragedy is that Antoine and the legion of children like him will be dropouts, if not tomorrow's prison inmates.[3]

As Reyhner (2008) points out, the conflict between those who teach for achievement and those who teach for understanding has been raging for more than half a century.[4] However, the crisis has deepened in the decade since teaching for mastery became a national policy under the mandates of No Child Left Behind (NCLB). The federal *Reading First* program committed over $6 billion to literacy programs such as *Open Court* that emphasized direct instruction in basic skills. A study for the Institute of Education Sciences (IES) at the U.S. Department of Education showed that decoding skills did improve but that early mastery does not correlate with long-term student achievement. In fact, *Reading First* students failed to show improvement over children in other programs in terms of comprehension—acknowledged to be the most important of *Reading First*'s five goals.[5]

WHAT IS THE CONNECTION BETWEEN LEARNING TO READ AND LEARNING TO THINK?

Fortunately for the Antoines of the world, the Balanced Literacy approach has emerged as middle ground between those who teach for mastery and those who teach for understanding. It calls for a strategic approach to literacy instruction, using skills of decoding and comprehension as needed.

- On one hand, there is a need for explicit instruction to help emerging readers master the basic skills of using alphabet and phonic knowledge to decode, as well as developing vocabulary and using language arts conventions. A given skill may be targeted for mini-lessons using direct instruction; still, children are encouraged to develop a menu of approaches that they pick from strategically.
- On the other hand, comprehension is also understood to be a basic skill that should be developed from the earliest stages. Emerging readers need explicit guidance in how to discover the complex web of connections that give meaning to a text as well as many opportunities to struggle and to experience the feelings of competence that come once they have broken the code.
- The goal of instruction is to get children to the point where all of the discrete skills have been mastered sufficiently so that the reader can call on them strategically. Thus "good readers" are engaged in problem solving about the best mix of decoding and context clues that will allow them to understand a tricky passage.

What Kind of Connections Are Worth Thinking About?

The Public Education and Business Coalition (PEBC) in Denver has been especially influential in spelling out specific strategies that teachers can model and use to develop such comprehension skills. Keene and Zimmerman's (1987/2007) *Mosaic of Thought* was among the first to discuss intentionally using open-ended questions before, during, and after the reading. Routman (1999), as well as associates of PEBC, including Harvey and Goudvis (2000/2007), Miller (2002), and Buhrow and Garcia (2006), have provided further discussion of comprehension strategies, based on their own rich practices and reflections. In recent years, Boushey and Moser's (2006, 2009) Daily Five approach has become popular. While they do not ignore the role played by mechanical features of literacy such as decoding and spelling, all these experts see mastery over these skills as being in service to the essential heart of literacy: meaning-making.

Moreover, they recognize that meaning-making calls for engaging the learners/readers in significant problem solving in order to make connections between their own experience and prior knowledge and what is happening in the text or story. They speak of modeling and teaching young readers how to *activate schema,* that is, to become conscious of four different kinds of connections:

- *Text-to-self*—links between what is happening in the story and the reader's own experiences or emotions. When I tell a Cinderella story, especially in an inner-city school, both boys and girls will make comments about how they have felt the painful loss of a parent's protection; others talk about how it feels to be left out from a party or special event that everyone else is excited about.
- *Text-to-text*—comparisons between stories or texts that have similar plots, themes, or character types. Antoine's question about the material the slipper was made of is representative of how natural this kind of question is when children are exposed to variants of popular stories. At the same time, those who have a habit of inquiry find connections between stories that are quite unrelated on the literal level. Many stories offer evidence that it takes courage to persevere when others are being cruel or threatening, but that in the end, persistence and goodness are likely to prevail. Cinderellas have that kind of courage, as do many other fairy-tale heroes and heroines; but Charlotte and Wilbur in *Charlotte's Web* do also. In fact, there are many real-life people such as Martin Luther King and the child Ruby Bridges whose stories bring the same lesson to life. In effect, text-to-text connections can extend the text-to-self connections into an ever-widening web of meaning.
- *Text-to-world*—complex relationships between what is said or happens in the text and the reader's prior knowledge or understanding associated with a discipline. For example, Antoine's solution to the slipper problem indicates understanding of the relative properties of glass and of gold.
- *Text-to-graphics*—connections between the text and illustrations or the reader's visualizations. Read-alouds, oral storytelling, and texts without illustrations invite mental pictures and images that draw on personal experience as well as learned prior knowl-

edge. Antoine's reference to the rocky, twisted path clearly indicated that he was visualizing and that doing so was key to his problem solving. In Chapter 5, I look more closely at the importance of graphics in making meaning in picture books, including informational texts.

What's the Connection Between Literacy and Literary Understanding?

Generally speaking, *literacy development* is understood as a finite goal—once the level of proficiency known as fluency is reached, instruction in the mechanics of reading stops (though conventions of spelling, punctuation, and grammar may continue to be taught for writing). Beginning with middle and upper elementary classes and on through the highest academic levels, the emphasis tends to shift to understanding and expressing *literary* appreciation. As Antoine's experience shows, poor readers are often barred from engaging in this much more interesting discussion and meaning-making.

There is another complication that goes back to the tension between direct instruction and constructivist approaches to learning. As Sipe points out in *Storytime* (2007, pp. 36–81), there is a spectrum of beliefs as to what it means to be an expert reader in literary terms. At one end, there are those who believe that authors embed a "true" meaning in the text that the good readers will recognize by putting together what the literal level of the text says with what can be inferred. Such discussions rely heavily on leading questions, yet they do allow for some problem solving as readers follow different paths to the "right" answer. At the other extreme, structuralists argue that the author's intended meaning is of less importance than the reader's "construction/deconstruction" of personal understanding.[6]

Sipe (2007) argues for a middle ground: *a balanced approach to literary understanding*. Like Keene and Zimmerman (1987/ 2007), Harvey and Goudvis (2000/2007), and Miller (2002), he argues that good readers are constantly connecting the text to their own experience and prior knowledge—ultimately, the greatest reward of reading is finding important meaning in the books and stories we willingly consume.

Sipes's (2007) research shows that at all levels of literacy skills development readers can and should be encouraged to develop *literary understanding*. Even young children at the pre-emergent stage of literacy can make sense of the stories they read or have read to them. The more opportunities learners have to explore and discuss books and stories, the more motivated they are to "break the code" of basic skills. Conversely, the more children like Antoine are restricted to basic skills, the less likely they are to see reading and writing as anything but an onerous chore.

What's the Connection Between Classroom Climate and Thinking?

My interactions with Jenny's classroom came though my involvement with Erikson Institute's New Schools Project. I was one of several consultants investigating whether (a) increasing student engagement and (b) strengthening the classroom climate would have a positive impact on learning.[7]

For several years I focused on how engagement and climate might correlate with the distribution and the quality of classroom conversations. I collected data, using a modification of CLASS: Classroom Assessment Scoring System (Pianta, La Paro, & Hamre, 2007). The descriptors provided for "Instructional Support" were particularly useful in identifying what teachers and students were doing to enhance or to stifle concept development, quality of feedback, and language modeling. In effect, I was looking to see if the classroom climate was more likely to support a "growth" or a "fixed" mindset, as defined by Dweck (2007).

The data included what kinds of questions were asked (closed, leading, open); who asked and who answered questions; and the degree to which discussions were sustained with feedback loops. In classrooms like Jenny's results like the following were obtained:

- *Open-and-shut closed questions* about the literal level of plot and vocabulary predominated.
- The few *open-ended questions* used were phrased in very general or abstract terms that left the children confused. Rephrasing to clarify the question seldom took place.
- Little *wait time* was allowed for children to ponder or to formulate their thoughts. Most often, teachers labeled answers as "right" or "wrong" and moved on, in a kind of verbal ping-pong.
- There were few or no *feedback loops* that moved the interchange from teacher question/student answer to a sustained discussion involving several participants.
- Both questions and answers were almost always *controlled* or *owned* by the teacher.

However, in other classrooms (including one down the hall from Jenny's) where open-ended questions were common, children could support their answers, share questions and observations, and pose clarifying questions and comments. Instead of constant restless, disruptive behavior and classroom management problems, children and teachers alike in these well-functioning classrooms were interested in learning—and their overall achievement was higher. The conclusion is obvious: *The degree to which children show evidence of learning and of constructing understanding directly correlates to the degree to which children are engaged in thinking and authentic problem solving.*

WHY IS CRITICAL THINKING SO CRITICAL?

Any discussion of the relationship between learning, thinking, and child development must consider Bloom's *Taxonomy of Educational Objectives* (1956). It was issued just about the time that the Russian launching of Sputnik raised questions about the quality of American education; not only was there a strong push to improve science instruction, but there also was a move to be *more scientific about education*—as the very use of the word *taxonomy* might indicate. Just as life forms are classified from paramecia to primate—from the least to the most complex—Bloom identified six levels of thinking that he saw as having a hierarchical order. His descriptions follow the same trajectory Piaget (Piaget & Inholder, 2000) and Vygotsky (1978) first identified as characteristic of learning/meaning-making as the child grows to maturity. We begin with the *concrete*; from hands-on understanding we progress through the *pictorial* stage in which the understanding translates to processing mental images; eventually we are capable of highly *symbolic* and abstract concepts. As Bloom himself and many others since have noted, this trajectory fits nicely with the progression from *closed* through *leading* to truly *open-ended* questions.

But what about "Ontogeny recapitulates phylogeny"?—the phrase from high school biology that has always delighted me—does it hold true for thinking? Does every lofty thought develop in the same way: beginning from a concrete perception and slowly complicating itself into a highly abstract construct? If we consider the course of rich classroom conversations, the evidence is actually against such a locked hierarchy.

The etymology of the word *conversation* offers us a rich image of what is involved: the prefix *con* comes from the Latin for "with"; the root word is the Latin *versare*, meaning "to turn." So a good conversation is a kind of wandering as we *turn back and forth* with the thought expressed by one leading to a response that triggers yet another rejoinder.

And, as any good knight errant knows, wandering is not purposeless; it is an attempt to find a path that will lead us to our goal—for the knights, to do one good deed and then another and thus continually prove themselves; for the learners, to arrive at a deeper understanding of something and then something else again. In the *Mathematics in the City* project, Fosnot and her colleagues have replaced the traditional linear model of the learning trajectory with one they call the "landscape of learning" (Fosnot & Dolk, 2001).

> When we are moving across a landscape toward a horizon, the horizon seems clear. Yet we never actually reach it. New objects—new landmarks— come into view. So it is with learning. One question seemingly answered raises others. Children seem to resolve one struggle only to grapple with another. It helps to have horizons in mind when we plan activities, when we interact, question, and facilitate discussion. But horizons are not fixed points in the landscape; they are constantly shifting. (p. 18)

Suggesting that *Yeh-Shen* was a story cousin of one the children knew well set a horizon; Antoine's concern about the glass versus golden slipper led the discussion into a previously uncharted but very productive path—one that gave Antoine a rare experience of competence. Inviting this "usual suspect" student to wonder gave us all something to ponder at a quite high level of thinking.

Table 3.1 summarizes key characteristics of the landscape through which thinkers wander as they wonder. Bloom's six stages have been combined into three levels of inquiry;[8] developmental considerations about the movement from concrete to pictorial/ abstract/symbolic thinking are also indicated.

What's the Difference Between a Hierarchy and a Ladder?

Table 3.1 is not meant to represent a hierarchy—with the implication that authentic quality learning only takes place at the highest level. The problem with Level 1 inquiries arises when an assumption is made that (a) this level doesn't call for real thinking; (b) this level is as much as young children can handle; and (c) inquiries about hows, whys, and wherefores can only be permitted after proficiency at this level is established.

Rather the image of a ladder is meant to convey that good thinking and rich discussions range and move about in the same way that a builder moves up and down a ladder, fetching materials from below to put in place above. Quality intellectual work means that (a) there is no single path to a right answer and many problems have no single solution; (b) support for the highest order of thinking involves examples, clarifications, and connections that use evidence from Levels 2 and 1; and (c) for young

TABLE 3.1. Climbing The Ladder of Inquiry to Higher Learning

	Level of inquiry	Developmental Trajectory
3	*Evaluating/Synthesizing Inquiry:* explores fully open-ended questions	*Abstract, Symbolic*
	• Emphasis on why questions, questions that make text to self, text to text, text to world connections • No single right answer; in fact, responses are often varied and may lead to a new direction • A good response will be supported with examples, connections, etc. • Response involves discussion/conversation as the responder expresses, clarifies, and extends thinking • Calls for active listening and facilitating on questioner's part; questions may need to be rephrased or prompts given	• At all stages of development, this kind of inquiry tends to elicit high engagement and satisfaction, as the inquirer "owns" the discussion and is constructing understanding; such inquiry typically meets the criteria for quality intellectual work and may be seen in play. • The 5–7 shift marks the transition from early to mid-childhood, as children develop increasing ability to abstract and to reason. • Before and into the early part of this phase, children's evaluative statements tend to be based on a specific concrete factor. • Between 7–12, children's ability to generalize and enage in abstract thought goes through another significant development.
2	*Analyzing/Inferring Inquiry:* explores leading to open-ended questions	*Pictorial*
	• Emphasis on how, why, and some what questions, includes comparison/contrast, categorizing • No single right answer but a "good" answer may need to include a certain amount of information/facts in support • Response involves discussion/conversation as the responder expresses, clarifies, and extends thinking • Calls for active listening and facilitating on questioner's part— questions may need to be rephrased or prompts given	• At all stages of development, the ability to visualize, create images, and draw inferences is an intermediate stage between abstract and concrete thinking and understanding. • Young children still in the concrete stage of development are very capable of analyzing and applying; their explanations tend to reflect direct experience or literal details rather than concepts. • As they reach the end of the 5–7 shift, children are able to make more complex inferences about character, motivation, cause and effect, etc.
1	*Knowledge and Comprehension Inquiry:* tends to use closed questions	*Concrete*
	• Emphasis on what, where, when questions that can be answered by direct reference to the text. • At lowest level, open-&-shut closed questions call for yes/no or single word responses & are asked to test recall • Level 1 questions can be unlocked-closed questions that call for visualizing, recalling, describing, and sequencing. • Level 2 & 3 Inquiries require basic comprehension and knowledge as part of checking facts, building support for an idea, clarifying, and creating connections. • In a conversation/discussion, this level of inquiry calls for active listening and facilitating by rephrasing or offering prompts.	• Young children at the concrete developmental level need extensive opportunities to explain and "unpack" the literal level of meaning. • Novice learners at all stages of development need time to make sense of the concrete and pictorial levels as a foundation to strong conceptual understanding at the symbolic level. • Fully mature learners often move quite quickly from the concrete to the symbolic in their areas of expertise. At all stages of development, when open-&-shut closed questions are used exclusively or extensively, participants feel little ownership of the inquiry; learning can be inhibited by anxiety and negative disposition.

51

children and novice learners, it is essential to establish a strong understanding at the literal comprehension level; doing so can call for complex
thinking and problem solving.

What Kinds of Questions Move Us Up and Down the Ladder of Inquiry?

Three questions that we often addressed in my many years of classroom conversations about *Cinderella* stories might demonstrate how rich
literary conversations range up and down the ladder of inquiry.

Is This Story True? This question is often the first to be asked after a
powerful myth or a tale like *Cinderella*.

- Unquestionably, evaluating whether or not a story that has
  mythic dimensions is "true" is a Level 3 inquiry. It involves
  profoundly abstract considerations about the nature of truth,
  as well as about deeply held beliefs and values. Children—like
  Antoine—who find hope or resilience in the way a character
  responds to a challenging situation they identify with are especially concerned that this story be "true."
- The younger the child, or the more novice the learner, the more
  time it is likely to take for the Level 1 thinking. Well into the
  first grade, much of the discussion of folk and fairy tales is spent
  differentiating between those things that happened in the story
  that are or are not "true" in the sense that they "can"or "cannot" happen in our everyday world.[9]
- For novice learners at any stage, being able to visualize what
  happened or what is being described calls for Level 1 thinking/
  problem solving. Antoine, for example, arrived at his conclusions by visualizing what would happen to a glass slipper on
  a rocky path. He was asking a more complex Level 2 question
  when he demanded whether a "true" Cinderella could have
  something other than a glass slipper.
- With experience in literary discussions, the group can move
  rather quickly to text-to-self connections as they consider what
  might be "true" about the ways in which the characters in a story
  feel or the motives they have; often this discussion is at Level 2,
  as group members analyze and compare their own experiences
  with what happened in the story or with what a character felt.
- As children become more capable of abstract reasoning, they
  tend to move from seeing a Level 2 point of comparison to Level

3 probing of why bad things happen or people act as they do. Such text-to-self connections can be quite intense. They may move away from the story to generalizations about human nature or to deepening self-understanding.[10]

- Text- to-world connections also can come up in discussions of how elements or details in a story from another time or culture might reflect realities of that setting. When those points need clarification, the discussion might well be at Level 1 comprehension/information or Level 2 comparison. However, these discussions also can move up into Level 3; for example, considering the Cinderella figure as an abused child or exploring the source of her resilience are issues that are at the heart of human experience, whatever the historical or cultural context.

How Do We Know This Is a Story Cousin of Cinderella? Immediately after a telling of *Yeh-Shen, The Rough-Faced Girl* (Algonquin), *Mufaro's Beautiful Daughters* (African), *The Talking Eggs* (Cajun), or any other variant of the Cinderella story, there is an animated discussion of what elements of the story made the listeners realize that this was a "story cousin." Observations are recorded on a graphic organizer such as a Venn diagram or chart. This is a text-to-text discussion that fits solidly in the Level 2 Inquiry category, as it calls for comparison/contrast and analytical thinking. Students can support their answers with a wide variety of evidence:

- Younger children tend to rely heavily on Level 1 knowledge as evidence, saying such things as "Both stories have the mean stepsisters and stepmother" or "Both have slippers at the end but in *Cinderella* it's glass and in *Yeh-Shen* it's gold." However, even Level 1 evidence can have complexity; for example, children have noted that one group of stories follow the general outline of Disney's Cinderella; but there is another set of stories in which the Cinderella figure succeeds in a series of tests that the stepsister(s) fail, including *Mufaro's Beautiful Daughters, The Talking Eggs,* and *The Rough-Faced Girl.*
- As the children's ability to generalize increases, the evidence they give to explain similarities and differences moves to Level 2 as they analyze and consider character motivation and point of view.
- Very often, that discussion leads into Level 3, evaluating and synthesizing, as the children begin to explore themes or to explain why they think that the Cinderella(s) deserve to triumph at the end.

What Picture from the Story Comes Into Your Mind When You Shut Your Eyes? This strategy has proven to be a very effective open-ended question after finishing a powerful story, such as one of the Cinderellas. After a minute or so, I call on volunteers to share their mental pictures. On the board, I draw a "story line" with beginning, middle, and end, and we make a notation, indicating where each picture would fit.

- This is very much a Level 1 comprehension activity that exercises the children's ability to visualize and sequence. Some children will picture a tiny detail while others concentrate on a major event or character. Inevitably these pictures depict the entire story line. Furthermore, the sequencing can be deeply engaging and call for serious thinking and problem solving. Thus it's usually easy to say whether a picture shows something from the beginning, the middle, or the end; but children will debate fine-tuning whether a picture belongs right before or right after another.
- At the same time, the mental image reflects a significant text-to-self connection for each listener that can easily reflect Level 2 or 3 thinking. As teachers who adopt this strategy say, it guarantees that there will be no wrong answers: Every child's response is valid, has deep meaning for this child, and is richly unique.
- Furthermore, the conversations in which these images are shared often act as the seeds for a deeper level of discussion that quickly moves up into Level 2 or 3 inquiries as meaning is co-constructed through a conversation between the children, the teacher, and the text.

As we have seen, focusing on meaning is dynamic. However often a rich story is revisited, the conversation keeps on going, digging deeper or wandering into new territory. Good teachers guide these conversations so that the emphasis is on what happens in the children's minds and hearts, rather than on what happens in the story, while fully recognizing that *what happens in the children is mediated by what happens in the story*. The desired outcome is not a right answer but an answer that the learners have constructed as the result of a disciplined inquiry and that they can defend as making sense.

WHAT HAPPENS WHEN TEACHERS GIVE UP ABSOLUTE CONTROL OF QUESTIONS AND ANSWERS?

We might say that teachers like Jenny fail precisely because they are so focused on control and on the logistical business of their job. In contrast, teachers/learners with a growth mindset measure their success by how effectively they set into motion the gradual release of responsibility from teacher to learner(s).[11]

Imagine what engineers would call a fulcrum and children would term a seesaw. The teacher is perched at one end; the learners at the other. At first, everything is being done on the ground by the teacher—the learners, up in the air, observe. To use Barbara Rogoff's (2003) wonderful phrase, the learners are paying "keen attention" to exactly what it is that an expert reader/writer does. The teacher might be using a think-aloud to scaffold them, sharing a text-to-self connection she noticed between *Yeh-Shen* and how bad she felt about not being invited to a party as a child.

Gradually, the teacher invites the learners to share their own thoughts and connections. The balance of the seesaw begins to shift and move toward equilibrium as the children "pitch in" (Rogoff's phrase again). Increasingly the responsibility for the questions and the responses shifts to the learners, with the teacher acting as a facilitator or monitor. Eventually, it is the teacher who is in the air, keenly observing the learners doing their quality intellectual work—engaged in explorations that will result in discussions, products, or performances that have meaning beyond the classroom.

Just as those on the seesaw rejoice in the constant shift in the balance, so do engaged teachers and learners repeat the process again and again, as new strategies are introduced and new texts are encountered. As I show in Part II, the *Gradual Release of Responsibility* (GRR) model provides an effective structure for explicit instruction in skills and strategies within and across the disciplines.

However, well before Pearson and Gallagher (1983) formulated the GRR, there was a strong tradition of belief that effective learning and teaching follow this kind of trajectory. That same tradition does not see learning and teaching as limited to the classroom, but as something that goes on in homes and workplaces throughout a lifetime. The apprenticeship system that informed the development of craftsmen in the Middle Ages—and that Halpern (2008) argues should become a model for twenty-first-century secondary education—uses this trajectory.

How Might Guided Participation Be Seen as a Way of Releasing Responsibility?

In fact, it goes back even further. As Barbara Rogoff's studies illuminate, this model is at the heart of the teaching/learning dynamic that has gone on since work began. Rogoff (1991, 2001) uses the term *guided participation* in her sensitive analysis of what can happen with participation in a learning community. When Mayan women weave as they interact with their children tumbling about nearby, they are engaged in a learning/teaching dynamic related to what happens as middle-class parents join their children in building Legos, or as university professors involve graduate students in their research. The key elements are closely related to those we have been looking at as characteristic of quality intellectual work:

- Authentic work must be involved; the outcome must have value beyond skill development. More than that, the outcome must be a product, performance, or discussion that furthers one's needs and goals.
- Teacher and learner alike must be engaged; both have a stake in the learner's developing expertise.
- Teacher and learner alike explore through a guided inquiry: At the modeling stage, the expert does the work as the learner observes; slowly the learner joins in; the initial careful monitoring gradually diminishes until everyone is satisfied that the learner is capable of doing the work competently and independently.
- There must be a constant evaluation by both parties as to exactly where the learner is in the movement toward competency and what the next step should be. This evaluation is grounded in mutual respect and does not imply that the learner is deficient but rather is engaged in the process of becoming competent. Furthermore, in this model, even the greatest experts are in the process of getting better.

Why Should We Keep Questioning and Conversing?

In my 30 years of oral storytelling, I saw myself as a member of these classroom learning communities; the stories were tools the children and I used to carry on an extended conversation about topics and issues that we all found meaningful. We all were engaged in quality intellectual work; inevitably I went away with a new insight—often enough with one as striking as Antoine's.

However, in order for this important work to take place, adults and children must be regularly engaged in rich inquiries and conversations that emphasize good questions rather than right answers. If we want to keep the Antoines of the world in school and doing quality intellectual work, two things should happen when finishing a good story:

- Our first question should always be: What questions or thoughts do you have?
- Our first response must be to listen with keen attention and to converse about their thinking.

TRY AND APPLY

Journal on reflections to the following eloquent example of the teaching/learning dynamic as guided participation from *The Quilters: Women and Domestic Art: An Oral History* (Cooper & Allen, 1999).

I'm eighty-three and I've done a heap of quilts, girl. But I remember, like it was yesterday, my first quilt. Mama had one of them frames that swung over the bed and there was always a quilt in it. She quilted for the public, to help pay our way. Now, we might take one out late one night when it was finished and wait till mornin' to put the next one in. But that was as long as it ever was.

Mama was a beautiful quilter. She done the best work in the county. Everybody knew it. She never let nobody else touch her quilts; and sometimes when she was through quiltin' for the day on a job that she liked a lot herself, she would pin a cloth over the top of the quilt so nobody could look at it till she was done.

I always longed to work with her and I can tell you how plain I recall the day she said, "Sarah, you come quilt with me now if you want to."

I was too short to sit in a chair and reach it, so I got my needle and thread and stood beside her. I put that needle through and pulled it back up again, then down, and my stitches were about three inches long. Papa come in about that time, he stepped back and said, "Florence, that child is flat ruinin' your quilt."

Mama said, "She's doin' no kind of thing. She's quiltin' her first quilt."

He said, "Well, you're jest goin' to have to rip it all out tonight."

Mama smiled at me and said, "Them stitches is going to be in that quilt when it wears out."

All the time they was talkin' my stitches was gettin' shorter.

That was my first quilt. I have it to still look at sometimes. (pp. 52–53)

1. Think about ways in which the quilting Sarah and her mother might
   - Meet the criteria for authentic work?
   - Illustrate the gradual release of responsibility from modeled to shared to independent?
2. Read a version of the Cinderella tale or reflect on the story as you remember it; come up with 5–10 points that you wonder about. Don't limit yourself to what is in the text but feel free to go from trivial to profound. Review your questions to see where they might fall on the Ladder of Inquiry.
3. Choose one inquiry that you find especially compelling and find some people to discuss the question with you. Take time at the end to consider what kind of thinking went on during your conversation and how your understanding might have changed as a result of it.

CHAPTER 4

How Can We Play with *Abiyoyo*?

The SIP of Play and Quality Intellectual Work

The children in a first-grade classroom in a rough neighborhood on Chicago's South Side were unsettled. One boy was especially disruptive after witnessing a shooting that hospitalized his mother and baby sister. The teacher asked me to come in with a story that might help the classroom climate.

I decided to do an oral storytelling of *Abiyoyo* (Seeger, 1986) and follow up with literacy activities that might help the children sort out their feelings of fear, anger, and helplessness. In the story a young boy and his father get "ostracized" by the townspeople, who are fed up with the annoying noise the boy makes playing his ukulele and by the tricks the father does, making things disappear with his magic "zooping" stick. When the horrible monster Abiyoyo stomps in to destroy the town, the boy comes up with a plan that will save everyone. He uses his ukulele and sings a song that features the name of the monster. Abiyoyo is so pleased that he dances faster and faster as the boy increases the tempo of the song. In the end, the monster falls to the ground, allowing the father to "zoop" him away. The story ends with the townspeople welcoming back the two outcasts as heroes.

The children loved the story and spontaneously joined in the singing. No sooner had I finished than they wanted to hear it again. I suggested that they join me in acting it out. My policy is to say that everyone chooses the role they want—if we have 6 or 10 of one character and none for another, that's fine. I played a narrator role.

In the first round, virtually everyone chose to be the monster; 3 boys decided to be the boy and only one was willing to be the father with the zooping stick. No one wanted to be the townspeople, so I took that part. Even though the class had not done dramatizing before, even the fiercest Abiyoyos observed the rule of no touching, though facial expressions and gestures could be as nasty as possible.

The reenactment didn't take very long, so we regrouped and talked about how the acting out went. There was some unresolved discussion when I wondered aloud if the boy and his father deserved ostracizing and who should get the most credit for saving the town: the boy with the idea and the song or the father with the zooping stick? At that point, the boy playing the father reported it was fun to zoop everyone. Everyone was eager to do another performance; I reminded them they could change roles if they wanted. This time around, most wanted to be the father (the girls and I agreed this character could also be a mother), about 4 chose to be the boy (or girl), just one continued as the monster, and again no one bothered with the townspeople.

In the debriefing discussion this time, we talked a little about how Abiyoyo felt when he heard his name as a song and a little more about who was the most powerful in the story; while more children had thoughts, no hard and fast conclusions were reached.

We also talked about what they imagined the monster looked like since oral storytelling leaves those details to the mind's eye. That led to another follow-up I had suggested to Ms. Holly: Each child drew the nastiest monster they could imagine and then wrote a sentence describing at least one ugly detail.

When I returned two weeks later, all the children remembered the story in detail—one little girl earnestly explained what it meant to be ostracized. They were eager to do more acting out and I was curious about what the role distribution would be—this time, the majority were quick to chose to be the boy/girl; others were the father/mother; only one was willing to be the monster. When I laughed about being the townspeople by myself again, several girls quickly offered to help me.

By now, the children were using their own words, so the narrator became a minor role. In the wrap-up conversation, they also had much more to say about how the monster Abiyoyo might have felt bad since everyone was afraid of him, about how it was the boy who had the good idea, and about how the father's tricks were a little mean if they happened to you, even though he thought they were funny.

This Case in Point offers a counterpoint to that in the previous chapter. While Jenny had "allowed" me in, Ms. Holly had "invited" me and took notes as she observed how I was interacting with the children. Furthermore, when we debriefed, she asked for tips that would help her facilitate dramatization and writing activities in ways that engaged the children as deeply as they had been with *Abiyoyo*.

HOW CAN PLAYING WITH RICH STORIES IMPROVE WHAT HAPPENS IN THE CLASSROOM?

My advice to her was very similar to the points that Jenny had not been receptive to: begin with a carefully chosen rich story and guide the learners into constructing the meaning for themselves, rather than directing them to a predetermined interpretation.

Ms. Holly and I talked about how *Abiyoyo* addresses a central social-emotional issue for children—and adults: How can I defeat or at least escape from the destructive forces in my life?" This question is embedded beneath the surface allure of monsters and magic so that digging deeper into the meaning seems like play, not like a didactic lesson.

Nonetheless, the children were being engaged in a *literacy* lesson. Instead of being quizzed on comprehension, the children were invited to represent their understanding of the story by acting it out. In doing so, they gave strong evidence they had fully mastered Level 1 story elements including the list of characters, plot sequence, setting, and key vocabulary. At the same time, the repeated enactments and follow-up discussions became extended conversations—with one child making an observation, with another joining in or me asking for clarification or confirmation of what was said. And, as happens with good conversations, there was much moving up, down, and around the Ladder of Inquiry described in Chapter 3.

Asking the children to discuss and draw what a monster like Abiyoyo might look like was a way of *activating their schema* about monsters, to use the Balanced Literacy terminology. Since it gave ownership of the problem to the children, it also proved to be a very engaging Level 1 comprehension activity. Chatting quietly as they labored over their drawings and sentences, even the worst "troublemakers" were intent on how they might put themselves into the picture. Some of the girls designed quite hip female monsters, decked out with hairstyles and clothes they themselves admired; the boys did their best to make their creatures gory. Any number included some kind of weapon or force shield in their drawings.

Ms. Holly and I also discussed the importance of giving children time to construct their own deep level of understanding of the story instead of the usual practice of telling and then quizzing them about the moral of the story. While the pressure of meeting school and district requirements made it feel risky to "loose so much time" with one story, Ms. Holly could see that doing a literacy activity like this once a week or so could have significant payoffs. She had been struck by the absence of disruptive behavior during the activities as well as by the way the classroom atmosphere was much more settled afterward. Furthermore, the level of discussion throughout the activities as well as the sentences the children produced were of a noticeably higher quality than their usual work.

The higher quality of the work reflects the higher degree of engagement—which in turn owes much to the fact that they were exploring a rich story. Many young children combat their feelings of powerlessness by being drawn to monsters; these children's lives were much more embattled than normal so that most of them were initially eager to take on the role of Abiyoyo and to be the one whose destructive anger strikes fear into others instead of being afraid and hurt as the victim of that anger.

Wondering and wandering, the children moved back and forth from the literal level of descriptions to constructing text-to-self connections between the story and themselves. Between the acting out and the conversations, the children were processing and digging deeper. They became more aware of the differences in the way the boy, his father, and the monster were "bad." The boy's plink-plank-plunk noise might be annoying; having a chair zooped out from under one at the end of a tiring day might be funny for those watching but would be upsetting to experience as the victim; but there is no question that it would be terrifying to watch Abiyoyo thumping toward the town, gobbling down all large and small living things in its path. Eventually, they recognized that you can't really out-monster destructive forces; as for the zooping stick, it only works if the monster is already down, and monsters by definition aren't pushovers.

The fact that the majority elected to play the boy the third time around was good evidence that the children understood that it is the boy who finds a way to channel and regulate the very qualities that led to being ostracized. He is the one responsible for defeating the most undisciplined of monsters—and thus for changing the community's reaction from rejection to celebration of the two outcasts. In other words, the boy is the most powerful character in the story and therefore the most desirable to be. This is the moral of the story, of course, but because the children had constructed it for themselves, it had enormous staying power. When I checked back with her a month later, Ms. Holly was impressed with how the highly unsettled atmosphere had disappeared, that the children were still referencing the story, and she had even heard someone use the word *ostracize* during play.

WHY IS PLAY QUALITY INTELLECTUAL WORK?

The repeated reference to *play* throughout the discussion of *Abiyoyo* is deliberate. Just as good texts are the best tools for learning, the most effective strategies for facilitating the learning involve play.

Clearly, the kind of play I am referring to is not the idle fun or diverting amusement that is commonly associated with the term. I am talking about what Piaget and other major authorities on cognition and education mean when they say that "play is children's work" (Bruner, 1987, 1992; Hirsch-Pasek et al., 2009; Katz, 1998, 2010; Katz & Thomas, 2003; Paley, 1993, 2005: Piaget & Inhelder, 2000).

What's the SIP Principle?

In this perspective, the essential characteristics of play map precisely with those that define quality intellectual work. I've taken to calling this the SIP principle. SIP play and quality intellectual work/learning can be characterized as:

- Satisfying
- Intentional
- Problem solving

Satisfying: I've said that quality intellectual work must be engaging and result in work that is intrinsically rewarding, with feelings of competence and confidence high on the list of rewards. All of these elements are highly *satisfying*. In the same way, once a session of playing house, a daydream, or a chess game loses its intrinsic reward and stops being satisfying, it is no longer play; more often than not, the activity is abandoned at this point.

There is good reason to use words such as *satisfying* and *engaging; fun* isn't nearly strong enough to describe the outcome of good work and play. There may be smiles; but if you observe children—or adults—at play or doing work they love, the expressions on their faces and the intensity of their involvement make it clear that they are serious about what they are doing.

Intentional: This term is fast approaching buzzword status in education circles. It is meant to convey that lesson planning is a strategic process. Instead of blindly turning to the next page in the teacher's guide, intentional teachers begin by identifying specific learning goals and then looking for texts and activities that are appropriate and engaging for their particular classroom (Epstein, 2007; Miller, 2008; Mooney, 2004).

So, too, expert players are always intentional: constructing models, engaging in dramatic play, or playing games with rules all call for *strategic thinking*, that is, for deciding which option is most likely to lead to a satisfying result. At the same time, playing calls for negotiating skills as one tries to get others to go along with a proposed turn in the story line or game plan. When players no longer have any voice in calling the shots, as it were, they are likely to take their balls and stomp off.

Problem solving: Authentic quality learning takes place when the learner is engaged in *authentic* problem solving:

- *The problem has to be defined specifically,* in terms that are actionable, that is, in a way that several possible responses or solutions can be identified/ hypothesized about: The characters in the story have a problem—Abiyoyo is coming. Their choices are to run away or to try to defeat him—choices that correspond to the primitive flight-or-fight instinct.
- *A strategic choice* is made as to which option is the most promising to pursue, and a plan of action is developed. In *Abiyoyo*, the boy devises and carries out his plan to use music to make the monster fall to the ground so the father can use his zooping stick.
- After trying out *the chosen path*—including all the on-the-spot adjustments to difficulties that emerge—it is time to evaluate whether or not the solution reached is satisfactory.[1] With Abiyoyo zooped away, the townspeople accept the boy and his father back into their community.

The first step—really focusing in on a problem statement that is specific—highlights one of the most intriguing aspects of play: You have to know something before you can play. Thus you can't play a game without having a general sense of the rules; the more you play, the better you learn the rules; and once you really understand them, you can begin to develop strategies.

In the same way, the heart of play is all the strategizing and negotiating that goes into successful problem solving. For dedicated gamesters, the English schoolboy motto holds true: It doesn't matter whether you win or lose, it's how you play the game. The best games are those that call for increasing the ability to strategize, given the variables and constraints of the problem situation. Children building with blocks or playing house are engaged in posing problems and resolving them in ways that open new ones; they are experiencing the same intense engagement felt by a chess player evaluating the far-reaching consequences of his next move.

What Makes Play Such an Important Factor in Quality Work?

It's not just gamesters and young children who take their play seriously. Early childhood specialists see Piaget's statement as foundational: "Play is the answer to the question, How does anything new ever come about?" (Piaget, 1962, p. 32). For constructivists, play and work in early childhood are synonymous. Only when children are deeply engaged in exploring and evaluating discoveries in which they are invested will they show the persistence and make the connections that are characteristic of true learning (Brown &Vaughan, 2009; Elkind, 2007; Hirsch-Pasek et al., 2009; Miller & Almon, 2009).

The same kind of strong connection between play, creativity, and learning is made when Csikszentmihalyi (1997, 1998) talks about "flow" or Diane Ackerman (2000) defines "deep play."[2] These discussions of play as an adult activity might use the technical term *autotelic*—that is, to be totally absorbed in doing something for its own sake. What they are describing is the SIP of play.

For both young children and adults, while play draws on Level 1 knowledge, the act of playing calls for a complex network of Level 2 and 3 analysis and synthesis—of generalizing, connecting, and applying prior knowledge to resolve a new situation and then evaluating the result.

- The problem situation is open-ended; even in a game with rules, there may be a set way to win the game, but the exact mixture of skill and strategy that prevails changes each time.
- Adult artists, researchers, or chess players, like preschoolers absorbed in imaginative play, are constantly refining their ability to make and manipulate mental representations, particularly within the discipline of their expertise, be it engineering or pretending to be a superhero in action. In order to do this kind of mental gymnastics it is important for basic Level 1 information to be deeply imbedded in long-term memory so that it can be retrieved effortlessly and the focus stays on the higher-order thinking (Willingham, 2008/2009). In other words, engaging learners in inquiries and explorations that meet the SIP principle makes memorizing or "learning by heart" advantageous rather than a drill-and-kill experience.

How Does One Kind of Play Differ from Another?

As is true for thinking, there are a number of taxonomies for play. Variables include the nature of the activity, the participants (solitary or social) and the context, including cultural dimensions. Table 4.1 shows one widely accepted structure that distinguishes four different stages/types of play that follow a developmental trajectory.[3]

As effective as they can be for quality intellectual work, we will not consider the fourth category of play listed in the table, "Games with Rules." Instead this chapter will focus on intentionally playing with stories incorporating elements of functional, constructive, and dramatic play. As we saw with *Abiyoyo,* such play allows for social-emotional learning at the same time that it addresses learning within the disciplines. The strategies outlined below focus on developing skills related to language and literacy development in ways that call for wandering, wondering, making connections, and problem solving—that is, in ways that are much more efficacious than drills that kill the spirit of play.

WHAT IS THERE TO LEARN FROM DRAMATIC PLAY?

Arguably, the most tragic and troubling consequence of No Child Left Behind has been the heavy-handed suppression of free-flowing constructive and imaginative/dramatic play. Exiling blocks and housekeeping from early childhood classrooms means short-circuiting the children's capacity to move beyond the recognition of a problematic situation to turning it into a problem to be solved. The negative impact of that loss can have lifelong consequences for social-emotional as well as cognitive growth.[4]

Developmentally, it is not appropriate to strongly focus activities with younger children on the highly symbolic systems involved in reading and number operations. It is much more appropriate to assure that 3–6-year-olds develop a high degree of competence in playing around with language and with what it means to be a competent and confident social human being. Such a foundation means they will be well-grounded in the habits of mind and the essential life skills Galinsky (2010) identifies at the point when their capacity for generalizing and abstract thought is at a level that allows them to successfully take on the cognitive demands in the disciplines.

What Social-Emotional Learnings Come from Dramatic Play?

Playing house or office or pretending to be firemen or superheroes offers children a chance to *try out* what it means to successfully live as a "grown-up."[5] This exploration often involves an intense negotiation with important others about the characters and story lines the players will imaginatively establish. Because the social-emotional stakes are very

TABLE 4.1. Types of Play

Type	Characteristics and Examples
Functional or sensory play: Begins in infancy and constitutes the predominant play throughout earliest childhood. Continues through adulthood and may be a significant factor in helping concentration. Closely related to Concrete Understanding/ Level 1 thinking.	*Characterized by:* positive sensory stimulation, often with repetitive motions. Very young and young children do water and sand play, swing, cuddle, bang or drum on things etc; In adulthood, people doodle, fiddle or fidget, whistle, hum, play background music, and a wide variety of other self-soothing sensory activities, including smoking and gum chewing.
Constructive Play: Begins with toddlers, with preschoolers merges into dramatic play. Continues through adulthood. Closely related to Pictorial/ Schematic Understanding/ Level 2 thinking.	*Characterized by:* using materials to build or construct an object, including use of construction toys such as blocks, modeling with clay, drawing/painting, dressing up or making costumes or props, creating dioramas, making working models of machines or objects. In children: By 4 to 5 can use directions, follow a model or make a plan. In adulthood many hobbies and some professions fall into this category, including model building, woodworking, sewing/quilting, handcrafts.
Sociodramatic/Imaginative Play: Stage 1: Uses objects/set text Stage 2: Let's pretend Begins with preschoolers and is a central focus at least into middle childhood. Continues through adulthood. Closely Related to Symbolic Understanding/ Level 3 thinking	*Characterized by:* While actions and movements may be involved, this is primarily a mental activity, with significant social-emotional involvement. In children: Sometimes the child will use an object that is very reminiscent of another—e.g., a stick as a sword. In fully developed dramatic play the child is able to imagine everything—from the props to the situation that is being acted out; the story line may shift quickly. In adulthood is done as daydreaming, visualizing, reminiscing, or participation in simulation games and activities.
Games with Rules: Begins after onset of the 5–7 shift stage when child can generalize enough to understand rules and the concept of winning and losing. Can involve elements of the other three types of play.	*Characterized by:* May involve cognitive and kinesthetic dimensions. In all cases, a game has preset materials and may involve playing pieces; when the set goal has been reached, the game is over; may be solitary or involve two or more players. Play includes thinking, conversations, and negotiations around rules and strategies. Continues and takes on increasing importance through later childhood and adulthood. Most adults take this kind of play very seriously.

high, children are careful to *pretend*. The distance between something that is inescapably real and something that seems "as if" it is real becomes a safety zone. Children take comfort in the distinction between the truth of what they feel and the conscious make-believe of their role or actions.

In psychological terms, acting "as if" provides a way to acknowledge troubling and painful issues but to displace them into a situation or role that allows perspective and flexibility. Instead of despairing about one's ability to cope with a threatening condition in one's life, the player asks, "What could I do if a monster came?"—then freely imagines an answer. An important feature of sociodramatic play is that it is *not* governed by rules, nor does it involve winning/losing. If somehow it moves in a direction that is threatening or if the players are no longer satisfied, this episode of play is easily abandoned.

By the same token, the issues of identity at the heart of imaginative play are complex. Children will return to the same problem situation again and again, trying on different characters and solutions, sometimes mentally playing out possibilities in their own minds and other times interacting with different configurations of playmates. As Logue and Detour (2011) show "children's pretending to act aggressively is not the same as acting aggressively" and in fact such play can develop children's social skills and give them ways to show courage in the face of danger.

Imaginative play is also an important way for young children to engage in higher-order thinking while staying grounded in the concrete (Gopnik, 2009). As Dockett (2001, p. 38) points out, pretending is a complex activity—not only are children conscious that they are pretending, they also are adjusting their actions to accommodate the perspective of the others. Such perspectivism strengthens the social-emotional as well as cognitive rewards of play, and contributes to the older learner's ability to make inferences or find complex connections.

Rich stories allow the same kind of displacement and "as if" thinking found in imaginative play. As we saw with the children dramatizing *Abiyoyo*, a good story is worth returning to again and again. Sometimes, children will play with how they might put themselves into it directly, experimenting with how it feels to be Abiyoyo, or the father, or the boy. Other times, they play with how the story might be told differently, selecting out the characters or problem situations that hit closest to home.

What Makes Children's Own Stories Such Good Tools for Literacy Development?

Early in her career, McArthur Genius award winner Vivian Paley took on a serious study of the dramatic play going on in her early childhood pre-K and kindergarten classrooms. She quickly realized if she was to learn from it, her role was not to interfere or orchestrate the play but to keenly observe (to use Rogoff's lovely term) and to reflect. Her sensitive readings about the crucial role of dramatic play in social-emotional development are chronicled in her books, including *The Boy Who Would be a Helicopter* (1991) and *You Can't Say You Can't Play* (1993); after retiring, she crystallized her important discoveries in *A Child's Work: The Importance of Fantasy Play* (2005).

As her understanding of the important work children are engaged in as they play deepened, Paley began to find strategies that would support children's growth by giving them ways to think about and learn from their own stories. As part of her daily routine, Paley invited children to dictate their stories and then later to involve the whole classroom in acting the stories out. While there are ground rules about respecting oneself and others in the acting-out phase, Paley insists that there are no rules about what makes a "good story" other than the fact that it be the one the child wants or needs to tell. Language and grammar are recorded and read exactly as they are produced. (Paley's own books are the best source for understanding the dynamics of her form of story dictation and dramatization.) Patsy Cooper (1993, 2007, 2009) provides a systematic look at the logistics of implementing the strategy in classroom.

However, as Cooper (2007, 2009) continued to research what happens in classrooms that use Paley's methods, she established that this system of story dictation and dramatization has direct benefits for children's literacy and language development.[6] Children carefully monitor how the teacher takes the words they say and puts them on paper; later they see their words come to life as the text is acted out. Children who are not ready or who are struggling with decoding tasks know that they are doing what full-fledged readers and writers do. They are making meaning in a way that is satisfying, intentional, and replete with significant problem solving. The path to full literacy may call for some labor, but the intrinsic delights and rewards are likely to motivate even very challenged learners to persist.

WHAT ARE INTENTIONAL WAYS OF PLAYING WITH STORIES TO LEARN?

Settings that promote quality intellectual work use an array of strategies that intentionally structure and orchestrate learning in playful ways throughout early childhood. As the title of the excellent book by Van Hoorn, Nourot, Scales, and Alward (2006) indicates, play belongs at the "center of the curriculum," even in primary school. As children mature, they don't lose the need to play, including the need to do text-to-self dramatic play with stories. However, as they move into primary school classrooms and beyond, it is appropriate to increase the emphasis on cognitive growth and academic competence.

How Can Sensory Involvement in Play Enhance Word Study and Language Development?

Finger plays, action songs, and movement activities do much more than sugarcoat language and literacy development. Research by neuroscientists such as Hannaford (2005) and Sousa (2005) make it clear that effective learning involves complex coordination between the brain and the rest of the body. Music and movement and visual perception all have a strong positive impact on reading (Hansen et al., 2002, 2007).[7]

- Nursery rhymes, songs, rollicking read-alouds like Doctor Seuss—along with rhyming games and playful production of nonsense words and onomatopoeic sounds—are all linguistic forms of functional play and thus very effective ways to develop phonemic awareness. The increasing emphasis on such fun-for-the-tongue activities in early childhood settings reflects the significant role literally playing with the sounds of language has for language and literacy development.[8]
- Finding ways to include the sensory/kinesthetic component also has a value-added impact on Level 1 tasks such as developing word knowledge: we saw how first graders readily defined and continued to use and understand *ostracized* several weeks after they first heard the word. In a third-grade bilingual classroom, a discussion of *Abiyoyo* led to generating a list of vivid words to describe movement—with the extra challenge that the word should begin with *s*. As each word was recorded, the teacher or a child demonstrated the movement; later they played a game in which others tried to guess which term a child pantomimed. Effortlessly, *slink, stomp, slouch,* and *shuffle* entered into everyone's vocabulary.

These few examples show another kind of connection that is effective in building vocabulary. Lists of words in basal readers, phonics programs, and spellers are typically chosen because they all illustrate a targeted decoding skill (short vowels, blends, and so on). It makes more sense and makes the learning task easier to study new words whose meanings are related to one another or a topic in some authentic way. Again, the staying power increases when the children are actively involved in generating those lists and finding ways to represent the words.

At the same time, "translating" the verbal text to sound or movement offers a higher-level problem to solve that can give staying power to meaning. Van Hoorn et al. (2006), Bernstorf (2004), Spolin (1986), and Katz and Thomas (2003) provide a wealth of movement and music strategies that call for the full SIP of play across the curriculum.[9] One striking example can be found in research on the Chicago-based group *Reading in Motion,* which systematically incorporates music and movement into literacy instruction. At the end of 3 years, children involved in this program were three times as likely to be reading at grade level as the control group.[10]

How Can Constructive Play Promote Content Area Learning?

In our opening case study, before they drew Abiyoyo, the children conversed about images that came into their minds when they pictured a "monster." The descriptive words or phrases they suggested were recorded and left posted for reference later, when they would write a sentence to go with their pictures. Everyone agreed that *ugly* wasn't specific enough; with little prompting, the children came up with vivid descriptors: *fangs, red piggy eyes, tiger-sharp claws.*

The discussion that led to the drawings turned a fairly prescribed vocabulary/writing activity into a form of constructive play so engaging that even a child who usually spent his time agitating others worked intently for 15 minutes on his picture—in fact, he moved himself to an isolated desk so he wouldn't be distracted or tempted to distract others. Especially for those whose literacy skills are emerging, drawing in response to a story is an effective way to develop imaging/visualizing skills.

Similarly, having children make puppets or masks is one way to help them think about the personality or "character" of story characters. Making props for a dramatization or a story or putting together displays or dioramas engages them seriously in problem solving about the task, while pushing them to dig deeper into the meaning of the story. So, too, the children involved in building a strong house in Chapter 1 had a SIP experience: They had the satisfaction of successfully *solving the problem* that was set by being *intentional* about which materials they chose and how they put them together.

How Many Ways Can a Story Be Acted Out?

Teachers sometimes find taking part in school assemblies is anything but an SIP of play for them or for the children. Their reaction is justified—if it's the teacher who does all the work of selecting the text, assigning roles, figuring out the props, and monitoring the learning of lines. However, those who have had the children actively engaged in problem-solving all aspects of the production are likely to feel very differently—as are the children.

In fact, the field of creative dramatics offers a variety of effective ways to "play" with texts that develop children's literacy and literary skills as well as support learning across the curriculum. As the key resources for the field make clear, these strategies can be tailored for use at all levels, from early childhood into secondary education.[11]

While not all forms involve performance in front of an audience, it is always important to follow up creative dramatics activities with a reflective conversation; there is much food for thought as the group wanders and wonders in response to open-ended questions: What did you like about what happened? What did you notice about what others did? What might you do differently another time?

There are three major forms of creative dramatics that I discuss here.

Narrative pantomime. As the leader reads a text aloud, participants silently act out the text, relying on movement and body language.

This strategy is productive throughout early childhood, even into adulthood, as a small- or whole-group activity. After one round, allow time for debriefing as to what went well and what might be done differently—and why—and then repeat the activity. Repetitions can take place in the same session or over the course of several days. "Doing it again" should be very much seen as part of the fun; it gives everyone a chance to play with different representations of the action.

Learning dynamic. Participants develop listening and visualization skills as well as vocabulary as they exercise kinesthetic and linguistic intelligences. Because this technique literally brings the action to life, participants often develop a much stronger understanding of the passage than they can get from silent reading or listening.

- This can be especially advantageous for second language learners and those with expressive language issues, as it gives them an opportunity to literally translate back and forth between words and actions.

- This is an effective way to reinforce procedural skills. Introduce a procedure by having the students mime as you read a "how to" or instructions to an activity or game. To help students evaluate their own "how to" writing, ask them to see if a partner can successfully act out what they have written.

Tips and Tricks

- Initially you may want to select a short passage from a favorite read-aloud or from the reader and then build up to longer passages.
- To sharpen listening skills do not preview the passage but have participants try to immediately "translate" the words into actions.
- In debriefing discussion, highlight the different ways individuals found to use body language (facial expression, gestures, and so on) to show emotion or mood. Emphasize that there can be a variety of acceptable responses; however, stress accuracy to the text, especially in later repetitions. (For example, when the text says "hop," the motion should be different from "jump" or "skip.")

Enactment of a set text. After hearing or reading a story or an account of a historical event, the group acts it out as an improvisation; scripts and props aren't used, though the group does plan what they will do. The term *enactment* helps distinguish this strategy from a play or a performance; it is a technique to support meaning-making for the participants, not entertainment of an audience.

Children who are management problems, especially the class clown types, often excel in enactment—the positive reinforcement of the experience can help self-regulation as dramatizing *Abiyoyo* did for the first graders.

There are several ways to handle enactments in a large classroom of children for a story that involves a limited number of characters:

- A large group can be broken into several smaller ones; as each group presents, the others are the audience; the debriefing discussion is done for the whole group.
- Many years ago, I developed the system described for dramatizing *Abiyoyo*. The rule is that everyone gets to choose the role they want, even if that means a shy child asks to be part of the setting, such as the remote cabin to which the father and boy

are exiled. The multiple Abiyoyos or ukulele players act in parallel, with a firmly enforced ground rule of no touching. Leaving the children free to choose which character they want to "try out" means that everyone is free to construct their own representation of the character, to make personal connections that lead to increased understanding.

- *Learning Dynamic:* In addition to speaking and listening skills, enactment is a powerful way to develop high-level thinking and comprehension; it can be used at all levels, beginning before children are able to read and continuing through the school years.
- As they plan and improvise their own representations, children get deeply engaged with all levels of meaning of the text and making the full array of text-to-self/text/world connections.
- Suburban and inner-city third graders who had heard about Rosa Parks since pre-K ended up with a profoundly different understanding of segregation when they literally experienced what it felt like to be arbitrarily ordered to the back of bus –or to be the one to do the ordering or make the arrest.[12]

Tips and Tricks

- Introduce enactment techniques with brief familiar stories or situations or with stories taken from a textbook or read-aloud.
- The adult facilitator may need to play a significant role in orchestrating the first enactments. Thus the first round of *Abiyoyo* was done largely as a narrative pantomime; by the last one, the children were fully in charge.
- Focus on the activity, not on logistics such as choosing roles; it's usually enough to remind everyone that there will be another round.
- Be sure to build in time for debriefing. As the group discusses and evaluates the reenactment, looking for what was well done and what might be changed, they are coconstructing a much deeper understanding of the meaning, including all the text-to-self/text/world connections.
- With experience, the group can be broken into clusters; give each group planning time to consider how they want to represent the text. Sometimes all groups will work on a single story and compare interpretations. Other times each group may be given a different scene of the story or be challenged to do their part under some constraint—so one group pantomimes, another

does a musical version, a third is asked to create puppets. Clearly, meeting the challenge calls for problem solving and negotiation between group members.

- Having children do oral storytelling, using their own words and voice, is another form of enactment that is both engaging and highly productive, as Hamilton and Weiss's (2005) excellent handbook shows. MacDonald (2005) is just one good source of appropriate stories to use.

Reader's theater: Reader's theater is distinct from enactment in that typically it does involve rehearsals and performance and participants don't have lines to memorize, although they do need to read fluently from a script. Working in partners, small groups, and sometimes whole groups, children begin with a read-through of a script that is at their reading level; they continue to revisit the script, working to read it with expression as they present it to their peers or for an audience. Props remain minimal.[13]

- *Learning Dynamic:* Reader's theater develops fluency as a SIP. As partners or groups explore the tone of voice and pacing their characters would actually use, they are engaged in problem solving and meaning-making. When classmates or visitors burst into applause, the performers reap the intrinsic reward of a job well done.

Tips and Tricks

- While reader's theater scripts are widely available on the Internet, many teachers find that the students are more engaged and reap greater benefits by developing their own scripts.
- Writing and performing their own scripts helps make sense of the conventions of written English. Quotation marks become indicators of a change of speaker. Punctuation marks are helpful cues to guide whether the voice should rise or fall at the end of a sentence. So, too, writing the script brings out the difference between using a narrator and creating dialogue that conveys the action and emotions.
- Virtually any text can be presented as reader's theater; Katz and Thomas (2003) offer many rich possibilities for presenting poetry–whether recited by individuals, done as a choral reading, set to music, or accompanied by dance and movement. Other ways to use this modality can be found in Johnson (1998) and Karelitz (1993).

- Reader's theater productions are an excellent way to make assembly or parent night performances an integral part of the classroom learning. At this point, a few props or backdrops might be added, especially if their preparation adds to student learning. Alternatively, the performance might be produced as a radio play or as an audiobook.

HOW CAN PLAYING WITH A STORY TURN READERS INTO WRITERS?

The creative dramatic strategies outlined above involved constructions and enactments that got the children directly involved in playing with story elements such as characterization, setting, and plot, as well as with language. If this play has been rich, the children will be motivated to play with the story as storytellers and writers. The key to success goes back to what I told Ms. Holly: It comes down to a sense of ownership. Choose a rich story that the children are likely to care about; the more the story means to them, the harder they will work at telling it in their own way. If they know that their work will be celebrated, they are likely to make it a SIP—satisfying, intentional, problem-solving.

Innovations on Classic Tales

Many classrooms—including those in the *Stone Soup* project detailed in Chapter 1—find all kinds of learning gets triggered by looking at different versions of a single classic tale. Children readily analyze and compare multiple versions; with just a little guidance, they can classify the different tellings into those that follow the traditional story and those that "play" with the story in terms of:

1. *Character/characterization.* Sciezka's *The True Story of the Three Little Pigs by A. Wolf* (1996) is a wonderful but rather sophisticated example of how one's perception of a story can shift radically depending on point of view. In contrast, *The Three Little Wolves and the Big Bad Pig* (Trivizas, 1997) inverts our presumptions about the good guys/bad guys in the same story.
2. *Setting.* Emberley and Eglieski move the *Three Billy Goats Gruff* and the *Gingerbread Man* to the inner city; other classic tales change the setting from a generalized woods to anywhere from the American Southwest to Alaska or Hawaii.

3. *Mode of representation.* Almost all the classic tales have been turned into songs or rhymes; a few have been done as comics, or graphic novels. In other cases, characters from one tale show up in another, as in Fearnley's *Mr. Wolf and the Three Bears* (2002).

This kind of analysis tends to be so engaging that children themselves will suggest that they could do their own versions of the story. In some cases, everyone is free to choose which one or two of the elements they want to use for their story. Other times, they decide to see what happens if everyone agrees to come up with a new setting or a different mode; they then problem-solve what kind of changes that entails. So, too, depending on age and ability levels, the activity can be done individually, with partners, or by the whole group as a shared writing.

Other Innovation Strategies

Beginning with E. B. White's immortal *Charlotte's Web,* the last 60 years has seen a steady stream of gifted authors whose books address the social-emotional benefits and challenges we all face. Some are peopled by a variety of animals who express their love and imagination, who feel hurt, loss, anger, and fear, and who demonstrate empathy, courage, and joy as we humans do. Others feature children and adults, with settings that range from contemporary to long ago in history, and reflect anything from twenty-first-century America to lifestyles and beliefs from the full range of human cultures.

Preschool and kindergarten classrooms discover great things happen when children are invited to create a page for a classroom book, modeled after a read-aloud that was purposefully chosen to link with the curriculum. Many classrooms will give children cotton balls and glue to make a page showing the child's response to *It Looked Like Spilt Milk* (Shaw, 1993). To reinforce number sense, each child might draw and label a page based on *Ten Black Dots* (Crews, 1995) or *12 Ways to Get to 11* (Merriam, 1996). Or give a positive spin to David Shannon's *No, David* (1998) by having children draw and dictate text for a classroom rule book entitled *Yes, David.*

Collecting the pages together and adding a cover and title page is easy to do; the real payoff comes when the book goes into the classroom library or multiple copies are made to send home; the children have tangible proof that they are indeed readers and writers—and likely to remain so for a lifetime!

In primary school, children end up thinking deeply about character and plot when they are challenged to write a new ending for a story, or to recast a picture book or a chapter from *Charlotte's Web* or another chapter book as a diary entry. This activity takes on even more force when small groups share their work and discuss how their ideas were the same or different and then consider the insights they now have about what the story means.

WHAT STORIES ARE GOOD TO PLAY WITH IN A CLASSROOM LEARNING COMMUNITY?

This chapter has explored how playing with a story can lead to quality intellectual work. The focus has been activities that promote literacy/literary understanding. In Part II we will be looking at examples of ways to use high-quality picture and chapter books at the heart of discipline-specific lessons or curricula, including math, science, and social studies.

In all cases, what makes stories such good tools for play and quality intellectual work comes from the way they address the significant social-emotional dimension of learning. In earlier chapters we examined the importance of the learner's engagement and sense of ownership with the learning task; without a positive disposition, the brain's capacity to reason and learn is literally blocked.

The activities used with *Abiyoyo* allowed the children to play with social-emotional issues, but the explicit literacy focus of the tasks helped maintain appropriate boundaries. It is important to remember this caveat: Explicitly addressing individual issues related to uncontrolled aggression, bullying, abuse, loss of a significant figure in one's life, or sibling rivalry can quickly turn into therapy—possibly a kind of bibliotherapy—and is best handled by trained facilitators working with selected individuals rather than by a general classroom teacher.[14]

There is another equally challenging issue. As many of the teachers I have worked with are painfully aware, many classrooms have highly prescribed curricula, especially in literacy and math. Given that the selections from basal readers are fixed, the teacher's instructional decisions and intentionality must focus on choosing ways to introduce or extend the story so that the SIP principle gets acknowledged.

However, as Ms. Holly found with *Abiyoyo*, and other classrooms did with the *Three Little Pigs* and *Cinderella* tales, revisiting a thoughtfully chosen read-aloud over several days and with a variety of activities can have a strong impact. The trick is to make a point of *regularly* selecting interactive read-alouds that allow for addressing issues of classroom management and climate and supporting the learning community. These texts should be ones that

- Include elements that can open up an inquiry grounded in one of the disciplines—including literacy, math, social studies, and science.
- Have social-emotional significance that will engage the students and motivate them to explore and play with issues related to the responsibility humans have as social creatures to respect others, despite differences, and to behave in a way that protects everyone's emotional and physical safety.

Folk and fairy tales, as well as a wealth of contemporary children's literature, meet these criteria. Numerous examples are given throughout this book. Programs such as *Making Meaning* and *Being a Writer* from the Developmental Studies Center use carefully selected trade book read-alouds to systematically develop comprehension strategies and writing skills while developing social values and practices found in well-functioning classroom learning communities.

Ultimately, however, it is the responsibility of the individual teacher to establish well-defined goals, including social-emotional learning as well as those that address the "big ideas" of a discipline. Working from those goals and reflecting on the specific needs and interests of the children in this particular classroom learning community, the teacher then must take on the seriously playful task of choosing texts and activities that will lead to quality intellectual work.

TRY AND APPLY

1. Find a version of the classic children's stories or a high-quality contemporary work of children's literature that speaks to an issue currently relevant to your classroom community. Analyze how the work "plays" with story elements.
2. Go on to develop an activity/lesson or series of lessons that uses the SIP principle. Identify the specific type(s) of play involved in the activity (functional, constructive, dramatic). After implementing your plan, reflect on what evidence of learning came out of the play.

CHAPTER 5

What Makes a Good *Goldilocks?*

Assessing the Quality of Picture Books

In multisession professional development projects done with Hug-a-Book and with the StoryBus[1] we examine multiple versions of a single story such as the *Three Little Pigs, Goldilocks,* or *Cinderella* and discuss how even when the basic plot is the same, the wording and illustrations give each version a unique spin. The whole professional learning community gets engaged in a rich discussion of what makes a high-quality work of children's literature. To get some sense of the process, take a few minutes to look at one page from three different versions of Goldilocks shown in Figure 5.1 and mull over these questions:

- If you could choose only one version, which it would it be and why?
- How might each version invite or inhibit open-ended wondering and wandering about questions such as "What kind of child is Goldilocks?" or "What do you think about the bears?"
- How effectively does each use illustrations and features of print to support and extend the story as told by the text in a distinct way?
- What indications do the illustrations provide about the setting, including the historical time period?
- What details in the illustrations or feature of print convey humor, irony, or other indications that make it clear this is not meant to be a scary story?
- What do the gestures and facial expressions suggest about the characters?
- How are features of print used to create emphasis or meaning?

FIGURE 5.1a. Three *Goldilocks* Texts (Aylesworth, 2003).

"And someone's been sitting in my chair!"
said the mama bear in her medium-sized voice.

"And someone's been sitting in my chair!"
cried the baby bear in his wee, small voice.
"And they broke it all up!"

WHAT MAKES A TEXT A GOOD TOOL FOR LEARNING?

My carpenter brother Peter is fond of saying, "A poor workman blames his tools." He's right, of course. Yet he would be the first to declare that a true craftsman begins by carefully *selecting* the tools—looking for those that are well made and that are most suited to the job at hand. Only then can one go on to skillfully using them.

For anyone who consider stories to be among the most powerful tools for teaching/learning, this means being very mindful in selecting texts/stories.[2] Given the avalanche of juvenile texts available, it is important to establish clear criteria that will help us winnow out the very best.

FIGURE 5.1b. Three *Goldilocks* Text (Buehner, 2009).

Then Goldilocks looked over at the little wee chair for Little Wee Bear and grinned.

"But *that* chair looks like it's just right.
I'll jump me up an appetite!"

She climbed up on the little wee chair. She jumped, and the chair bounced. Goldilocks jumped and bounced, jumped and bounced until she jumped right through the seat of the little wee chair.

"Oopsy-daisy! What a mess!" She giggled. "Bounced a bit too much, I guess." But she hopped right up when she saw the three bowls of porridge on the table and started skipping rope again.

In early childhood classrooms (pre-K–third), texts often present themselves as picture books. The discussion that follows owes much to the important book-length studies of picture books done by Nodelman (1988, 2003), Jalongo (2004), and Sipe (2008). While this class of books is our primary focus, the considerations we are bringing to bear apply equally well to more complex text forms, including chapter books, collections, and informational works. However, before looking at the issue of quality, it is important to clarify the different ways texts can be structured.

FIGURE 5.1c. Three *Goldilocks* Texts (Ransom, 2005).

Then, Goldilocks sat in the smallest chair. It was just right. But she was too heavy, and the little chair broke!

Después, Ricitos de Oro se sentó en la silla más pequeña. Estaba perfecta. Pero ella era muy pesada ¡y la pequeña silla se rompió!

19

HOW DO TEXT STRUCTURES AND GENRE IMPACT READING FOR MEANING?

Even very young children who are familiar with books realize that you *can* tell a lot about a book by looking at its cover! The title and jacket illustrations and a quick flip through the pages provide many clues as to what kind of text is involved. A fairy tale that features pigs, wolves, or bears invites a very different set of expectations and questions than an informational picture book that looks at how any of these creatures lives in nature. We shift to yet another mindset when responding to a poetic text or to a chapter book.

So, too, as far as picture books are concerned, it is often problematic to distinguish between fiction and nonfiction. It is more meaningful to make a distinction between texts that have an informational structure and those that have a literary structure and then to subdivide each, using genre classifications.

What Are Informational Text Structures?

The accepted definition of literacy calls for reading and writing for a variety of purposes, including information and pleasure, with the implicit suggestion that information and pleasure are distinct categories. The fact is, many children and adults find that reading and writing about science or history or another "nonfiction" area is deeply meaningful and pleasurable. Indeed, some children find developing expertise about a topic such as dinosaurs, ancient Egypt, or recycling is more satisfying and creates a stronger sense of competence than talking about a fairy tale.

Thus Balanced Literacy programs and advocates have taken to pairing the term *informational texts* with nonfiction (Burns & Flowers, 1999; Duke & Kays, 1998; Jalongo, 2004). In fact, since 2001 the ALSC (Association for Library Service to Children) has issued the Robert F. Sibert Medal for distinguished books in this category. While the Sibert Medal excludes poetry and other traditional literature, it considers all other forms that use text and illustrations to present factual material.

At the same time NCTE (National Council of Teachers of English, 2011) annually gives out the Orbis Pictus Award for Outstanding Nonfiction for Children as a way of "promoting and recognizing excellence in the writing of nonfiction for children."[3]

Recent research identifies two populations for whom informational books are especially valuable tools.

- There is strong evidence that boys often prefer picture books that feature information over storybooks (Hall & Coles, 1997; Sullivan, 2009).
- English language learners also benefit from the way that informational texts emphasize specific, concrete vocabulary that can be linked to illustrations. New language learners often find it easier to develop and represent understanding about this kind of material than to make and express inferences about character or motivation in a story. Rojas (2006) gives a striking example of how a Spanish-speaking father and son found new ways to communicate with each other through a science project. Duron-

Flores and Maciel (2006) indicate ways to match English language learners' levels to developing science vocabulary; Celic (2009), Hartman (2002), and Buhrow and Garcia (2006) also indicate specific strategies.

How Can We Judge the Quality of the Information?

In an informative text the emphasis is on conveying accurate information and concepts about the natural world as well as aspects of social sciences.

- In high-quality informative texts information is detailed and accurate and is structured in an engaging way. The text has a clear flow, with transitions and examples or explanations that are at a developmentally appropriate level.
- At the other end of the spectrum, the information is highly generalized and may be inaccurate; the structure of the content can look random, with poor transitions from one point to the next; explanations and examples are missing or are done in a way that may be too complex or too simple-minded for the targeted audience.

As the ALSC definition indicates, a broad variety of text structures fall into the "informational book" category, and the quality within any of these genre varies just as widely.

- Using a *narrative* "story" structure is very typical of nonfiction genres such as biography and history; so, too, children's books about a region or culture may be built around the life of a representative child who may be an actual individual or may be a compilation that represents typical experiences. An increasing number of science picture books use a similar structure that uses a representative creature or a story framework to convey factual information.
- *Q & A formats* in which factual information is "chunked" around a series of questions has been a trademark of British publishers Usborne and Dorling-Kindersley. The structure is closely related to that used in field guides. Both formats are now often used for informational books issued by educational and trade publishers alike.
- *Concept books* such as alphabet and counting books or books about colors, shapes, and other basic concepts are another large category of informational texts for children.

What Are Literary Text Structures?

We tend to think of *fictional narratives* and *poetry* as the basic categories of literature; however, *personal essays* should also be included. Picture
books that combine illustrations and text to reflect on or present an idea
or experience that has strong social-emotional impact fit this category. *On
the Day You Were Born* by Debra Frasier (1991) has become a classic of this
form; it is one of many nonnarrative celebrations/musings on the parent/
child love.

However, by far the greatest numbers of literary texts in children's
literature are *stories*—that is, works with a *narrative structure* that puts emphasis on the interplay of characters, plot, and setting.

This structure applies across the many genres of children's literature,
each of which has its own set of conventions and expectations. By kindergarten, children who have regular exposure to stories bring what we
could call a *schema* or story map that mediates their response. Thus, while
they may not be able to name the genre as such, they know that different
kinds of stories "work" in different ways.

1. In a *fairy tale or fantasy*, things happen by magic. The magic
    might involve special powers, the granting of wishes with a flick
    of a wand, or some kind of transformation—but in any case, as
    much as we might wish or hope it was, magic is not a feature
    of our everyday world. While fairy tales like *Cinderella* are set
    in "once upon a time," fantasy worlds like Narnia may have
    decidedly otherworldly features.
2. *Myths and legends*, including pourquoi and trickster tales, often
    include magic, but these stories are specifically about how
    features of our world and universe or of animal characteristics
    came to be as they are. Very often these stories are rooted in
    cultural beliefs.
3. We can also distinguish another category of *childhood classic tales*
    that are set very much in the "once upon a time." In this group,
    there is no magic, although things are not as they are in the
    world around us. For example, animals may talk, interact with,
    threaten, or aid humans, as they do in *Goldilocks* or the *Three Little
    Pigs*, the African-American Brer Fox tales, or in animal fables.
4. *Realistic fiction with animal characters* is yet another class of stories,
    the animal characters operate in settings that look very much
    like the world around us; these mice, squirrels, rabbits, and
    other critters confront issues with parents, siblings, and friends
    that are remarkably similar to those a young child confronts on

a daily basis. Rosemary Wells and Kevin Henkes are two masters of this genre.

5. Of course, a huge number of narrative texts fall into the category of *realistic fiction*. They feature ordinary, human girls, boys, and adults meeting and resolving the large and small challenges life deals out. These may be set in the contemporary world; when placed in the past, the work is often called *historical fiction*.

WHAT MAKES A TEXT INVITE QUALITY INTELLECTUAL WORK?

Whatever the structure or genre, three dimensions need to be considered when evaluating how likely a text is to promote quality intellectual work:

- Literary quality
- Equity
- Developmental appropriateness

Many of the examples in this discussion will reference the *Goldilocks* story. However, the criteria themselves apply to a wide range of texts. The very best and the worst books fall cleanly to one end of the spectrum or the other on all the dimensions. However, the majority of texts will show a more varied profile. Ultimately, the decision as to whether or not to use a particular work in a classroom will take into account the quality profile along with considerations such as availability and the potential it has for connecting to what is currently happening in the classroom learning community. Table 5.1 lists elements of the quality profile for "Best," "Good," and "Worst" books on the spectrum.

What Defines Literary Quality?

As we indicated in the previous chapter, it is not necessary to reach an expert level in *literacy* skills before engaging in the meaningful exploration of the *literary* qualities of texts. Sipe (2007) collected extensive data of kindergarten and primary classroom discussions of picture books; his analysis shows the complex meaning-making children are engaged in involves simultaneously

- Mining all that is between the covers of the book—from structure to language and expression to illustrations and other features of print.

TABLE 5.1. Elements of the Quality Profile Across the Spectrum

Element	"Best" (Read again and again and again)	"Good" (Definitely worth reading again)	"Worst" (Not worth reading again–or ever)
Text: story line and characters	Characters are well developed and appealing; the story line invites prediction but also allows for variation. (The illustrations add to this element in picture books.)	Characters are presented in a way that may have some appeal; story line is predictable.	Characters are wooden or generic; story line is contrived, very predictable, and/or obviously didactic.
Text: problem / theme	Theme and story line pose problems that are engaging and compelling in terms of human experience and are resolved in a genuine way that invites reflective thinking and responses. There is plenty of material for the conversation to range up and down the Ladder of Inquiry.	Theme and problem situation touch upon issues that are important to young children, but in themselves do not really open up questions or conversations that will go up and down the Ladder of Inquiry..	Theme and story line offer a superficial problem or may make a real-life issue seem trivial, driven by didactic point, or oversimplified. The resolution is also contrived and trivial; it does not result from the characters' motivation or behavior, or show anyone really thinking about the problem. It does not acknowledge that solutions may be complex.
Text: language	The language and expression of the text is of high quality, with strong imagery, vivid word choice, and pleasing rhythm; it enhances literacy skills such as responding to imagery, language development, and phonemic awareness. Language is a joy to read aloud and invites joining in.	Language is acceptable; does not have high "fun for the tongue" appeal; tends to lack strong imagery.	Language of the text has no strong appeal and little to no imagery; language may be choppy, sing-song, formulaic, or use clichés.
Illustrations	The illustrations and other graphic features show an individual style and are appealing, and enhance the meaning of the text. Cf. Nodelman: the best picture books have 3 stories: "the one told by the words, the one implied by the pictures, and the one that results from the combination of the other two."	Illustrations and graphics are acceptable but lack a distinctive appeal; there may be some interplay between the text and illustrations in terms of meaning making, but it is minimal.	Illustrations are very conventional, without distinction, and may depend heavily on animated (TV) conventions or stereotypes.
Socio-emotional/ cultural/ diversity sensitivity	The text offers a productive way to explore feelings and social interactions with family, friends, and community, including afflictive feelings. It conveys respect for self and others, celebrates diversity, and may explicitly convey that sameness and difference are positive features of our lives.	The book offers some acknowledgment of human emotions and diversity, but does not offer rich material to explore these issues.	The book gives a superficial or stereotyped approach to explore feelings and interactions. It offers a simplistic, moralizing, right/wrong approach to social-emotional issues or questions of diversity.

- Connecting what they find to their own experiences—with other books, with their lives, as well as to other things they know.
- It follows that texts that are best suited to act as tools for quality intellectual work must offer rich resources to mine. They must be of high literary quality—a dimension that is in itself multidimensional.

1. Basic narrative elements. These include plot, characterization, point of view, setting, and theme. As we have seen, both informational and literary structured texts very often are narratives. Whatever the structure, high-quality narratives have:

- *Plot/story lines* that unfold in an interesting manner and pose problems that are engaging/compelling in terms of human experience and that are resolved in a genuine way that invites reflective thinking and meaningful connections with one's own thoughts and experiences.
- *Well-defined characters* whose words, thoughts, and actions suggest personalities and motivation.
- Other elements such as point of view and setting are developed in ways that enrich meaning. First person, third person persona, or multiple points of view may be used to create irony or support insights into theme or character.
- *Themes* that emerge from these elements are rich and invite reflection and make connections to individuals' experiences and understanding.

2. Language and expression. It doesn't matter if a text is literary or informative, narrative, reflective, or poetic; high-quality language and expression employ the following:

- *Vivid, robust vocabulary* and compelling images that evoke sensory impressions of how things look, sound, smell, and feel, often triggering emotions and association from personal experiences.
- Effective expression that uses language features such as *rhythm, rhyme, repetition,* and *varied sentence structures* to convey meaning and create emphasis. High-quality texts echo the sounds of speech or the music of language.

These features play an essential role in moving the words off the paper into our hearts and minds. They invite the reader to engage in higher order thinking skills such as inference and making connections; the tone and voice reflect the targeted purpose and audience for the text.

At the same time, rhyme, alliteration, and rhythm are so much fun-for-the-tongue that texts with these language features easily become engaging opportunities for developing literacy skills such as phonemic awareness and word study.

3. Illustrations and graphics. Perry Nodelman's *Words About Pictures* (1990) literally opened the eyes of many to the tremendous impact illustrations can have on the meaning-making process in picture books.[4] In their discussions of what makes a high-quality picture book, Jalongo (2004) and Sipe (2007) concur with Nodelman's statement that picture books have three stories: "the one told by the words, the one implied by the pictures, and the one that results from the combination of the other two" (Nodelman & Reimer, 2002, p. 295).

That combined meaning has the most resonance when the illustrations and graphics meet the following criteria for high quality:

- The illustrations and other graphic features show an *individual style,* and are *appealing.* At the highest level, the illustrations have aesthetic merit as art work.
- Whatever the style, the illustrations and graphics should enhance *the meaning of the text and contribute to tone and mood.*
- *Features of print* such as arrangement of text on the page, varying fonts, font sizes, and using boldface all contribute to creating emphasis and meaning. These text effects can contribute to emerging literacy development by reinforcing phonemic awareness and repetitive language structures as well as by supporting book-handling skills.

What Does Literary Quality Look Like in Informational Texts?

In keeping with the focus on *Goldilocks,* we can use two informational picture books about bears in nature as examples of high literary quality.

Structure and language in informational texts: Jonathan London's *Honey Paw and Lightfoot* (1998) follows a mother bear and her cub through their first year in the Western wilderness. Although the two are given names, everything we are told about these creatures conforms to what wild bears do so that the book is much more accurately classified as informational than as fiction. The naturalist Jim Arnosky uses a similar structure in his picture book, *Every Autumn Comes the Bear* (1996). Both books effectively convey accurate information about the life cycle, habits, and behaviors of wild bears by creating a vivid sense of a single representative mother and cub in their natural setting.

So, too, in these high-quality informational texts, it is also easy to find passages that could be used in a minilesson on phonics or as a model for a writer's workshop exploration of vivid language. Notice how delightfully just one sentence from London's *Honey Paw and Lightfoot* plays with the /s/ and /sh/ sounds: "*Swoosh*, Honey Paw and Lightfoot plunged down the slopes, skidding to a stop in a shower of slush."

Graphics in informational texts: Graphics play a crucial role in informational texts. Studying naturalistic illustrations, photos, and diagrams can literally allow the reader to "see" what the written text is trying to convey; graphics can be essential for understanding a process or forming a mental picture of an unfamiliar creature or object.

In the two bear books, the illustrations in London's version are more naturalistic than in Arnosky, whose watercolors have an impressionistic feel, but both help us literally see how wild bears look and act. The photos, highly naturalistic illustrations, and chunked text, labels, and captions in Seymour Simon's *Wild Bears* and *Amazing Bears: Eyewitness Junior* issued by Dorling Kindersley provided an easy-read Q & A format book that many children were able to use on their own.

Features of print, including graphic organizers: Charts, tables, and Venn diagrams literally draw out the difference between "big ideas" and supporting information; so, too, they visually organize comparisons and contrasts. At the same time, other features including labels, captions, and highlighted terms draw attention to key terminology.

Again, as Opitz and Guccione (2009), Buhrow and Garcia (2006), and Rea and Mercuri (2006) point out, such graphic features are particularly significant aides for second language learners. Explicit instruction in how all of these features provide clues to meaning is important. Even so, whether or not one knows the English for terms like *snout, claws, fur, rearing up on two legs*, or *lumbering around on four legs*, a few photos is all it takes to have a good sense of what a bear looks like and how it moves. Representing that understanding by doing a drawing is just as valid as passing a vocabulary test.

WHAT ROLE DOES EQUITY PLAY IN CHOOSING BOOKS?

We have already indicated how illustrations and graphic features can be effective tools to ensure equity for the children of color, including the many whose first language is not English. Using Spanish or other language versions of a text is one way to assure that children can focus on making meaning of the story instead of struggling to understand the meaning of words in another language. In the many cases in which the other language version is not available, doing a "picture walk" before and then again after reading can be an effective way to preview and then review a text (Barone & Xu, 2007). The emphasis should be on meaning rather than details of vocabulary. For example, a Spanish-speaking pre-schooler showed she had a clear sense of the important meaning when she said the bears were eating *sopa* instead of *porridge* and that Papa's was hot because he had dosed it with chili sauce.

However, differentiating between linguistic and conceptual challenges is just one aspect of equity. If we are to support children in becoming responsible citizens of the world, we must be as exacting about the quality of the attitudes that a text promotes as we are about its language and structure.

- High-quality texts convey respect for self and others and celebrate sameness and difference as positive and productive, including diversity that reflects cultural, ethnic, or gender differences.
- Poor-quality works ignore or misrepresent information about other cultures or groups; implicitly or explicitly they may promote one culture over others or use stereotypes.

There is another possible way to look at equity in *Goldilocks*. From Southey's original version in 1837, there's an inherent irony in this story: The bears, if anyone, must be considered the ones outside the mainstream culture; one could even say they are characters of color. However, they are the ones who insist on "civilized" behavior and whose glaring presence wakes Goldilocks up, as it were, to the consequences of her willful, childish actions.

This last point suggests another important issue of equity. It was the late 1980s before persons of color began to be seen on a regular basis in children's trade books. Even decades later, Flournoy's *The Patchwork Quilt*, which was published in 1985, remains one of the relatively few picture books that show a solid, two-parent, mainstream American family of color. Most often, what is depicted reflects demographic and historical stereotyping—American Indians in headdresses and breechcloths, African Americans escaping slavery, or contemporary poor children of color valiantly overcoming obstacles posed by their impoverished homeland or their poor urban settings, more often than not through their talent for sports or music.

As Mendoza and Reese (2001) point out, it is not enough to sprinkle in references to persons of color, those from other cultures, or those with disabilities; rather, we need to be satisfied that the texts used in our learning communities will bear scrutiny when examined in the light of such questions as:

- Are characters "outside the mainstream culture" depicted as individuals or as caricatures?
- Does their representation include significant specific cultural information? Or does it follow stereotypes?
- Who has the power in this story? What is the nature of their power, and how do they use it?
- Who has wisdom? What is the nature of their wisdom, and how do they use it?

The inequity goes both ways—neither Whites nor children of color are likely to see evidence in books that poverty does not equate with race and that standing up for what you believe in, being empathic and caring, and learning to regulate your behavior goes across all demographic and cultural lines.

Goldilocks is an interesting story to consider in terms of equity. Even in recent years, very few versions portray Goldilocks as a person of color. *Leola and the Honeybears* by Melodye Rosales is one exception. However, the text makes it very clear that little Leola is deliberately ignoring the rules about proper behavior her grandmother has drilled into her. She, like all the traditional blonde and blue-eyed Goldilocks, clearly comes from a background with solid values and clear expectations about what it means to be well brought up.[5] In an interesting way, judgments as to what kind of child Goldilocks is and how she behaves are likely to shift radically if she is shown as a poor, possibly homeless, child—then her behavior makes perfect sense.

Equity would be well served if there were, on one hand, more stories about underclass Whites and, on the other, a significant increase in stories showing middle or professional class African American, Hispanic, Asian, and Muslim people. These works also need to show the full range of family structures, without either stereotyping or being didactic about possible gender roles. In all cases, the higher the literary quality, the more likely these texts can help *all* children construct meaning that will connect to their lives and expand their understanding.

It may well be that the outpouring of stories featuring animal characters acting as ordinary contemporary humans in the more recent decades may be a response to this need. From the wonderful tales spun by Rosemary Wells, Kevin Henkes, and Mo Willems to TV animation characters such as *Arthur*, more and more picture books show a rainbow of rodents and mammals going to school together, struggling with adverse emotions such as anger and sorrow, and discovering ways to show and receive the benefits of friendship and belonging.

IS HIGH QUALITY THE SAME AS DEVELOPMENTALLY APPROPRIATE?

Teasing out what makes a book high quality is very different from saying that a given book will appeal to everyone or that it can be used productively from early to late childhood. As a general rule of thumb, the following points should be considered when deciding if a particular text is likely to be a good tool for learning.

- Literary and informational texts with plots, concepts, and characterization that rely heavily on prior knowledge, cause-and-effect logic, inferential thinking, or complex motivation are wonderful tools for use in elementary school. However, these characteristics strongly limit their appeal and usefulness with younger children.
- Pre-K children often cannot sit through text-heavy books, however wonderful the language. This is especially true for large-group settings. If the illustrations are effective and if the story is not too complex or is familiar, it may be possible to do a fast-forward paraphrase of the text.

Perhaps no group of tales illustrates these rules better than the "classic tales" genre to which *Goldilocks* belongs. Three- and four-year-olds, for example, take the problems faced by Goldilocks quite literally. They are not particularly troubled by the fact that humans and bears are leading very similar lifestyles, including their family structure, homes, clothing, and food.

However, between the ages of 5 and 7 young children's ability to generalize and to abstract develops significantly. Not only can they distinguish between fantasy and reality, they also begin to understand irony, to recognize others' point of view, and appreciate jokes. Thus, while preschoolers are likely to be confused, primary-age children find versions such as *Goldilocks Returns* or Margaret Wiley's portrayal of the bears' home as a real lair amusing—and they can apply the point it suggests about perspectivism to their own lives.[6]

WHAT DISTINGUISHES ONE GOLDILOCKS FROM ANOTHER?

As I have shown, the literary quality of a text is not tied to a single element such as language, illustrations, or character and plot. It lies in the interplay between them. When there are multiple versions of a story, or several stories that are related in some way, exploring the text-to-text connections can deepen the meaning-making. However, the effect is the greatest when the texts have solid literary quality.

The *Goldilocks* story is an excellent case in point. For close to 200 years, this tale has been a staple text for young children. In the countless editions that have been published, only a few alter the basic plot structure. In each, however, the language and the graphics do affect our understanding of other narrative elements such as point of view and setting. However, these elements have even more of an effect on characterization and theme. Specifically, they offer different takes on the question that I would venture is at the heart of young children's fascination with this story: "What kind of person is Goldilocks?" For a child beginning to emerge from early childhood, that question is indistinguishable from "What can I learn from her story about the kind of child I want to be?"

What Kind of Child Is Goldilocks?

Keep this question in mind as you look again at the three versions of *Goldilocks* given in Figure 5.1. Even a single page is enough to show that the language and illustrations for each create a different take on the nature of Goldilocks's character and whether she offers a model one can identify with, want to emulate, or decide to see as an example of how not to be.

In Figure 5.1a, the Aylesworth telling, illustrated by Barbara McClintock, shows the bears as a proper Victorian family living, as Goldilocks does, in a well-appointed house. His text uses the narrative voice of an oral storyteller to make sure we realize that the human child Goldilocks is not nearly so civilized as the owners of the house she invades. Repeatedly he lets us know that her curiosity is so strong that it overrides her doing what she has been instructed is expected of a well-behaved child. This version is one that uses a change in font size to call out the difference in each of the bears's voices.

In contrast, in Figure 5.1b, the Buehners' author/illustrator team shows Goldilocks as a thoroughly modern member of the "me" generation, complete with a sense of entitlement; she's a borderline ADHD jump-roper who sings a little rhyme as she wantonly destroys Baby Bear's belongings. Several primary classes found parallels between Buehner's *Goldilocks* and other beloved classics of childish misbehavior: *The Cat in the*

Hat by Dr. Seuss and Sendak's *Where the Wild Things Are*. These stories and their characters allowed the children to probe the importance of respecting others and their property, as well as of thinking before acting, without having to point any fingers at themselves.

In Figure 5.1c, Ransom's bilingual version presents the story straightforwardly. The clear, rhythmic prose calls out the verbal repetition that compliments the strong pattern of the plot[7]—with the booming "Too . . . something" for Papa Bear, a mild "Too . . . something the opposite" for Mama, and a squeaky "just right" for Baby Bear. The illustrations are fairly commonplace, but we can see from the expression on Goldilocks's face that this little girl had no intention of breaking the chair; she sat down because she thought of it as "just right" for her.

What Happens When You Take the Wonder Out of *Goldilocks?*

As powerful as the Goldilocks story is, it is possible to kill it. That is pretty much what happens with *Super Why: Goldilocks and the Three Bears* (2009). This book is an offering of the *All Aboard Reading* series, showcased on a PBS Kids television series that features four SuperReader characters and two brothers, Whyatt and Jack. Like *Dora the Explorer* and *Blue's Clues*, these cartoons claim to develop young children's problem-solving and literacy skills. Unfortunately, they give a distorted picture of the meaning-making process that engages lifelong learners and readers.

The tie-in with television may build in some appeal for fans, but the plot is very difficult to follow for anyone unfamiliar with the shows. In this case, the Goldilocks story isn't even alluded to until halfway through; the main plot tries to get Whyatt to clean up after himself. All in all, the characters are one-dimensional; the didactic tone is so labored that it smothers any invitation to think in terms of themes or deeper meaning. The illustrations are cookie-cutter animation with poor picture-text match. The language is stilted, and between rebuses, boldface, and shifting font size, the print is hard to follow.

How Can Questions Open New Ways to Play with a Story Like *Goldilocks?*

Perhaps the greatest weakness of the Super Why version is that it fails to offer a SIP: in fact, this version is not satisfying precisely because it doesn't create any opportunities for intentional problem solving, since the problems and questions that it poses are completely closed.

It also doesn't offer an opportunity to genuinely play with the meaning. When Nodelman talks about the three stories that coexist in high-quality picture books, he makes it clear that the first two—the story told by the words and the one implied by the pictures—are there in the book. However, the third one is the *work*—or we might say, the *play*—of reader/ listener. Inevitably the way anyone combines those first elements depends on the prior experiences and the kinds of concerns or questions that individual is bringing to the task.

The enduring power of a story like *Goldilocks* comes from the way it embeds a Level 3 open question. Just as *Abiyoyo* gave Ms. Holly's classroom a way to play with the threat of monsters, *Goldilocks* can be seen as an exploration of the advantages and disadvantages of growing up. She, like the children most fascinated by her, is just emerging from early childhood. On one hand, getting older means greater independence: She can go off by herself; she can decide what she will eat and what she regards as comfortable. On the other hand, getting older also means greater responsibilities and higher expectations. She is too big for baby things or to act like a baby, though both still have appeal. She is supposed to be well-behaved without being told. She is expected to respect others and their belongings. If she transgresses, there are likely to be consequences that are not so pleasant. The stories provided by Ayleworth, Buehner, and Ransom's versions are rich ground for the playing with this dilemma.[8]

Other versions explore a different feature of play: perspectivism— that is, the ability to understand that others may have a very different point of view from one's own as to what is "just right." Ernst (2003) has Goldilocks returning as a busybody adult to make things right by redoing the bear's house to suit her standards—Mama, Papa, and Child Bear are just as pleased to see the back of her as they were years before. Wiley (2008) has the three bears live in a proper lair, sleep on piles of leaves and sticks, and eat insect and leaf-rich porridge. Goldilocks assumes she is doing right when she puts things in the kind of order humans like—though the bears make it clear she has messed up.

A quite different path to wonder and wander about came when our 3-year-old granddaughter Simone announced that she knew what the problem with *Goldilocks* was. She pointed out that if the three bears had "blowed" on their oatmeal like they should have, they wouldn't have gone out for a walk, and Goldilocks would never have broken into their house. Of course there wouldn't be a story either, but she was demonstrating a wonderful capacity for satisfying, intentional problem solving, with a scientific bent.

Her remark got her physicist grandfather asking his colleagues and students, What kind of scientific explanations could account for the fact that the biggest bowl of porridge was hot, while the middle-sized one was cold, and the littlest one in-between? That led to animated discussions of the laws of thermodynamics and the importance of variables such as the time of serving, the materials from which the bowls were made, and environmental factors such as nearby fans.

WHAT IS GOOD WORKMANSHIP WITH GOOD TOOLS?

In a previous chapter, we looked at how quality intellectual work calls for putting the emphasis on *what happens in the children*, rather than on *what happens in the story*—while fully recognizing that what happens in the children is mediated by what happens in the story. As our study of *Goldilocks* shows, that mediation involves specifics of how the story is told and illustrated. Clearly, the potential for good work is maximized if the story is presented in a way that meets standards for high quality.

That is different from saying that a given version of a story like *Goldilocks* is the absolute best any more than a single book or story is better than all others. There are many texts that meet the standards for high quality and that trigger rich conversations that lead to quality intellectual work. In the end, while some readers may lean more toward one version than another, the classroom community might well decide that they want to keep three, four, or many more different *Goldilocks* in their classrooms, to visit again and again, digging deeper each time. Which ones we use as teaching/learning tools depends on many factors, including personal taste.

That's another point of equity we should be emphasizing in our classroom communities: Everyone is entitled to preferences and opinions; however, one is also responsible for being able to support one's thinking using thoughtful criteria as well as for respecting the legitimacy of other perspectives and preferences.

TRY AND APPLY

1. Create a set of three to five books that are closely related to each other, such as versions of a common story, or a set of books related by plot or theme. A few possibilities are listed in the next item, or use another cluster of books you see going together in some way. Specify an age or grade level and use the rubric in Table 5.1 to evaluate each in terms of the different dimensions.

2. Using the criteria discussed in this chapter, compare and contrast related texts, indicating how you might use them together or whether you see one as more suitable than another

for a given age or project. Choose from the following sets of books or create your own set.

a. *The Mitten*—versions by Jim Aylesworth, Jan Brett, Alvin Tresselt; *The Missing Mitten Mystery* by Steven Kellog; *The Mitten Tree* by Candace Christiansen; *Animals in Winter* by H. Bancroft.

b. *Stone Soup*—versions by Marcia Brown, Heather Forest, John Muth; *The Real Story of Stone Soup* by Y. C. Compestine; *Cactus Soup* by Eric Kimmel; *Growing Vegetable Soup* by Lois Ehlert.

c. Stories about names: *My Name is Sangoel* by K. L. Williams; *The Name Jar* by Y. Choi; *Chrysanthemum* by K. Henke; *Tikki Tikki Tembo* by Arlene Mosel; *My Name is Yoon* by H. Recovits; *Miss Alianeus* by D. Frasier; *If Your Name Was Changed at Ellis Island* by Ellen Levine.

d. Apples and pie: *The Apple Pie That Papa Baked* by L. Thompson; *The Apple Pie Tree* by Zoe Hall; *Bring Me Some Apples and I'll Make You a Pie* by R. Gourley; *Down the Road* by A. Schertle; *The Story of Johnny Appleseed* by Aliki.

Part II

DISCIPLINED INQUIRIES

CHAPTER 6

How Long Is *Tikki Tikki Tembo?*

What's the Problem with Naked Numbers?

When I stopped by to remind a kindergarten teacher that I would be telling *Tikki Tikki Tembo*, Ontario wondered if I could do a math story instead since she had been told to do more number work. I told her not to worry—it was easy to find math in this story.

Ontario's class delighted in joining me in reciting Tikki-tikki-tembo-no-sa-rembo-chari-bari-ruchi-pip-peri-pembo's name repeatedly as the story tells how a Chinese washerwoman learns the drawbacks to giving such a long name to her older son. Chang, her second son, calls for help when his brother falls into the well, but precious time is lost when all the adults insist that Chang use his brother's full name. While the boy is rescued, it takes him a long time to recover.

I then used the overhead to help the children literally see the difference in the length of the two brothers' names. On a sheet of grid paper, I filled in one square for each letter of the abbreviated version Tikki tikki tembo; in another column I did the same for Chang. Everyone readily saw which name was longer and which was shorter without doing any counting.

I then asked the children to predict if their own names were closer in length to Chang or to Tikki tikki tembo's. Even Faytheolonis and Zaccariah didn't quite reach the 15 letters in the older brother's name. However, many began calculating that their name would be longer than Chang's while a few realized they had a name that was even shorter!

When I came back the next week, Ontario told me she and the children were still talking about names, making all kinds of comparisons. She showed me the bar graph they developed for display on the hall bulletin board (Figure 6.1). She reported happily

FIGURE 6.1. How Long Are Our Names?

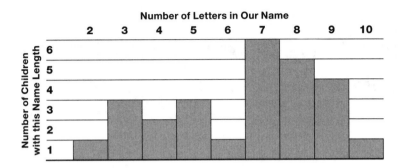

that now the other kindergarten class had begun to work on their own graph, to see how the results would compare.

"I've done all kinds of literacy things with *Tikki Tikki Tembo*," Ontario told me. "But I never thought of using it to get the kids having fun counting and measuring. This kind of math sure beats doing worksheets."

WHERE'S THE STORY IN MEASUREMENT?

In the 15 years since this interchange, I've heard many teachers agree that stories and math both become more interesting when connections are made between them. All kinds of questions emerge when a group of children in a primary classroom—or of adults in a workshop—use connecting cubes to build their own "name tower" using one cube for each letter. All ages are equally engaged and intrigued. Each time, the data that emerge are different—as are the conversations that explore all that the data reveals and suggests. However, a good conversation only gets going if the participants are genuinely interested. Look, for example, at Figure 6.2.

Imagine being asked to put the six stacks in order from shortest to tallest. There's no need to count the cubes; we just have to visually compare them—to be absolutely sure young children might move those that are the same length side by side. In any case, no real problem solving is involved and there is little incentive to think any more about it. Ten is a naked number; it doesn't represent anything of interest.

However, if these towers represent names, especially those that are of some interest, it is a different story; or perhaps it is more accurate to say that if the towers represent something meaningful, they begin to suggest stories and thus to *trigger conversations* about the problems these stories might pose.

FIGURE 6.2. Comparing SIX Name Towers

- If I say that the towers represent the number of letters in the names of my granddaughters, one wonders what the names are; when I reveal that in order of age, the girls are called Mireille (rhymes with hooray), Savannah, Ava, Tyra, Simone, and Saskia one might want to rearrange them to see how the age order compares to the length-of-names order.
- If I add that we joke about how my second son, Michael Sebastien Collingwood Berry, deliberately gave his daughters very short names, it is easy to identify which towers belong to them—as well as which is the older of his two. If I add that the two longest names belong to the oldest son's family, there's enough information to order all six by family.
- Since the fathers are all brothers, the girls have the same last name. So, if the name towers included both first and last names, each of the towers would be 5 cubes taller than shown; however, their *relative* order would be the same.

These comparisons are a kind of play that gives some reason to order and reorder the stacks. In fact, further discussion about what can be learned from all these playful comparisons can lead to a much deeper understanding of key concepts of measurement.

Can You Measure Without Numbers?

You may have noticed that all the comparisons of name towers involved virtually no mention of numbers and absolutely none of *inches, feet, pounds, grams, quarts, liters,* or any other standard unit—although most people assume such conventional units should be included in a definition of measurement.

In the real world, however, many measurements are only concerned with establishing whether things or sets of things are "bigger" or "smaller" or "just the same/equal" without going into the issue of how much/how many more (or less). The idea that comparison is at the heart of measurement is often missed.

In the world of mathematics, *measurement is always a comparison*, made in reference to a specified attribute (length, weight, capacity, volume, area, and so on). According to circumstances, the comparison can be made in one of two basic ways.

- Measurement can be done as a *direct comparison*, in reference to a particular attribute. Just as it was easy to visually order the name towers, it is often possible to compare size or quantity directly. Putting things next to one another makes it easy to order by length. A balance visually indicates that the item in the lower scale is heavier—has more weight than that in the one that rises up. More often than not, in a direct comparison, there is not only no need to count, it may not be possible to do so. Imagine that instead of name towers made up of stacking blocks, we cut out strips of paper of five sizes and then compared them. We could still put them in order from smallest to tallest.
- Yet there are many cases in which it simply is not possible to directly compare items or to define an attribute in an item. Then the comparison is between the item and the number of units used to represent the attribute. For example, we can say Mireille's name tower is 10 units long and Ava's is 3 units long, making Mireille's 7 units longer than Ava's.

What's Important to Understand About Units?

Perhaps the most critical thing to understand about units is that anything goes—the only requirement is that the chosen unit can meet the purposes for which the measurement is being made

At times, it is most convenient to use an *arbitrary unit*—many people will pace out the measurement of a room to get a good approximation of its size. Children enjoy finding out their height in paper clips or even measur-

FIGURE 6.3. Name Towers Using Different Units

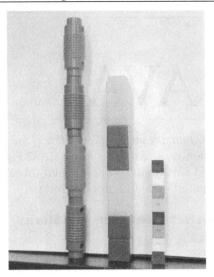

ing out a line of pennies. Other times, it's important to be able to communicate the measurement to others or to be more precise; that's when tape measures, yardsticks, scales, or liquid units are much more suitable; these tools are marked and calibrated with a widely accepted or conventional unit (inches/feet, centimeters, meters, ounces and pounds, or grams).

In all cases, there are three critical characteristics that must be observed when making a measurement.

- *The same unit must be used to compare the same attribute to make a "fair" comparison.* Figure 6.3 is another representation of the number of letters in the names Mireille, Savannah, and Tyra; in this case, the towers use three different sizes of units. The large cylinder units make Tyra's name look tallest; using two different sizes of connecting cubes makes it hard to see that Mireille and Savannah have the same number of letters.
- *When items are measured in terms of a unit, it is critical to name the number and the unit as well as the other attributes being compared.* My granddaughters' names make the point: Consider that Mireille and Savannah have the same number of letters in their names as do Simone and Saskia; Tyra and Ava's names are quite a bit shorter. letters. But how do their names compare if we measure by clapping the number of syllables? The comparisons now don't correspond at all to those that emerged when based on the number of letters. Tyra, Ava, Simone, and Mireille all yield two claps while Saskia and Savannah take three claps.

FIGURE 6.4. Names in Different Font Sizes: Ava in 48 Point, Savannah in 10
Point

AVA Savannah

- *The bigger the unit, the smaller the number of units that result.* What
  happens when we use different font sizes? Figure 6.4 shows
  how Ava and Savannah compare when three letters in font size
  48 are compared to eight letters in font size 10.

How Do Units Turn Naked Numbers into Stories?

I could summarize some of the examples just given by saying 15 is
more than 5, 10 = 10 or 10 – 7 = 3; however, such statements of comparison that are expressed in naked numbers have little interest. It is the unit
that tells the story embedded in all measurement problem situations. In
order to determine "What's bigger?" or "How big?" or "How much bigger?" there are problems to be resolved.

- What kind of bigger is at issue? The name towers illustrate how
  changing the attribute being measured can affect whether or
  not a direct comparison can be made; if units are called for, the
  nature of the attribute and the purpose for which the measurement is being made both influence what kind of unit is best
  suited. Furthermore, when standard units are being used, there
  still is a question about what unit is best. For example, one of
  the most delicious absurdities in Scieszka and Smith's *Math Curse*
  speculates about how many M&Ms it would take to measure the
  length of the Mississippi River. Clearly, a 1-centimeter piece of
  candy is much too small a unit to measure the 4,000 kilometers
  of the river.
- What *tools or procedures* will be used and what skills are involved
  in making an accurate or fair measurement? As young children
  directly compare name towers, many will need a reminder to
  check that both stacks match at the bottom—that is, a fair comparison has to observe a baseline. Young children are very likely
  to "fudge" the baseline to make their item look bigger. Tools
  such as rulers, tape measures, and commercial scales are fairly

easy to master; however, it can take intensive training to accurately use highly specialized scientific instruments.

HOW DO NAKED NUMBERS MAKE THE DIFFERENCE BETWEEN ARITHMETIC AND MATHEMATICS?

To this point, the discussion about the role of stories in mathematics has focused on measurement situations. There is a very human element to measurement. "What is bigger?", "What kind of bigger is in question?", and "How much bigger?" are questions of enormous concern to children. They tend to equate *bigger* with *more*—and in their minds, that means *better*. So in *Tikki Tikki Tembo* the old Chinese custom of giving a long name to honor the oldest son seems to make sense.

However, the tale ends by challenging the *bigger* = *better* equation. The difference in the time taken to say the two brothers' names and thus how long it took to rescue each makes it clear that not all *biggers* are better. The last line of Mosel's telling makes the point: "And from that day to this, the Chinese have always thought it wise to give all their children little, short names instead of great long names."

The more the discussion goes on, with questions and comments from the group and perhaps a few facilitating ones from the teacher, all kinds of inquiries might be played with: Do we agree that it is "wise" to give short names? Is it fair to honor the oldest son more than the second one? But it is also quite easy to move from the story to math: Do our names fit the Chinese customs? What kind of patterns or comparisons will we see when we make name towers and compare them? Now, the children are exploring measurement—one of the major content areas of school mathematics.[1]

However, there is a sense in which all situations that include counting and numbers are a kind of measurement. When we ask, "How much/How many?" we must say, "How much?/How many—of what?" Asking that question means there is a story waiting in the wings.

So, What Is the Problem with Naked Numbers?

The school experience of math tends to be an endless succession of tasks and tests to determine how quickly and accurately naked numbers can be manipulated: that is, counted, added, subtracted, multiplied, and divided, including complex problems that involve formulas using one or more of these operations.

This emphasis is problematic on several counts. On one hand, young children are often deeply engaged by what Ginsberg identifies as "play centered on mathematics."[2] Issues of "how many? or "how many more?" are part and parcel of many play situations and negotiations.

At the same time, the latest brain research argues against overreliance on rote memory for number sequence, math facts, or algorithms such as borrowing and carrying. Rote memory and drill can lead to getting information into long-term memory, where it can be retrieved rapidly, so that calculations can be done without distracting from the problem situation. However, if the information was learned by rote so that it functions as labels, but the underlying conceptual framework or meaning is not there, one's ability to retrieve it strategically is restricted. For example, the times tables may have been drilled in order, so that one has to run up from 1 x 6 to 9 x 6 in order to retrieve that you will have 54 bottles of soda pop if you get 9 six packs (see Willingham, 2008/2009).

In fact, early school experiences tend to emphasize arithmetic rather than mathematics. What makes these arithmetic chores so onerous is that they are endless cases of naked numbers, stripped of their stories. All we hear is 3 + 3 or 3 x 4 or even 2714 ÷ 3; never are we told exactly what the "3" things are. School arithmetic suppresses the fact that *there is no such thing as three!*[3]

By primary school, we are so used to thinking of counting as a fixed sequence of number words or symbols that we don't realize *three* and *3* are *only symbolic representations of the attribute that indicates quantity*. Number is specifically a mathematical attribute—the mathematician's name for it is *numerosity*. Just as there is no such thing as *green*—just many, many things that have a color that is on the green spectrum—there is no such thing as 3—only *threeness*. A collection of three wild elephants and three scary mice may differ radically in size, but they are equal in terms of number/numerosity.

What Happens to the Story When Numbers Are Recognized as Adjectives?

Because adults don't recognize numbers as adjectives rather than nouns—as *attributes* rather than *units*—it's not surprising that children are easily confused.[4] In order for young children to develop a deep understanding of numbers—that is, to develop *number sense*—it is essential that they experience counting and operations as linked to *sets* and that they are helped to see that each set can be described, with the *number representing an attribute of a unit*.[5] The process is parallel to the way very young children's language develops. At first, they use the generic term *water* to ask for something to drink; soon they can specify a favorite beverage such as apple juice, milk, or orange soda pop. In the same way, number sense develops as a result of many experiences that establish that the statement

3 + 4 = 7 is symbolic; it is an abstraction that describes many different situations, such as the following:

- Suky Ray has 3 letters in her last name and 4 in her first name, making 7 letters altogether. She likes to think of her name as representative of herself as a low-maintenance, compact person.
- Suky decided to pack only purple clothes for the weeklong road trip she was about to take with her best friend. They were planning to drive west from Chicago to Denver; estimating 4 days would be spent traveling, she figured that 3 full days would be devoted to her family in the Mile-High City.
- On the first day out, the friends snacked on 3 oranges and 4 apples, consuming 7 pieces of fruit in all; 3 apples and 4 oranges were left for the second day; Suky wondered if they would finish all that fruit before hitting the Denver city limits.

While writing out 3 + 4 = ? three times in a row seems silly, clearly, there are endless possibilities for telling the story behind the naked numbers. Since Suky is named in each of these examples, each seems to be a different aspect of a single story. Notice that the somewhat chatty narrative offers additional details that build out the *story*, although they do not affect the *numbers* involved. However, the details do change *our perception of the units*. They also can illustrate how all possible stories about 3 + 4 = 7 must fall into one of two types of relationship between the units/sets; an algebraic expression of the two situations is:

1. 3 *unit a* + 4 *unit a* = 7 *unit a* : that is, 3 of a given unit and 4 of the same unit equal 7 items of the same unit.
2. 3 *unit a* + 4 *unit b* = 7 *unit c:* that is, 3 of a given unit and 4 of a different unit equal 7 items of a unit that includes both *a* and *b*.

By and large, the second problem situation produces more interesting stories—there are so many possible ways that *unit c* can be named so that it includes both *unit a* and *unit b* and each possible solution opens up different questions. Oranges and apples are both kinds of fruit but by no means the only fruits that might be in the bowl. If Suky had packed mangos and breadfruit, *unit c* could be specified more closely as *tropical fruits*; strawberries and raspberries could be termed *berries,* a subset of fruits. But why, we might wonder, would there be only 3 or 4 berries available— that might be a feast for a mouse but not a human—unless Suky and her friend were dieting.

So, too, there are all kinds of potential questions about her travel plans including which of the many possible routes they will follow. Do they intend to do some sightseeing on the way, taking local highways, or will they drive straight through on the interstate? Each of these questions/stories could be translated into a very different number sentence/problem statement and each of those might tell a host of different stories.

This kind of playing with the idea of composing and decomposing sets can be found in wonderful picture books like Paul Giganti's *How Many Snails* or *Each Orange Had 8 Slices*, Donald Crew's *Ten Black Dots*, Eve Merriam's *12 Ways to Get to 11*, or *Anno's Counting Book*. Having seen and explored story problems like this makes it easy to get young children creating their own entries for a classroom book in a way that number facts flash cards never could.

We are back to the same point: When problems are reduced to bare number sentences, the story gets lost—along with a strong incentive to find the answer or to see it as meaningful—or even vaguely interesting.

WHY IS IT IMPORTANT TO LEAVE THE STORY IN MATHEMATICS?

Before school spoils the fun, young children experience mathematics as a continual SIP of play: a *satisfying* and *intentional* way for them to *problem-solve* many situations and ideas they wonder about. They tend to be preoccupied with comparing themselves to others—always assuming bigger is better. However, equally often, they evaluate toys or everyday objects, asking inherently mathematical questions such as "How many are there?" "Do I have more?" "How many more do I need?" "Did I get a fair share?" So, too, as they navigate from one place to the next, within a room or building or outside, and as they build with blocks and other construction toys, they are doing geometry—they are exploring movement and direction and the attributes of three dimensional shapes.

Unfortunately, all too often neither their parents nor their teachers recognize the mathematics all around or they dismiss it. Instead of embracing all this rich play and problem solving, they equate mathematics with arithmetic. Especially in early childhood settings, the distaste many teachers feel for the subject means they spend minimal time on it; for the most part, what they do comes straight from a scripted curriculum. They themselves do not understand enough mathematics to teach for understanding.[6] The consequences are serious.

How Can Playing with Mathematical Ideas Impact School Success?

Brain research indicates that early emphasis on the mathematics all around us is highly advantageous as a predicator of later school success; in fact, it is arguably the best measure, much better than early literacy skills.[7]

However, the research makes it crystal clear that the advantage comes from laying a strong foundation in early childhood for developing mathematical thinking; it is not the result of arithmetic drills, just as early alphabet knowledge is not a good predictor for comprehension skills. When the National Research Council reported that "well before first grade, young children can learn the ideas and skills that support later, more complex mathematical understanding" (Cross et al. 2009, p. 2), what they meant is that well before first grade, children can develop *problem-solving skills*; they are capable of persistence and flexibility as they explore and reflect on mathematical problem situations that arise naturally in play and everyday experiences.

The purposeful thinking they do as they experiment, observe, and evaluate engages them in conversations and questions that support language development—in ways far richer and with more staying power than chanting the alphabet or doing phonics worksheets ever could. If this kind of approach continues well after first grade, the positive effect on school achievement in all areas, including mathematics, can continue to be dramatic—for good reason. Not only is there a strong correlation between positive attitude and achievement, but quality intellectual work is far more efficacious for learning than rote drill.

This is the point Van den Heuvel-Panhuizen and Buys (2008) make when arguing for the importance of young children having fun with measurement activities, as well as for being involved and motivated by the way the problems are presented. "If these factors are positive, the insight into all sorts of aspects of measurement will undoubtedly develop more swiftly" (p. 40).

What's the Difference Between Mathematizing and Arithmetic?

The importance of these factors is not confined to young children. It underlies the constructivist approach to learning. This philosophy is articulated by the Freudenthal Institute, which has directed mathematics education in the Netherlands since the early 1970s. The Institute sees teaching mathematics as a "human activity . . . the focal point should not be on mathematics as a closed system but on the activity, on the process of *mathematization* . . . the students come up with mathematical tools which can help to organize and solve a problem set in a real life situation" (Van den Heuzel-Panhuizen, 2000, pp. 3–4).[8]

The idea of *mathematizing* comes up with increasing frequency in current discussions of mathematics education in the United States. Cross et al. (2009) describe mathematizing as happening when children can "create a model of the situation by using mathematical objects (such as numbers and shapes), mathematical actions (such as counting or transforming shapes), and their structural relationships to solve problems about the situation" (p. 40).

More fancifully, we might think of mathematizing as a kind of magic wand which, when waved, reveals the formal mathematics inherent in a problem situation and allows us to focus on the mathematical thinking that will result in a solution. The problem might be one that arises in everyday life or in dramatic play.

What Makes Story Problems Meaningful?

Still another way to define *mathematizing* would be to say that it looks for the mathematics embedded in stories. It is ironic that those who have a negative attitude toward mathematics tend to find story problems particularly distasteful. After all, it is story problems that call for thinking and problem solving. Once math facts have been learned—usually by rote—it takes no thought to solve pure number problems, as tedious as it may be. In contrast, story problems call for the same kind of strategic decisions that were identified as part of measurement. We have to think through what we want to know and decide which of the four basic operations or what formula is best suited to give a good solution, as well as to know which numbers to plug in.

In too many classrooms, the emphasis is heavily on arithmetical number problems, stripped of their stories. The stories that do show up in math textbooks are reduced to bare bones, identifying little more than numbers and units. Just as we saw with cube stacks and $4 + 3 = 7$, the more inviting the story, the more likely it is that it will lead to mathematizing, along with the rich problem solving and learning that result.

Fortunately, there has been an increasing recognition that literacy, mathematics, and thinking don't all have to be at odds with one another. In fact, Hyde (2006) and Siena (2009) have done wonderful jobs of investigating and explaining how the open-ended questions and conversations that are crucial for developing mathematical thinking are closely related to those that are posed to stimulate understanding/exploration of texts in general, using the kinds of comprehension strategies that work. Hyde, for example, has transformed the popular KWL strategy (*What do you Know, Want to know, and what have you Learned*) into a mathematical format that he calls KWC:

- K calls for identifying what is *Known* for sure in the problem statement.
- W asks for a good statement of the problem, identifying the unknown element—that is, precisely what does one *Want* to figure out or find out.

- C looks for the special *Conditions,* rules, or tricks that one should watch out for.

Hyde gives examples of how to use the KWC strategy to effectively structure a discussion of a mathematical problem situation. Instead of just looking for numbers, the teacher guides the conversation toward visualizing the real-life problem situation; children are encouraged to pose their own questions, explain and support their reasoning, and represent the problem with manipulatives or drawings (pp. 20–39).

Taking the time to mathematize in this way brings even bare-bones stories to life. At the same time, it adds a whole new dimension to beloved read-alouds such as *Tikki Tikki Tembo.* Furthermore, strategies such as KWC can be especially important for poor readers, second language learners, and those with other learning or language challenges.

Further testimony to the power of leaving the story in mathematics has come through Cathy Fosnot and others involved in the very successful Teachers College Math in the City program who are working closely with the Freudenthal Institute. All their lessons begin in real-life story problem situations—the teacher's role is to guide them as they develop their ability to solve these issues by being mathematicians—not just getting right answers on arithmetic problems.

How Is Mathematical Thinking Related to Higher-Order Thinking?

In our discussion of higher-order thinking we saw how the movement up, down, and around the Ladder of Inquiry corresponds to movement between Concrete-Pictorial-Symbolic modes. However, this developmental path has special relevance to mathematics. In order to engage the learner, we need to begin with a well-defined, concrete, real-world mathematical problem situations, such as "How do the lengths of our names compare?" The problem might arise in the context of children's play or it may be one that we pose, building on the interests and needs of the learners, including questions triggered by a story.

- Exploring the problem and possible solutions is an intermediate stage—it calls for generalizing in a fairly concrete way. Problems that concern "What's bigger?" call for different procedures than those that ask "How many?" or, for that matter, "How much bigger in what kind of dimension?" Learners who have had many experiences with interesting, authentic measurement situations may begin to mathematize that question themselves. Many will find that the best way to clarify the problem and arrive at some way to solve it is to use concrete manipulatives, drawings, and discussion—in other words, to literally play with the story. Very young children and those with little experience thinking mathematically might need guidance to realize that they can figure out the answer by doing some kind of comparison—directly by building name towers or indirectly by simply counting the letters.

• Only after many experiences, accompanied by good conversations that explicitly reinforce the mathematizing, can children begin to construct for themselves the "big ideas" associated with a given content strand of mathematics. As the capacity for symbolic thought develops, as they continue to gain experience, reflect, and see connections between different kinds of mathematical problems, children go on to construct a richer, more complex understanding of mathematics on the conceptual, symbolic level.

• If their inquiries are deeply grounded, it is likely that each newly constructed understanding will trigger further inquiry and lead to "digging deeper." At the same time, as facility with mathematical thinking increases, the less complex concepts and procedures will move into long-term memory.[9] Then it becomes increasingly possible to function at the abstract/symbolic level, without having to dip down as explicitly to the concrete problem situations.

Nonetheless *a ladder* continues to be a better image than *an ivory tower* to describe how higher-order mathematical thinking involves moving up and down and around the different levels. As the Cross et al. (2009) point out, very young children are capable of higher-order mathematical thinking as long as their inquiries have a concrete ground to begin from.[10] At the same time, the greatest mathematicians are always finding their kind of problem in the world around them. Biologists looking at the structure of many natural phenomena including certain plants and shells were able to mathematize their findings as they established that these structures can be represented by the Fibonacci series of numbers.[11] Primary school students are likely to be engaged by exploring those structures, as well as the remarkable story of the boy who discovered the series, as they read and study the way those structures are represented in the picture books, *Wild Fibonacci: Nature's Secret Code Revealed* (Hulme, 2005) and *Blockhead: The Life of Fibonacci* (D'Agnese, 2010).

HOW CAN WE KEEP THE STORIES IN MATHEMATICS?

The idea that mathematical thinking calls for dynamic movement up, down, and around the trajectories makes texts and stories especially powerful tools that can be used in a variety of ways.

On one hand, we should make a habit of *mathematizing high-quality texts*. When choosing read-alouds or texts and stories to use across the curriculum, look for ways to invite mathematical thinking and problem solving from the texts.

- Concept and informational books may have a direct mathematical focus. Counting books, for example, are among the most popular categories of concept books. However, there are a wide variety of ways in which these books play with number sense.[12] Many informational books, especially those with a focus on science, have many mathematical problem situations built in, including issues around measurement.
- Stories and tales will often have mathematical problem situations embedded in the plot. *Tikki Tikki Tembo, The Knee-High Man* (Lester, 1992), *Two Ways to Count to Ten* (Dee, 1990), *Two of Everything* (Hong, 1993), and *How Big Is a Foot* are just a few examples of folk tales about measurement that can be mathematized.[13] *Those Shoes* (Boelts, 2007) explores how the difference between what we "need" and what we "want" complicates value as measured by cost and availability. *Grandfather Tang's Story* (Tompert, 1997) features the Chinese game of tangrams. Shirley Raines and associates (1989, 1999, 2000) have compiled several anthologies of extending activities, including math, that are based on children's stories. Whitin & Wilde (1993, 1995), Burns (2004), and Burns and Sheffield (2004) all provide many excellent discussions of specific works of children's literature that can be used to explore key mathematical concepts.
- The more intentional the teacher is, the more effective the learning. In other words, the books and stories from everday life should not be chosen at random but should be part of a thoughtful sequence—curriculum, if you will—in which the learners are guided through a particular landscape yet allowed to wander. The deep patterns and interconnections between the different strands of mathematics can be lost when one day the teacher brings in a book that helps develop number sense and the next turns to one that explores shapes in a completely unrelated way.

- All of these texts are ones that get the value-added effect discussed in Chapter 4: the mathematical "big idea" problem situations such as "What's bigger?"and "Is it fair?" all have important social-emotional dimensions. As they figure out how to solve the mathematical problem, the classroom learning community can also play with text-to-self connections that may support understanding of themselves and others

- The problem solving in these texts may literally involve "acting out" the mathematical situation; kindergarteners and first graders whose number sense is fragile benefit from enacting *The Door Bell Rang* (Hutchins, 1994) so that they see and feel how the number of cookies each child gets shrinks as more children arrive. Those who are beginning to understand division as partitioning a set into equal subsets might write innovations on the story, beginning with a different quantity of items that need to be divided into a fair share.

- As Whitin and Piwko (2008) point out, all poetry has a mathematical element in that poems are patterned. Piwko had second and third graders write poems about geometrical shapes, based on Margaret Wise Brown's *The Important Book.* As the children edited and consulted with their families about both for poetic richness and accuracy of their definitions, they developed a deeper understanding of the mathematical properties of geometric shapes and the all-important personal connections the shapes had for them.[14]

On the other hand, it is equally important to *put stories back into arithmetic.* If children are to develop fluency in number operations they need to be comfortable with using the comprehension strategies Hyde and Siena recommend for making sense of math story problems and to ground the mathematics in the everyday problems that Math in the City uses. However, it is also important for them to have many opportunities to construct stories that could underlie arithmetic problems.

- Such stories might happen as a quick math minute, when a class is invited to generate different tales to fit a number sentence, such as $3 + 4 = 7$.

- Alternatively, children might be challenged to make up problems, building on a popular story. A preschool classroom created their own book, *What We Found in the Three Bears' House.* One especially charming page declared, "I saw three refrigerators. A great big fridge for Papa; a middle sized one for Mama and a bitty one for baby."

Building mathematics lessons for children or workshop participants out of a story is not just a "cute idea"; it is the best way I know to get participants involved in constructing for themselves key mathematical concepts, such as those about measurement that we looked at earlier in the chapter. No prodding is necessary—the story comes out of the book, and moves into the group's hearts and minds. As they wonder, reflect, make connections, and mathematize, they become engaged in quality intellectual work.

Try and Apply

Use one of the books from the list below or another of your choice to practice "mathematizing"—finding the mathematical thinking/problem situation in the book. While counting books or other concept books may seem straightforward, they can target quite a range of "big ideas" from simple counting to number patterns and operations (McDonald, 2007; Shatzer, 2008). A suggestion as to what mathematical content area could be found in the work is given in parentheses.

Suitable for early childhood developmental levels (pre-K, kindergarten, first grade)

- *Caps for Sale,* E. Slobodkina (Think about rational counting, use of graphs)
- *Goldilocks* (any version) or *Three Little Pigs* (Think about sets, sorting, and patterns)
- *The Growing Story,* Ruth Krauss (Think about measurement, rates of growth, size)

Suitable for full range of developmental levels (second to fifth grade)

- *The Doorbell Rang* by Pat Hutchins (Think about fair share, fractions)
- *Two of Everything* by Lily Hong (functions, number operations)
- *Grandfather Tang's Story* by Ann Tompert (Think about geometry, patterns)
- *The Ten Mile Day,* by M. Fraser or *Henry Hikes to Fitchburg* by D. B. Johnson (Think about measurement—time, money, distance)

CHAPTER 7

How Did the Sun and Moon Come to Be in the Sky?

Playing with the Amazing Facts of Science

Several years into our Stone Soup collaboration, the team of Hug-a-Book consultants and lead literacy teachers from the three network schools asked participating classrooms to do something with *pourquoi tales*—myths and legends that offer explanations for the origins of phenomena in the natural world.

Since many classrooms were planning a field trip to the aquarium, I repeated the same activity in about 20 classrooms, from K to sixth grade. In all cases, I brought in a large piece of chart paper on which I had drawn the outlines of a large traditional African dwelling as well as three sizes of self-stick notes. Contrary to my usual practice, I didn't launch immediately into the story. Instead, I asked the children to tell me what kinds of creatures they knew about who lived in or near water. For each, we would decide if its size made it appropriate to record its name on a big, medium, or small sticky note.

The notes were posted on the blackboard, loosely clustering those who lived in the water (fish, whales) apart from those who lived half in one and half in the other (reptiles/toads) with those who lived near water and depended on it for their food (seals and penguins). In the older primary and middle school classrooms, I challenged them to classify the creatures even more exactly—which were fish? mammals? crustaceans? reptiles? In all cases, suggestions snowballed with one suggestion triggering another; children eagerly shared any expertise they might have about the classification or habitat of water creatures. No two classroom lists were identical, although hammerhead sharks, killer whales, polar bears, seals, and penguins were universally popular.

The oral storytelling began once everyone had named a creature. The tale *Why the Sun and Moon Live in the Sky* was collected by E. Dayrell from Western Nigeria. It links issues of "fairness" with equity in friendship. Sun and Water are best friends who live in different houses, but Sun wonders, "Why must I always go to your house? Why won't you come to mine, the one I share with my wife, the Moon? Do you not respect her?"

Water quickly replies he would love to come but he has many creatures that depend on him and so he can only go places where all of his people can accompany him. Sun and Moon decide this is a good excuse for building a larger house—one to which all Water's people will be welcome.

At this point, I posted the house; as I recounted the arrival of Water and of his people who absolutely must stay with him to live (fish, sharks, whales), I moved the related Post-its into the house, beginning at the bottom. As the story goes on, those who live in both water and land arrive and, finally, those who live on land. Each time, the water rises and Sun and Moon need to move up to make room until finally the story concludes: The sun and the moon were forced to go up into the sky, where they have remained ever since.

Inevitably, this was a very interactive storytelling—the children were the ones to direct me as to which creature(s) needed to be moved into the new house of Sun and Moon. They also kept a sharp eye that I kept moving Sun and Moon above their guests.

It was delightfully unclear as to when the story began or ended—in every case, the session could be best described as a conversation. The children had much to say about how some creatures literally breathe water and others need air. Disagreements about classification sent individuals racing to reference books to support their point. I ended up learning along with the students—for example, the difference between a crustacean and a mollusk.

The Post-its were left in the classrooms for the children to continue to sort and discuss. Many teachers picked up on a suggested extending activity: individually or in pairs, children would become the "classroom expert" on one of the creatures identified in the pre-story activity. They would be responsible for two different kinds of representation:

- They would represent their creature as they "drew like a scientist"—carefully observing a model—or possibly find a photo, though drawing was strongly encouraged.
- On the back of the drawing or in a notebook they would record key information about their creature, including classification,

habitat, favorite foods, mode of movement (fly, swim, crawl). They researched the information using the resource books in the classroom library (this was before the Internet was available).

Many classrooms found ways to "go public" with the children's expertise. Some created wonderful bulletin board displays; others created a classroom book; still others included details in a newsletter home reporting on the aquarium visit. The teachers who had been preparing for the field trip expressed their delight with how the activity brought their science unit to life—weeks later, there were children making references to the creatures they had chosen to be an expert about.

WHY USE POURQUOI TALES IN SCIENCE CLASS?

The Stone Soup Network planning meetings were always lively and stimulating—precisely because the Hug-a-Book consultants and the six literacy leaders from the participating schools truly functioned as a professional learning community. Our initial discussions in this particular year took up the problem of how science often is lost in kindergarten and early primary because of the test-driven emphasis on literacy. Children got to third grade with limited experience of inquiring about the world around them, thanks in part to the text-driven, didactic science basal textbooks the schools used—if they used any. The group talked about including more informational books in the collection from which each participating classroom teacher would select 20 books. But we felt we needed some kind of focus to so that the teachers could continue to make connections between children, rich books, and the curriculum.

As the discussion continued, I remembered having done an annual series of *pourquoi legends*—tales about how things had come to be as they are now. In the years I had returned to the same 10 or 15 classrooms on a weekly or monthly basis, I would pick a topic, such as how the world began, the origin of the sun, moon, or stars, where fire came from; then I'd carefully choose legends related to the topic from different cultures. For 6 to 10 weeks we would converse about how these stories related to each other and about what we could learn from them. We noticed how geographical and environmental conditions got reflected in the stories that people told. The sun's heat and the need for rain was an issue in hot climates; the movement from winter to spring or the origin of fire was important in colder regions.

What Do Pourquoi Tales Wonder About?

My goals in those days weren't particularly directed toward science as much as toward fostering children's sense of wonder and appreciation of diversity. Together we learned to respect how much we could learn by looking at the same topic through a variety of lenses. In fact, we learned to look at the world around us much more carefully.

Unfortunately, today far too many children—and adults—have never taken note of how the sun moves across the sky or how the moon waxes and wanes; they haven't seen animals in nature to know that crows really are black or how strong a thread a spider can spin into intricate webs. However, every pourquoi tale ends with the same phenomena that we can see today, if we take the trouble to look; these stories are good evidence that our ancient ancestors were keen observers of the natural world, without the need of modern science for explanations.

Tracing the tales across the globe, a certain kind of character shows up again and again—a crafty "trickster" who sometimes used his or her powers for good, but just as often was self-serving. The character of the trickster never changed but the animal with which it was associated did— raven in the Pacific Northwest, coyote in the American Southwest, spider in the Caribbean and Africa, as well as fox and rabbit in a wide variety of cultures.[1]

Our Hug-a-Book collection already had a good number of single-story picture books and several collections of these world tales done by Gerald McDermott (1977, 1987, 1996, 2001), Verna Aardema (1992, 1994, 1998, 2000, 2008), Ashley Bryan (1987, 1999, 2003), and other gifted folklorists for children. We decided to continue to support this collection and to add more high-quality informational books about earth and sky sciences, insects, and life cycles. We then went on to develop workshops and consultations with the participating classrooms to explore how to bring science to life while engaging children in rich reading and writing activities.

Our Stone Soup Network was playing with pourquoi tales in the same decade that the Balanced Literacy movement was emerging and elementary and secondary science teachers were evolving a systematic approach to teaching/learning that has come to be known as Guided Inquiry. In all cases, the emphasis was on helping children focus on the higher-order thinking that comes from asking *why* and on constructing answers that involve moving up and down the inquiry ladder to gather the *how, when, where,* and *what* facts and conceptual frameworks that build support for their responses.

How Is an Inquiry Different from a Theme?

Pre-K and kindergarten teachers have long been free to organize their curricula as a series of themes—often doing a series of loosely connected activities about transportation and then moving on the next week to do colors. Under Lillian Katz's dynamic promotion of project-based learning and awareness of the Reggio Emilia approach, the "themes" moved from general topics to a series of activities that would investigate a well-defined problem that had engaged the children's interest. Thus, instead of "transportation," the children might spend a week or two building ramps from a variety of materials and racing toy cars and other objects down them to investigate "How can we make things go faster—or slower?" Conversation is a crucial element of the teaching/learning process in this approach; children are helped to hypothesize, to experiment, to use annotated drawings to represent what happened, to offer and clarify explanations, and above all to pose new questions (Helm & Katz, 2001; Helm & Benneke, 2003; Katz & Chard, 2000).

What Does It Mean to "Guide" an Inquiry?

As children mature and develop increasing cognitive capacity for generalizing (i.e., for abstract thought) it is appropriate that they are asked to take on increasingly complex learning in the disciplines. Thus in the primary grades the inquiries and investigations can and should be more *disciplined*, that is, more intentionally structured to dig deeper and deeper into a specific ideas about a topic.

Furthermore, the learning outcomes should include not just content information as "the facts," but also should help the learners construct a *conceptual framework* that shows how those facts are related to a "big idea" of the discipline. In other words, while the inquiry or investigation should be grounded in the *concrete*, it should also be structured to move up and down through mental representations (the *pictorial* stage) to more abstract understanding (the *symbolic* stage). As we have repeatedly noticed, a rich inquiry involves a question or problem that is open-ended, authentic, and engaging; that is, one that allows for ongoing conversations, facilitated by the teacher (Gallas, 1995; Kuhlthau et al., 2007; Michaels et al., 2007). As Roseberry and Hudicourt-Barnes (2006) and Duron-Flores and Maciel (2006) show, conversing about science in ways that include the students' observations and home experiences is a powerful way to celebrate diversity and to support language development in first and second language learners. They point to the power of "active word walls" that include graphics as well as definitions of terms being used in the ongoing science inquiry.

Once again, research on the brain and memory confirms why these strategies work. Drilling terms that have little or no meaning is tedious and is unlikely to establish their meaning in long-term memory. Since we can only manage about 6 items at a time in short-term memory, there is little staying power. However, linking meaning to multiple modes of representation and doing so in a way that actively involves the learners triggers positive chemicals and accelerates the rate that information takes to move from short-term to long-term memory (Sliva, 2003; Sousa, 2005; Willingham, 2008/2009).

While the demands of a standards/test-driven climate make it challenging to fit this kind of inquiry into primary classrooms, the power of good texts is such that intentional teachers can use them to guide their classroom communities toward rigorous learning, as the Case in Point activity at the beginning of the chapter indicates. It began with an open-ended invitation to the learners to share their prior knowledge.

- There was an opportunity for those who knew a lot and those who knew only a little to contribute; at the same time, the work already done to prepare the classrooms for the aquarium visit guaranteed that everyone was likely to be successful and engaged.
- The sharing was a conversation with other children as well as the facilitator, problem-solving around what size Post-it note should be used or about different ways in which a creature might be classified.
- Once the interactive storytelling began, everyone began to see the information from a new perspective; a different problem emerged as to which creatures should arrive when; that called for reviewing the decisions about size and about how closely dependent a creature was on water.
- Because the creatures in the story had come from the children's own suggestions, there was a sense of ownership as they chose one to become an expert about.
- The children who visited the aquarium were excited to see the real creatures they had been learning about and writing up for the classroom books and displays. Their pride and delight meant that the unit was brought to closure in a way that met the criterion of having meaning beyond the classroom. Best of all, teachers reported that enthusiasm for learning more about life in and around water continued long after the visit and the displays were over.

WHAT DOES IT MEAN TO REPRESENT LEARNING?

The activities around the pourquoi tale provided much richer evidence of what the children had learned than the usual multiple-choice/short-answer unit test ever could. Such tests are passive measures—they tend to look for "right" answers to closed questions as well as to privilege good memories and good spelling for those who are English language proficient. In contrast, the sea creatures activity called on all learners to actively construct responses that they could explain and support, using multiple modes to represent their thinking, including drawings, discussion, and gestures.

What Is Science When It's Not at School?

In effect, the activities described offered the children ways to play with knowledge about water creatures. Like the dramatizing and kinesthetic experiences we looked at in Chapter 4, making meaning of a text moved off the page into the learners' eyes and ears, into the movement of their bodies, and ultimately, passing through their hearts, deep into their minds. The learning and the representation of knowledge both bring into play what the Reggio Emilia movement calls the "100 Languages of Children" and Howard Gardner has defined as "Multiple Intelligences." Not surprisingly, advocates of both movements see learning as inseparable from play, in the ways we have been discussing (Chen et al., 2009; Edwards, Gandini, & Forman, 1998; Gardner, 2006).[2]

Sadly, just as we saw how naked numbers inhibit mathematical thinking, the focus on naked facts in schools squashes children's experience and interest in the real-world practice of science. The best scientists access the full array of the intelligences as they pose questions, hypothesize, design, and manipulate tools to collect data or test theories. So, too, the evidence that real scientists record in their lab journals and logs takes multiple forms: Words, sketches, diagrams, data charts, formulas, and sometimes even audio or visual recordings all help establish an accurate record of what was directly observed so that subsequent reflections on what was seen and how the phenomenon works or happened can be supported.[3]

How Do Scientists Construct and Represent Understanding?

In order to *teach* science for understanding from the earliest years, classrooms need to understand these essential features of what it means to *do* science.

- Scientific explanations are not simply a function of verbal intelligence. We have already seen that mathematics is the language of science, essential for all the measurement-based descriptions of the natural world. Visual-spatial intelligence comes into play with diagrams and carefully rendered illustrations or photos; the use of tools calls on the kinesthetic; the organization of scientific knowledge into taxonomies or other systems that classify and order is a function of the naturalist intelligence—in fact *all the intelligences have an important place in expressing/representing scientific knowledge.*

- It is equally characteristic of a true scientist that any given answer is the springboard to a new set of questions—one that pinpoints the problem to be solved in a more accurate way or that looks for a significant way to apply the newly gained knowledge. In effect, science is not about finding right answers; it is fundamentally concerned with the *progressive posing of better and better questions.*

- *Every child at play is a scientist; every scientist was once a child at play.* Along with being satisfying intentional, and problem-solving, a scientific inquiry must be informed by the kind of flexibility and perspectivism that see error as a gift and an opportunity.

WHAT DO SCIENTISTS THINK SCIENCE TEACHING/LEARNING SHOULD LOOK LIKE?

The way so many people leave school feeling indifferent if not negative about inquiry as well as about the nature and the validity of scientific knowledge is a real cause for concern—a concern that is addressed in the National Research Council report, *Taking Science to School* (Duschl et.al., 2007). It concludes that the immense changes in our understanding of what children know and how they learn calls for a shift from simple acquiring of knowledge of scientific facts to having them learn by actively engaging in the *practice of science*. Indications are that children are capable of a mix of concrete and abstract thought—they can move up, down, and around the Ladder of Inquiry. Furthermore, a child's knowledge and experience play a critical role in what they are capable of understanding, so that expectations/standards for what a child *should* know must take into account both chronological age and the age that a child is introduced to inquiry (pp. 2–3).

The bottom line of the report is a call for an emphasis in K–8 science instruction that honors four proficiencies in students:

1. Know, use, and interpret scientific explanations of the natural world.
2. Generate and evaluate scientific evidence and explanations.
3. Understand the nature and development of scientific knowledge
4. Participate productively in scientific practices and discourses (p. 2).

WHAT ARE WAYS TO DEVELOP AND SUPPORT PROFICIENCY?

Proficiency 1: Know, Use, and Interpret Scientific Explanations of the Natural World

A precocious 3-year-old cousin charmed adults by his preoccupation with what his 1-year-old brother knew. "What does Nathan know about orange juice?" he would ask, watching him reach for a sippy cup; or, *"What does Nathan know about blocks?"* as the baby gleefully knocked over a tower each time it was constructed. We do not need to read the National Research Council report (Duschl et al., 2007) to know that Nathan, like all very young children, knew a great deal about the natural world. However, his knowledge was *implicit*—that is, while the child uses the knowledge, it does not *get articulated* into words. In fact, such knowledge is *not acquired* through verbal explanations either—but through intense observation and interaction with the natural world.

For the young child, as for "real" scientists, this knowledge is not an isolated tidbit, taken out only when someone announces "time for science." It is continuous with their experience as a living, wondering being. The need to know is fed by intrinsic rewards that come from tangible evidence that one is capable of learning/problem solving and thus is competent—which gives a boost to one's sense of self-worth and efficacy.

Why are multiple intelligences so important in Proficiency 1?
While Proficiency 1 tends to emphasize developing Level 1 comprehension, it calls for doing so in ways that use what we have termed *unlocked closed questions*. Moreover, learners must be given ways to access the full array of multiple intelligences as they acquire, represent, and explain their understanding of the natural world. I discuss below just a few of the interactive strategies that use stories and informational texts to trigger and guide scientific inquiry.

How can Reading an Object support Proficiency 1? This strategy can be used either before or after reading a text or story that concerns a natural object.[4] Once the story has engaged the children's thinking, they are provided with a real specimen to observe closely and then to record their findings in a science notebook, using not only words but also pictures and measurement data.

- One kindergarten classroom wondered what persimmons were after reading *Dear Juno* (Pak, 2001). The teacher acquired a few of the fruit from an Asian supermarket for the class to explore and taste. She also shared some information she had found on the Internet. Together the class created a poster entitled "What We Know Now About Persimmons."
- To jump-start the FOSS science kit investigation of rocks, a number of classrooms I work with have adapted the following general plan.[5]
    * Read aloud and discuss: *Everybody Needs a Rock* by Byrd Baylor (a prose poem giving 10 "rules" for choosing a special pocket stone) or *Elizabeti's Doll* by Stephanie Stuve-Bodeen.
    * Bring in an assortment of rocks; each person picks one and then closely examines it, using drawings and words to record observable physical attributes such as shape; form; size in multiple dimensions including width, height, and diameter; coloration; and texture.
    * Introduce the rock: Learners introduce their rocks through a creative expression or representation such as a drawing, oral report, written description, story, song, or movement activity.[6]

Why is visual representation of knowledge so important? Children's work from Reggio Emilia exhibits and books provides irrefutable evidence that even quite young children are capable of graphically representing knowledge. Drawings, clay sculptures, weavings, and constructions all convey the children's understanding of natural phenomena, with minimal reliance on words.

The strategy of intentionally developing children's ability to use the basic science process skill of observation can yield quite precise graphic representations. For example, a third-grade science activity began with an interactive read-aloud of an informational book about spiders. Children then went back to their desk clusters and each drew a spider in pencil, trying to include as much detail as they could. The five children in each cluster compared their drawings and discussed differences and then did a second draft of the drawing. Then each cluster looked at a photo, again comparing it to their drawings; each then drew a final draft of the spider, using colored pencils this time. They were encouraged to label the body parts as well. Both the teacher and students found the difference between the first and final draft of the drawings a striking way to assess how much had been learned about spiders. This case was especially notable because it involved hearing-impaired and second language learners as well as typically developing children; it gave everyone an equal opportunity to develop and represent knowledge in ways that were not limited to verbal expression.[7]

How can amazing facts spark inquiry? This strategy is designed to engage interest and to provide direction for an inquiry into a topic for which there may not be a great deal of prior knowledge.[8] The "Who Lives in the Ocean?" inquiry might be launched this way:

- The teacher has preselected informational books, single-page articles about various sea creatures taken from the Internet, and other materials with good illustrations; she makes them available for the children to peruse.
- Each child (or pair) is instructed to skim the materials and to find three amazing facts; the teacher emphasizes that the only criterion is that the fact be amazing to the individual. Each fact is written on a separate card or sticky note.
- After about 15 minutes the group comes together to share their amazing facts. As one is read, the facilitator asks if anyone has another that is similar or seems closely related. Thus, if someone noted that blue whales are the largest living species of mammals, others who had facts about the size of other species would share their findings, and all the notes about size would be clustered together on chart paper posted for all to see.
- As more facts emerge, so do the clusters. A topic like sea creatures is almost certain to end up with a few broad categories such as relative size, eating habits, appearance, habitat, and classification.
- In the lively conversation that takes place in the sharing phase, the group's interests begin to emerge naturally, along with a more focused direction for the inquiry. If the areas seem to generate equal amazement, the whole group might be broken up into "expert" teams; each team decides on an inquiry focus and then reports back to the others when their investigation is completed.

This strategy is effective in the same way that the Case in Point activity was: it is very open-ended; every answer is right, so those who are afraid of giving a "wrong" answer are comfortable participating. At the same time, the community conversation ends up drawing virtually everyone in—including those whose initial interest in the topic was low.

However, it does call for the facilitator to be very intentional about the materials from which the facts will be culled. The reading level should be appropriate for the group. It is important to avoid overly dense texts—some teachers find it is best to include photocopies of a few pages as well as guides or whole books. This is a very effective way to incorporate and develop visual literacy skills for younger children, those with lower literacy skills, and English language learners. If they are provided with a high proportion of good illustrations with captions, they will find many things to amaze them—which they can express orally and represent using Post-its and sketches on the page itself.

Proficiency 2: Generate and Evaluate Scientific Evidence and Explanations

This proficiency refers to the familiar *doing experiments,* using *the scientific method* or *collecting data.*

What's the role of error in Proficiency 2? If science is to come to life in classrooms, we need to carry out activities in a spirit of inquiry and discovery. Rather than doing cookbook experiments, children need to get messy in the way real scientists do with wandering, wondering, and meaningful surprises as vital parts of the process. They need to get the intrinsic reward that comes with persisting through the gift of error—going back to discover if a result that doesn't match the hypothesis calls for reformulating the problem statement, taking into account different variables, or changing the methodology or perhaps redoing the experiment to correct careless procedures.

How can stories support Proficiency 2? As shown in the opening chapter's discussion of using the Three Little Pigs' houses to learn about the scientific method, authentic inquiries involve the learners in formulating problem statements as well as possible solutions. Linda Sweeney (2001) talks about the importance of using stories to do *systems thinking—* that is, to look for patterns in how things happen and in how problems arise as well to take systems into account when problem-solving. Her book *When a Butterfly Sneezes* looks at how this approach might work in 12 favorite children's stories. But here are a few examples of what happened in Chicago Public School classrooms:

- A few third-grade classrooms got intrigued by a different problem posed by the Sun and Moon story—they explored how different sizes and weights of objects affected how the water in a fish tank rose. This fit well into the physical science unit they were doing.
- Another year, several classrooms had selected Pamela Allen's delightful Who Sank the Boat? This offers a very engaging lead-in

to kindergarten and primary hands-on investigations to answer the challenge: "Can you make a better boat?" The science center included a dishpan with water for testing, a variety of materials to make boats, lumps of clay to act as test passengers, and a small collection of informational books on sinking and floating such as those by Niz (2006) and Nelson (2004). Partners or trios worked together and documented their efforts, using digital photographs.

Proficiency 3: Understand the Nature and Development of Scientific Knowledge

This proficiency operates on two different levels. On one hand, it is related to the *history of science*, which tracks and reflects on the growth of scientific knowledge over time, so that children appreciate how each generation builds on discoveries made in the past. *Snowflake Bentley* (Martin, 2009), *Starry Messenger: Galileo Galilei* (Sis, 2000), *The Man Who Walked Between the Towers* (Gerstein, 2003), *Rocks in His Head* (Hurst, 2001), or *Marvelous Mattie* (McCully, 2006) are just a few of the many picture book biographies of scientists and inventors that will help young students recognize that you don't need formal training as a scientist to *think* like a scientist—to use those all important science processing skills. While the message is implicit in such books, it is important to facilitate a discussion that will help children develop explicit understanding of how scientific knowledge is established and developed.

On the other hand, this proficiency also has a *personal application* level. Lifelong learners begin early on to understand that knowledge is a like an onion or an iceberg; an individual's growth of understanding is progressive and process-based. The more one knows, the better one's subsequent questions will be as one digs deeper.

How can stories support Proficiency 3? Once again, high-quality children's literature is a highly effective tool for developing this understanding. A book like Ruth Krauss's *The Growing Story* (2007) or her classic *The Carrot Seed* allow young children to literally follow along with the main character's discovery about what it means to grow bigger. The beautiful *Circles of Hope* (Williams, 2005) invites primary-age children to "unpack" how Facile builds on past failures and advice from others as he finally learns to how to plant a tree that will grow strong, as a gift for his baby sister.

Why is evaluation so important for Proficiency 3? Development of Proficiency 3 calls for consistently reinforcing the learner's *metacognition,* that is, awareness of what one knows, including how one has learned and how prior learning will contribute to learning more. One might say that *evaluation*—the third of our 3 E's, as well as one of the highest-order thinking skills—*is a function of Proficiency 3*. Once again, the implications for the classroom are significant. The focus for assessment should not be scoring correct responses to a standardized checklist of facts or skills; rather, teacher and learners alike should be constantly engaged in reflecting on how well the current inquiry is going—and if it is not going well, what can be done to refocus the question or to provide appropriate scaffolding.[9]

- The K-W-L strategy is a very effective tool to use in this regard. At the beginning of the inquiry, the learning community generates a list of what members believe they already *Know* about a topic; properly done, even when a misconception is stated, it goes on the list without any attempt to correct it. Concurrently, a list of what members of the community *Want* to know is also generated. Again, if someone identifies something that another claims to know, the item goes in both places. As the inquiry proceeds, both lists are constantly referenced. New learning or confirmation of something that was known gets acknowledged in a third prominently posted list that identifies what has been *Learned*. When the classroom is truly functioning as a learning community, with a positive environment, there is as much delight in recognizing and correcting a misconception as in new learning. Reviewing the lists becomes part of the closure activities of an inquiry.
- As shown in this chapter's Case in Point, pourquoi tales work well across an inquiry. They can offer an authentic way to confirm/assess acquisition of knowledge as effectively as they can launch an inquiry. Many years after the Sun/Moon activity, a third-grade teacher wondered if I knew a pourquoi tale that would give her students practice with asking good questions at the same time that it might help her assess what they had learned in the water cycle study they had just completed. I found a Papago/Tohono O'odham tale: The warrior Whirlwind gets sent away from his village because the chief's arrogant daughter accuses him of insulting her. Blind Rain must accompany the exile because Whirlwind guides Rain wherever he needs to go. As time goes on, the village is left without wind and rain; all the water resources dry up. Eventually the people beg the chief to bring the two back, but they only return after being sent for many times—and they just visit and then leave again. It is hard to get them back, the people say, so now Arizona is very

dry, with wind and rain coming only occasionally. Before beginning the story, I told the group that this was a legend about the
water cycle and they should listen to see how it fit with what
they had been learning.[10]

In the lively conversation afterward, it was clear that it was the story
as a whole that extended this activity through the cycle of Engagement,
Exploration, and Evaluation. Some of the discussion clearly had the at-
tractions of solving a puzzle as we talked about how it makes sense that
wind and rain are pictured as inseparable friends. As they eagerly pointed
to parts of the story that corresponded to the stages of the water cycle
such as precipitation, evaporation, and condensation, the children provided good evidence of having learned the scientific "Big Ideas" about
the water cycle. However, it was the social-emotional dimensions of the
story that kept the conversation dynamic. There was some debate about
the chief's daughter who had brought such trouble to her people, without having to pay any personal consequences. In effect, the story took on
double force because it got the children constructing their understanding
both in terms of the science phenomena and in terms of the interpersonal
dynamics.

Proficiency 4: Participate Productively in Scientific Practices and Discourses

Proficiency 4 calls for embedding the other three proficiencies into
regular functioning of the learning community. However, it specifically
reflects a concern that good inquiries are *disciplined*—that is, the learners
are intentionally guided into developing habits of mind and skills specific to the different disciplines. Thus, while all inquiries involve problem
solving, scientific problem solving calls for close observation of natural
phenomena; making predictions; generating, representing, and analyzing
data; and classifying, ordering, measuring, and representing observable
attributes of those phenomena.

How can writer's workshops turn into science? The National Science Foundation Elementary Science Integration Project (ESIP) has funded a variety of projects that promote connections between language arts
instruction and inquiry-based science in grades K–8.[11] A committee working with Wendy Saul, the director of the project, realized that the popular
writing workshop structure developed by Lucy Caulkins offered a model
of how to consistently support the basic skills of science inquiry. *Science
Workshop: Reading, Writing, and Thinking Like a Scientist* (Saul, Reardon, &

Pearce, 2002) offers practical suggestions, strategies, and examples of how Proficiency 4 can be sustained in early elementary school. NSTA Press has also issued a very valuable series of articles that feature actual classrooms and teachers: *Linking Science and Literacy in the K–8 Classroom* (Douglas, Klentschy, Worth, & Binder, 2006).

As useful as ESIP resources are, in some ways this is the easiest of the proficiencies to support—*if the classroom is committed to functioning as a learning community that does quality intellectual work*. As we have seen, real-world scientific practices and discourses are done as inquiry, directed toward understanding the workings of the natural world. Those workings, in turn, are closely interwoven with those of the human heart and mind—the stuff of stories.

TRY AND APPLY

1. Locate, read, and reflect on a pourquoi tale that interests you.
2. Decide on a specific science inquiry that it addresses and then consider whether you would use it to introduce, to develop, or to assess the children's learning.
3. Identify a cluster of 3–5 high-quality informational texts that can be used in the inquiry. You can browse through the holdings of a local library or bookstore; however, online booksellers and other Internet resources can be very helpful.
4. Identify which of the four proficiencies you could focus on, as well as a strategy, and draft a lesson plan.
5. If you are currently in a classroom, you might take one of the activities described in this chapter and tailor it for use in your classroom.

CHAPTER 8

How Do You Get from Patches to a Patchwork Quilt?

Reading an Object to Spark Inquiry Across the Curriculum

CASE IN POINT

In methods courses and professional development programs we often discuss how strategies, individual lesson plans, and extended inquiries must always be "tailored" to meet the specific goals, needs, and interests of the classroom learning community that is using them. In the example I relate here, first-grade and third-grade cross-curricular inquiries were launched by what might look like the same activity.

In both cases, the students were gathered in a circle around the classroom rug. All 20 third graders were in one group, but we broke the first graders into two groups of 14. Carefully unfolding and laying out a hand-sewn patchwork quilt top, I invited the children to examine a section near them for a few minutes, considering questions such as these:

- What purpose do you think this object serves? Do you have anything like it at home?
- How old do you think it is? What do you notice about how it might have been made?
- Do you think this comes from a store? Do you think it's valuable?

They were free to quietly discuss their observations with neighbors at first. After a few minutes, children shared what they noticed in a whole-group discussion. Many children recognized the object was a quilt—although they knew it wasn't finished yet because of the "messy" back. Most also thought it was old and that it didn't come from a store. A few had quilts made by a relative and others had special blankets that had been given to them. As the children made comments, raised questions, or supported their responses, everyone took a more careful look at the quilt top, both front and back. For the most part, I facilitated the discussion without contributing.

Within 10 minutes, however, it was time to move on. After complimenting the children on their careful observations and on the way they were able to back up their responses with thinking, I clarified for everyone that this was a quilt top that was not fully finished because it didn't have a middle or back piece and the layers weren't sewn together. I explained I had acquired it at a farm auction so that I wasn't quite sure who had made it for whom or why it wasn't completed. However, I did know that it was probably about 50–60 years old.

As I carefully refolded the quilt top, I mentioned it was valuable to me because it reminded me of things my aunties did when I was a little girl. I invited them to think about the different ways the quilt in the read-aloud we would do might be considered valuable. The first graders heard *The Patchwork Quilt* by Valerie Flournoy (1985) and the third graders *The Patchwork Path* by Betty Stroud (2007).

As soon as the story was finished, both groups excitedly made comments connecting the story with the quilt top they had just examined. Many wanted to look at it again and were glad to hear it would be staying in the classroom as part of a new inquiry project, one that would involve learning across the curriculum.

- In the first-grade classroom, the teacher wanted to address an issue that was very much a part of her classroom's demographics:
  a number of children in the class were being raised by grandparents or had grandparents in the household. Others indicated
  they didn't have many relatives nearby. But she wanted all the
  children to understand that just as there are many different family
  structures, there are many ways for a family to share its heritage.
  At the same time, she wanted to strengthen the home-school connection so that families were being celebrated, not just called in
  when a child had a problem. The controlling inquiry question she
  chose was: *In what ways are families like a patchwork quilt?*
- In the third-grade classroom, the teacher had just returned from
  maternity leave. She wanted to reestablish a positive climate that
  was governed by behavior that conformed to the acronym ASK:
  Appropriate, Safe, and Kind.[1] We decided to combine the idea of
  quilts as "show ways" to freedom via the Underground Railroad

with having each student make a quilt square that would be a "show way" to the ASK principle. The overarching inquiry question was: *What can we learn from Underground Railroad quilt codes about how to find a way to be Appropriate, Safe, Kind citizens of our school and world?*

WHAT'S THE STORY ABOUT TEACHING/LEARNING SOCIAL STUDIES?

Both the first- and third-grade inquiries involved literacy-based activities as well as math and science lessons. However, both primarily emphasized *social studies* and the many subdisciplines that constitute the study of humans in relationship with others and with the world. As is developmentally appropriate, the first-grade inquiry kept the focus on the immediate family and community while the third graders had a much larger scope.

Historical figures, events, and movements; geographical places and formations; economic practices and trends, as well as cultural beliefs and customs, largely do not move beyond rote learning until the capacity for abstract thinking has fully kicked in by the end of the 5–7 shift. However, both before and after the shift, rich stories and hands-on experiences can help make connections between events, feelings, and phenomena in daily life to something that took place long ago or far away.

All the important elements of a well-told story, including character, setting, and story sequence, contribute to these kinds of connections. Stories involve characters struggling to resolve problem situations; if the character is portrayed in a compelling way, one can identify with the sense of excitement, joy, loss, or danger the character experiences in a historical or cultural setting that is very different from one's own.

HOW CAN "READING AN OBJECT" HELP MAKE SENSE OF STORIES?

As effective as these stories are, there is still a level at which young children and novice learners at any age benefit from having some kind of hands-on experience that literally brings remote events and objects to life. Going to museums, especially living history museums like Colonial Williamsburg, can do this. Over the years, however, I developed an activity I call "Reading an Object," which is illustrated in this chapter's Case in Point.[2]

Initially, I periodically brought in something unfamiliar to show *after* a storytelling—for example, after telling the Greek myth of Persephone and the changing of the seasons, I passed around a pomegranate so everyone could see what it meant to eat just a few of the tiny seeds. However, I came to see an advantage to triggering wonder about an object *before* doing the read-aloud or storytelling. Teachers tend to take for granted that everyone knows enough about the quite ordinary items featured in many texts. Or, if something from a different culture or time is mentioned, it seems adequate to offer a quick definition along with a picture as part of "pre-reading." We overlook how meaningful it can be to dig deeper by intentionally observing something. Flournoy's *The Patchwork Quilt* along with Pinkney's illustrations meet all the standards for a high-quality book. Still, appreciation for how much work Tanya did and the power of a quilt as a metaphor of a family's loving relationships between generations takes on immediate force when there is an actual quilt top made up of many small pieces to see, to feel, and to wonder about.

Where Does Reading an Object Fit on the Developmental Trajectory?

One of the beauties of this strategy is that it is always developmentally appropriate. It triggers inquiry in a way that respects the two critical learning trajectories. On one hand, having the learners use their senses to explore a real object honors the C-P-S principle: Learning begins with the *concrete*, moves to the *pictorial,* and then is generalized and understood on the *abstract/symbolic* level. At the same time, as the object is handled, the learner may remember something they already knew about it or start to make connections. A kind of recognition begins that may grow in the conversation that follows. In effect, this process also honors the way that *receptive precedes productive understanding,* that is, we can understand what a word or idea means before we can explain in our own words.

As is true when the first questions and comments about a story come from the group rather than the teacher, Reading an Object leaves the learners free to wander and wonder in ways that make sense to them; while the teacher plays an important role in facilitating the discussion, the focus isn't locked into the teacher's questions or answers. Inevitably, the conversation and the connections are enriched. Even the teachers learn.

What Does it Mean to "Read an Object"?

The "rules" for Reading an Object are quite simple:

1. A real object connected with the story or topic is presented to the group of learners, along with an invitation to explore, make

discoveries, wonder, and share ideas about the purpose for which it is intended, the age, and the nature of the object.

2. While the invitation is phrased as an open-ended statement, the selection of the object and the focus suggested for the exploration is very intentional; it is directly tied to the nature of the inquiry that is being launched.

A few examples might help make the possibilities clearer.

- A math lesson for preschoolers and kindergarteners is done during an exploration of the theme "We are all the same; we are all different." Children are invited to turn to a partner and decide on one way in which the shoes they are wearing are the same and another way that they are different. Their ideas are shared with the whole group before a read-aloud of Ann Morris's informational photo essay, *Shoes, Shoes, Shoes* (1998). Immediately afterward, there's a lively discussion of how shoes can be the same or different in appearance, in reference to the job or the occasion for which they are being donned, or in reference to the culture of the persons wearing them. Even preschoolers are eager to explore different ways to sort their own shoes.[3]

- Two baskets are handed around, one filled with raw eggs, the other holding apples; the group converses about what it feels like to handle the two baskets, before listening to *Down the Road* (Schertle, 2000). A young girl is eager to be able to take on the responsibility of carrying home eggs from the general store; although she is careful, the eggs break; upset, the girl retreats to an apple tree. Her father joins her and helps her understand the importance of living with one's mistakes and learning from them. They go home with a basket of apples, and the family enjoys apple pie instead of eggs for breakfast. Adults in professional development groups as well as primary school children who have handled the eggs and apples move quickly to probing the difference between an intentional mistake and one that happens despite one's best efforts; the conversation deepens into consideration of what it means to learn from mistakes—of either sort.

- Third graders are given an opportunity to examine an old wooden-handled shovel; while most of them know what this tool is called, few have actually ever used one. They note the wood and the steel instead of plastic and point out marks of use as proof of its age. Immediately afterward they do an interactive read-aloud of *Miss Bridie Chose a Shovel* (Connor, 2004). From the first words of the spare text—"She could have picked a chiming clock or a porcelain figurine, but Miss Bridie chose a shovel back in 1856"—the group has a very concrete sense of how Miss Bridie's choice says a great deal about her personality as well as about the qualities that helped this young immigrant girl endure in a new world. They begin to speculate about what the other two choices might indicate. Later on in this social studies theme unit on emigration, they will read *The Lotus Seed* by A. Garland (1997), *Tea with Milk* by A. Say (2009), and *Going Home* by Eve Bunting (1998). The culminating project includes working with a partner to produce a book based on Miss Bridie, featuring another emigrant experience of taking things along and leaving things behind.

Why Use Reading an Object to Launch an Inquiry?

The last example suggests how effective it can be to launch an extended inquiry by "reading an object." The "digging deeper" into the meaning of a fairly ordinary object acts as a signal that the learners are going to be doing an in-depth exploration of a concept or an issue of which it is important to develop understanding—but that can be understood through a variety of lenses.

At the same time, discussion of the object might also work as the Amazing Facts strategy we discuss further in the next chapter; it gives the whole community a chance to explore and identify particular aspects of an inquiry that might be of greatest interest to the whole group or create a cluster of smaller "expert" groups.

HOW IS A PATCHWORK QUILT LIKE AN INTEGRATED CURRICULUM INQUIRY?

My interest in quilts began with going to farm auctions in northwest Indiana. I was deeply drawn by what my mother had called "dreams of beauty"—the many ways that hardworking women had found to turn the necessary into beautiful creative objects. I began to learn the names of the various patterns and the stories behind them and how to evaluate the materials, techniques, and skill that distinguish a really good quilt from a mediocre one; I also overheard snippets of the personal stories of the women who had made them. Around the same time, in the Britannica math project, one of the math educators pointed out how the rows and columns of quilt blocks are a natural *array* that can be used to understand multiplication. That gave me another excuse to build my collection of quilts and all kinds of books about them.

Soon I was incorporating quilts and quilt stories into pre-service and in-service teaching as well as into direct work in classrooms. Quilts proved to be a powerful way to look across the curriculum, offering rich opportunities to explore concepts related to mathematics, science, and social studies.

Mathematics: including *geometry* (shapes, movement, and direction); *patterns* (within a single block and/or the structure of the whole quilt top); *measurement* (area, perimeter, arrays).

Science: including *color theory* (colors as an attribute for establishing a pattern and design); *material sciences* (attributes of fabric types; methods used to join the quilt pieces and layers); *use of technology* (including sewing machines, measurement and design tools); *application of the scientific process* (the full process and problem solving involved in going from design to finished quilt).

Social studies: including *social history* (issues and understandings around frontier life, women's roles/bonding; the aesthetic element in domestic objects and tasks); *historical impact* (cotton as the preferred fabric type; cotton gin/slavery and Underground Railroad connection); *economic aspects* (women's doing quilts for hire; economic factors in slavery, share cropping; *cultural traditions* (African American; Amish; fabric artists).

One of the most striking features of a beautiful patchwork quilt is that although it is made up of small shapes cut out of many different fabrics, there is a strong impression of coherence created by the design. In the same way, while activities around quilts could be used to feed *any* of the discipline-specific goals/issues listed above, it is equally apparent that trying to stuff *all* of them into a single study is impossible. The structure of a well-designed, coherent inquiry honors two key planning principles.

Planning Principle 1: What's the Question?

A well-designed inquiry begins by identifying and then tailoring a good *question* with the following characteristics:

- *Specific* enough so the learners can see connections between the specific knowledge—including facts and skills about a topic—as well as how this information is connected to a larger conceptual framework; they can see that "facts" are the building blocks of the key "big ideas" of a discipline. Thus one might begin to see a relationship between the historical fact that many quilts are made of cotton to the economic fact that cotton was the cheapest and most widely available fabric, to the science fact that it is also very durable—all features which make sense in relation to the "big idea" known as the law of supply and demand.

- *Open* enough so that connections can be made and conceptual understanding developed across disciplines. The example above includes facts drawn from sciences and social science disciplines—at the same time, mathematical calculations and statistics are necessary to express these facts.
- *Engaging* enough to lead to quality intellectual work that reflects the needs and interests of the particular learning community. Both the first and third graders in the Case in Point above were deeply engaged by making their own discoveries about a quilt top; there was a noticeable difference related to developmental levels in the observations they made; so, too, the choice of the read-aloud that followed helped direct their interest in different ways.

While the general direction one wants an inquiry to go may be clear, crafting the right question can be a tall order. For many teachers, it calls for a fairly radical shift from beginning with a plan for student work to identifying the essential learning/teaching goals that the lesson or curriculum plan is meant to help the children construct.

However, beginning with the question is very much akin to the scientific method in which one first identifies a problem situation or phenomena, next considers the factors and variables that might be contributing to or causing the phenomena to be explained, and then designs and carries out an experiment that will lead to some conclusions.

In the business world, the concept of "Backwards Planning" has long been seen as strategic, especially in uncertain times. It clearly makes sense that marketing strategies should *follow from* rather than *dictate* marketing or sales goals, for example. The approach clearly makes equal sense in education—certainly, if the aim is to teach for understanding and not just to the test. Wiggins and McTighe (2005) and Tomlinson and McTighe (2006) have elaborated a whole procedure for curriculum planning using these principles that they call Understanding by Design (UbD). The templates they offer are very useful tools.

However, being keenly intentional means that such planning cannot be done by autopilot or by blindly following a prepared plan. Unquestionably, all kinds of ideas from other teachers, curriculum materials, past experiences, and current requirements will be part of the mix; however, in the end, teaching for understanding calls for careful tailoring: that is, reflecting on the specific needs and interests of the classroom learning community at hand and building them into the goals as well as the details of the implementation plan.

The third-grade classroom in the case study is a good example. I had been consulting with Chiquita, the school social worker, and Heather, the classroom teacher, about the increasingly negative dynamics in this classroom of students at risk academically and socially. Two social work interns were available to help us engage the children in developing positive behavior traits. The group was close to the point of no return if the many messages that they were "bad" didn't get recast. While their behavior may not have always been productive, these children, like all humans, needed to know that they were worthy of respect and that important adults in the school believed that they were capable of respecting others.[4] We wanted them to think about the importance of behaving in a way that was socially responsible, that met the standards for the ASK acronym: Appropriate, Safe, and Kind.

We all agreed that these restless 8–9-year-olds needed something to do; given that they had plenty of experience being perceived as "underachieving," it was also critical that the project would be seen as something special and noteworthy that they had been *chosen* to do. We would have to think through a series of experiences that would maximize the likelihood of success and build their sense of competence.

We also wanted to support the many efforts the principal of this school had made to help children caught in the cycle of poverty take pride in themselves as strong African Americans, fully capable of moving forward. As it turned out, I had recently acquired *The Patchwork Path: A Quilt Map to Freedom* (2007) by Betty Stroud to add to my collection of quilt stories. This book used quilts to celebrate the courage and problem solving needed to escape from slavery via the Underground Railroad. It gave a very concrete face to Jacqueline Woodson's inspiring picture book *Show Way* (2005), which uses a quilt to summarize her family's history from slavery to the modern day.

The team agreed that a classroom quilt was the kind of highly visible product that was needed. I would draw on my experience doing quilt projects in classrooms to set up the logistics. The classroom teacher saw she could tie in the math and poetry lessons she was planning, as well address history standards using material on the Underground Railroad. The social work interns would focus on the ASK traits. Even so, we still had an idea rather than a blueprint; before selecting or organizing specific activities or books, we hammered out our key objectives, shown in Table 8.1.

TABLE 8.1. Teaching Learning Objectives Across the Curriculum

What can we learn from Underground Railroad quilt codes about how to find a way to be ASK (Appropriate, Safe, Kind) citizens of our school and world?

Conceptual Framework Ideas/Skills	Inquiry Questions
Quilts as Constructions: Quilts are usually made of a number of blocks, each of which reflects a geometric pattern; these blocks are joined together in an array and may be separated by borders or strips. • Many quilt patterns use regular geometric shapes, with some patterns using related shapes (for example, a square may be made up of two right-angle triangles). • Quilt patterns can be constructed for a single block or multiples of the same block. • Color choice and shape play an important role in our perception of a quilt pattern. • Quilt pieces and the layers of a quilt can be joined in a variety of ways. • "How big" a quilt is can be expressed in terms of area and perimeter.	**Math:** How can the pattern of a quilt block be changed by changing the arrangement of the constituent pieces? **Science:** What importance do color and shape have in influencing our perception of a quilt block? **Science:** What are different ways fabric can be joined and what might be the advantages of each? **Science/Math** What kinds of measurement are important in making a quilt?
Quilts as Documents: The fabrics from which a quilt is made and the pattern(s) chosen are a reflection of the quiltmakers' personal interests and history. Groups or cultures may have a series of codes, or signals, that are understood within the group but are not obvious to outsiders. Quilt-block names reflect historical or sociological associations.	**History:** What was the Underground Railroad and what kind of codes and clues led to a successful escape via it?
Quilts as "Show Ways": As members of a community we often need rules and reminders to "show the way" to meeting our responsibilities and to assure that our rights are respected. This point has a particularly powerful resonance for the African American historical experience, including the Underground Railroad heritage. • As members of a community, we have rights and responsibilities; we owe each other respect in all situations by showing the ASK traits. • Maps provide a two-dimensional representation of movement and direction. • Maps can help us get from one place to another; the distance traveled may vary from quite close to very far away. • By observing carefully what we hear, see, and smell, as well as feel and taste, we can gain knowledge about our immediate environment.	**Social Studies:** Why is it important to take guidance from cultural and community leaders about how to lead our lives? What does it mean to show the ASK traits (Appropriate, Safe, Kind)? **Geography/Math:** What are different ways that a map can represent movement and direction? **Science:** How can our senses provide important information that keeps us safe as we move around an environment?

Planning Principle 2:
What's Involved in Mapping Out a Successful Project?

This principle involves a set of concurrent objectives:

- The overarching inquiry question should be broken down into a series of questions that will be addressed in individual activities/lessons and that reflect "big ideas" of the disciplines being addressed.
- Choices about specific activities/lesson focus and the sequence of the activities must be carefully structured; individual lessons should build up to a culminating project or performance that has value beyond the classroom—one that is a celebration of the learning that has taken place.

Once again, the critical point is that an authentic inquiry is much more than a collection of lessons/activities loosely related to a theme. It is not a coincidence that the ASK quilt turned out to be one of the most rewarding classroom projects I have done and that it also was one that evolved from rigorously intentional planning and implementation done as a professional community, including myself, Chiquita, and Heather. Just a few of the decisions we made in mapping out the project can illustrate how this worked:

- After the initial read-aloud, pairs of children were asked to become "experts" on one of the block designs mentioned in *The Patchwork Path*.[5] Each team was given preselected reading materials that would help them research danger signals escaping slaves had to be alert for as well as indicators for Underground Railroad stations. Some of the patterns were associated with spirituals such as "Follow the Drinking Gourd" that also were used as "codes." Heather used the texts of these songs to introduce the poetry unit she was doing.
- The project also dovetailed with several math topics. Early on, to reinforce the children's understanding of how a quilt was made up of constituent blocks and to give them experience of how geometric shapes are related (two right triangles can form a square or rectangle) and of how different patterns can be created by rotating or flipping shapes, we included an activity that called for children to reconstruct the "Shoofly" pattern using paper pieces. Toward the end of the project, we had the children discuss and determine the mathematical issues of the array in which the 21 squares should be arranged. While I anticipated

that 3 across and 7 down was more likely to "look right" than a 7 x 3 array, it was the children who figured out what the options were, chose one, and then decided how to distribute the squares according to theme (7 showed Appropriate, 8 showed Safe, and 6 depicted Kind).

- The social work interns spent 3 one-hour sessions asking the children to discuss and come up with examples from their own lives about what it meant to be Appropriate, Safe, and Kind. Each session had the students draw a picture and write a few sentences showing one of these examples. Later, each child chose one of his or her designs to draw with fabric markers on an 8-inch unbleached muslin square; these were backed on an orange and purple burlap (the school colors) and each child tied the layers together somewhere near their square.

Unquestionably, the greatest reward was seeing how the project truly paid off for the children. They showed enormous interest in detailed information about the Underground Railroad, a topic that had previously meant no more than reciting the name Harriet Tubman. Each child was photographed with his or her own square, and each drafted, edited, and published a one-page essay about it for a classroom book; individual copies were made for each child, the school principal, and the school library. Most meaningfully, Heather reported that her students were beginning to challenge each other about ASK when the "he said/she said" accusations started.

When we reported back to other teachers in the school about the project, Heather, Chiquita, and I unanimously agreed that the project was well worth all the work. We thought it would be great to do again; while the general plan could be followed, there still would be tailoring involved.

We thought the project might work better at the beginning rather than at the end of the school year; emphasis would move to creating the classroom community and establishing positive rules, rather than the kind of "damage control" we did. Some of the activities we did would have to be changed to reflect developmental stages and needs of the children. For example, first or second graders could also do an ASK quilt; however, they would need a great deal more support in the actual assembly, so a paper quilt might be better for them. But we were even more insistent that tying the Underground Railroad theme to ASK would not be appropriate for younger children. The topic is too complex; before children are solidly through the 5–7 shift, their sense of time and of history is shaky and the topic of slavery can be threatening.[6] At the same time, we felt the emphasis for younger children should focus firmly on the idea of the immediate classroom community. They need to make direct connections to their own experiences to realize that observing rules based on respect gives them rights as well as responsibilities—they themselves can feel secure that they will be treated in a way that is appropriate, safe, and kind.

HOW CAN A MATRIX HELP LEARNERS MAP OUT THEIR UNDERSTANDING?

As rewarding and meaningful as making a classroom quilt can be, there are many good reasons why a teacher would choose to do a very different kind of quilt project. For example, when the first-grade teacher who used the quilt Reading an Object strategy with Flournoy's *The Patchwork Quilt* looked through my collection of picture books that featured quilts, she found a good number that featured grandparents; she liked the idea of using them to explore how the story of every family is a unique blend of connections and relationships that stretch over time and place. She felt that having each child develop a collection of information and stories about his or her family would meet her goals much better than a classroom quilt.

Focusing in on her goals this way helped Chris narrow down the selection of books she wanted to use. Thus she loved the way *Luka's Quilt* (Guback, 1994) uses the story of how a grandmother and granddaughter come to understand the importance of compromise when two people who love each other disagree. However, the idea of quilts as containing old family stories isn't very strong in this work. *The Story Blanket* (Wolff & Savitz, 2008) is a lovely testimony to how stories can unite a community, but the focus on family isn't there, so she put that book aside as well.

In the end, Chris decided to focus on four books she would introduce as interactive read-alouds; each would be revisited several times, with discussions and extending activities. She sent home a letter listing the books and explaining how family members would work with the child to complete a Family Patchwork Portfolio, complete with a cover page that the child would design using a quilt-block pattern. The portfolios would be displayed on report card pickup day. Items included:

1. *The Patchwork Quilt* (Flournoy, 1985). *Portfolio page:* "What Might Go in Our Home Family Quilt?" List a favorite clothes item for each member of the household.
2. *The Name Quilt* (Root, 2003). *Portfolio page*: "Once When I Was Young." What's a good story about something that happened when an older relative was young?
3. *The Quilt Story* (Johnston & DePaola, 1996). *Portfolio page*: "What Do We Do at Bedtime?" Tell about your family going-to-bed routines.

4. *The Keeping Quilt* (Polacco, 2010). *Portfolio page:* "How Far Apart Is Our Family?" Count up how many family members, including parents, siblings, grandparents, uncles, aunts, and cousins live: (a) in your immediate household, (b) somewhere in Chicago, (c) elsewhere in the United States, (d) in another country.

As her plans came together, Chris realized that this project would be a perfect opportunity for her to try out the book matrix we had discussed in a professional development workshop. This strategy is a graphic organizer that acts as a map of text-to-self, text-to-text, and text-to world connections between a selected cluster of books. After deciding on a core set of books, the teacher draws up a list of 3–5 questions that apply to all of the books. The chart is done on large-size poster paper and kept up during the unit or project. After each book is read, children discuss and agree on the points that should be recorded for each question. Table 8.2 shows the matrix for this project.

Chris was delighted with how quickly the group began to see connections that moved not just across the row but also down each column, as each new story was read. They didn't need any prompting questions to get them discussing how *The Patchwork Quilt* and *The Name Quilt* involve grandmothers and granddaughters sharing family stories, even though Sadie was hearing stories about older relatives while Tanya's were about her immediate family. As soon as the phrase "tucking into bed" came up in *The Quilt Story*, someone related it to the same term in *The Name Quilt*. Later, they pointed out connections between Sadie's experience and the narrator of *The Keeping Quilt* in the way that the quilt helped them learn about older generations.

While she hadn't included them in the core books for this project, Chris had stocked the classroom library with other quilt books. She was delighted when two girls came to her with *Luka's Quilt* and explained they thought it ought to be included in the project as well—after all, it was a story about a grandmother making a quilt for a granddaughter. Chris had to agree and another row was added to the book matrix chart. The girls' action was wonderful evidence that the gradual release of responsibility trajectory was successful—they clearly had taken ownership of their own learning. The indications were just as strong that everyone was engaged in quality intellectual work.

WHAT CAN WE LEARN FROM PATCHWORK QUILTS?

The two quilt curriculums we've looked at in such detail are a kind of patchwork in themselves. Just as a riot of disparate flowered, striped, or

TABLE 8.2. Book Matrix for Family Patchwork Portfolio Project

Book Title/ Author	Who is involved in making the quilt?	Who is the quilt for?	What kind of "family stories" can be found in the quilt?
The Patchwork Quilt by Valerie Flournoy	Mostly Grandma and Tanya, other family members help	Tanya	Stories associated with the clothes the patches came from; the story of how the quilt got finished.
The Name Quilt by Phyllis Root	Sadie and her grandmother	Sadie, to replace one lost in fire	Stories of past incidents from older relatives
The Quilt Story by Tony Johnston & dePaola	Abigail's mother or grandmother	Originally for Abigail, but then for the child who finds it many years later	Stories about how taking something treasured like the quilt can help make you feel comfortable in a new home
The Keeping Quilt by Patricia Polacco	Great Gramma Anna	Newborn babies for 4 generations, down to the narrator's baby	Stories about how the family came to America and their lives there.

solid-colored fabrics cut into squares or triangles will come together when they are arranged in a quilt pattern, so, too, lessons involving a variety of disciplines, including literacy, math, science, and social studies can come together in an integrated curriculum. The more carefully the pattern has been thought through before the cutting begins, the more effective the result.

The highest quality quilts invite us to look closer again and again; each time, we might make another discovery about how the pattern plays with repeating a particular fabric or color. For example, no two quilts done in the Barnraising variant of a Log Cabin quilt are the same—one award-winning piece will look strikingly different from another. Each quilter makes complex decisions about which color tones and prints to use so that one half of each individual block seems light and the other dark; these blocks get arranged so that the dark and light interplay in the quilt as a whole.

Effective curriculums are designed in a similar way so that the learners come back repeatedly to the same elements, each time making a somewhat different discovery. Mies Van Der Rohe's famous dictum for architecture was "less is more." In curriculum planning it is also considerably more effective to "dig deeper" rather than to end up with broad and shallow learning.

Thus in the third-grade project Stroud's *The Patchwork Path* helped launch the unit, but as it continued, we came back to it again and again; the pattern the students experimented constructing in the geometry lesson was taken from it; the metaphor of having a map to help us negotiate through difficulties was extended from the Underground Railroad to the context of the students' own lives. In the same way, Chris felt concentrating on just a few books about quilts and family stories would make it easier for her first graders to make connections with their own families.

In many ways, a beautiful patchwork quilt is not just a metaphor for an integrated curriculum inquiry; it is an equally appropriate image to represent the complexities as well as the fundamental simplicity of the teaching/learning dynamic.

- We learn by inquiring, observing, reflecting, and making sense of the world around us.
- The more invested/engaged we are by a desire to understand a phenomenon or concept, the more likely we are to keenly observe, reflect, and ultimately learn.
- By and large, the questions that engage learners most intensely don't fall simply into a single discipline; they call for looking at an issue from a variety of lenses. While it is important that each lens is clearly focused, it is equally crucial that there is some kind of well-crafted unifying principle or question that brings the strands of the inquiry together.
- At the same time, the best inquiries are testimonies to the power of open questions—the more we learn, the more we want to know, and the better we are able to formulate the next question. Like scientists, we are constantly asking better and better questions.
- We need to be rigorous in "tailoring" an inquiry so that we are responsive to the needs, interests, and even the wonderful quirks of the specific learning community.

TRY AND APPLY

1. Identify a holiday connected to a historical or cultural event, tradition, or person. Taking into account the developmental stages and the home cultures of your classroom learning

community, brainstorm open-ended inquiry questions to explore related to the holiday. Decide on which one might be most productive in your classroom; then do these things:

* Craft a statement of the overarching teaching/learning goal for this inquiry
* Design a launching and a culminating activity that would make this inquiry qualify as quality intellectual work
* Outline how other disciplines including literacy, mathematics, and science might be integrated into the curriculum
* Identify a cluster of 4–8 high-quality stories or works of children's literature you could use to develop the inquiry

2. Write a reflection on how you might tailor one of the two quilt projects for use in your classroom. Alternatively, discuss why using quilts does not seem a productive focus for you or your students. Try to identify another focus you might use.

CHAPTER 9

Who's the Strongest?

What Makes Stories Such Effective Tools for Quality Intellectual Work

CASE IN POINT

I used the parable *Who's the Strongest* for a family literacy program that brought together families with young children, their home visitor caseworkers, the program administrators, and a funder or two.

I began by asking who liked to be strong, gesturing by showing my muscles. The children immediately raised their hands along with a few adults. Remarking that there are many different ways to be strong, I launched into the story of a poor rock chopper working in the hot sun who comes upon a genie trapped in a bottle. When he releases the genie and is offered a wish, the rock chopper asks to be the strongest thing there is; the genie tells him he has to be more specific. Remembering the strength of the sun, the rock chopper asks to be the sun. *Piffle, Paffle, Poof!* goes the genie and the man is delighted—until a cloud blocks the sun's rays; the rock chopper calls the genie back and asks to be turned into the cloud—only to discover that the cloud can be blown by the wind; when he becomes the wind he is dismayed to discover he has no power over the mountain. Children and some adults were soon joining in the *Piffle, Paffle, Poof!* of the genie, as well as mimicking his increasingly skeptical expression as the rock chopper kept calling him back. As I began to mime a mountain with a pain in its foot, several anticipated the way the story circled back to the beginning—once the rock chopper realizes that the mountain's pain comes from someone just like him chopping into it, he asks for one last transformation. Emphasizing this is the last time, the genie turns the rock chopper back into himself. All ends happily ever after, as from that day forward to this, he is proud to be the best

153

and strongest self he can be—as I assured each audience member that he or she would be just by doing their best to be themselves.

No sooner had I finished than several children demanded that I tell it again. I proposed an even better plan—we would tell it again together. Four groups of children and grown-ups would work together to present one scene of the story, using the materials that were provided for each group.

- Group1 would have one person narrate the opening while the others pantomimed to show the rock chopper discovering the bottle, releasing the genie, and requesting to be turned into the sun.
- Group 2 would draw a picture to show the story from when the rock chopper is the sun through his turning into the cloud. They could do one big mural or break their part into cartoon panels.
- Group 3 would use music and movement to show the segment involving the wind. They might make up a song or use the drums, shakers, and cymbals made from pan lids and tin cans and other everyday objects.
- Group 4 would make puppets to act out the last scene, using paper plates, large tongue depressors, paper bags, construction paper, scissors, and tape.

As I circulated, I assured everyone that what they came up with would be fantastic, clarified what they needed to do, and asked questions that would help them think through their plans. No one was exempt and no one was appointed to be in charge of the group. The administrator and the funder who ended up in the music group happily deferred to the young father who declared that they would do their scene as a rap.

I had asked a caseworker to get a digital picture of each family working together that they would take home, along with a short version of the story to read again and again, a certificate of participation, and two children's books.

After about 15 minutes, we gathered the whole group back and had our grand performance. As predicted, each group did spectacularly. We thanked the families for joining us and let them know that the way we had been playing with stories is a gift that keeps on giving—it's the best way for parents to help their children be successful in school! During the socializing and snacks part of the program, many commented on how they never thought about how easy it was to enjoy a favorite story, make music, or do simple movement activities with their kids.

WHAT DOES IT MEAN FOR A STORY TO ENGAGE LEARNERS IN A SATISFYING INQUIRY?

Who's the Strongest is the perfect example of the point made in the Introduction to this book: While there is good evidence that I am a good storyteller, the key to successfully engaging children's minds and hearts with stories is to be rigorous about *only using good stories*. In fact, I have spent much more time considering what would be the right story than I have in rehearsing it. Again and again, I return to a key point in Chapter 5's rubric for evaluating the quality of a text: The best stories are those in which the theme and story line pose problems that are engaging and compelling in terms of human experience and that are resolved in a genuine way that invites reflective thinking and responses. Once again, *Who's the Strongest* can help us dig deeper into the implications of this point.

Who's the Strongest is one of my personal favorite stories to tell; I chose it because it promoted the workshop focus on having parents read to their children. The story itself and the extending activities follow the trajectory of the 3 Es from Engagement, to Exploration, to Evaluation. At the same time, the issues the story raises call for the SIP that characterizes play and learning alike; that is, inquiries triggered by the story are conducive to Satisfying, Intentional Problem solving.

How Do Engaging Stories Support a Positive Disposition for Learning?

In the first chapter we looked at how all learning begins with a need to know; if the need is imposed by external factors and is tinged with negative emotions such as fear, anxiety, anger, resentment, or dislike, the brain's chemistry send emotions into overdrive and learning is inhibited. On the other hand, a positive disposition characterized by curiosity and seasoned with delight sets off the prefrontal cortex where thinking takes place. There is nothing like a rich story to spark engagement.

I usually frame telling this story as I did at the family workshop by asking, "Who likes to be strong?" This is one of the "big idea" questions that motivates a great deal of human behavior at all ages and stages. Young children who are just beginning to establish their autonomy are consumed by this question. Because they are still concrete thinkers, it makes perfect sense to them that strength and power are represented in the story by strong natural forces:

- Like the sun, there are times when they want to beat down others or send them fleeing for shelter.

- Like the cloud and the rains that it brings, at other times they want to be seen as someone who helps or offers relief, although that impulse can build into trying to establish control or feeling overwhelmed by a sense of being controlled, just as gentle rains can turn into storms and floods.
- In a similar way, the wind is a natural metaphor for comfort or for a sense of control, depending on how gently or hard it blows; it is easy to slip into seeing the appeal of being able to move others in the direction one thinks is best.
- Finally, at times, we want the security and solidity of being firmly established, like the mountain, impervious to all those other forces; it is equally important to have others who are solidly there for us. Nonetheless, the idea of being able to move about, of not being so stuck, can seem powerfully attractive.

More mature listeners are likely to move fairly quickly to see the parable as a metaphor for crucial abstract or metaphysical questions: *What does it mean to be strong? What are strengths that I aspire to? In what ways might I personally be strong?* These are not trivial questions with a single obvious response; as the story makes clear, the answer we arrive at in one set of circumstances may not be satisfactory in a different situation. In effect, the metaphorical nature of the story gives us a way to play with these questions.

How Do Rich Stories Engage Us in Problem Solving?

In earlier chapters we looked at the difference between teaching for achievement and teaching for understanding. While achievement depends on measuring up to someone else's standard, lifelong learners are empowered and feel a sense of ownership; they find it *satisfying* to take on problems—just as good play is satisfying even when it is challenging. And just as one episode of play often leads to another, so, too, solving one problem is likely to trigger another inquiry.

Who's the Strongest is literally structured as an inquiry into a fundamental human problem—one that does not have any over-the-counter prescription for resolving. The parable uses a circular pattern that makes it likely that the listeners will *coconstruct* the story as it is being told. Those who haven't heard the story before begin to make predictions as the story unfolds. When telling it, I let my body language and voice convey how each time the rock-chopper moves from great satisfaction to dismay. I build in a little pause that invites the listeners to anticipate what will happen next and to join in the refrains. It is clear that even those who are not yet actually reading are already competent in one of the skills expert readers at all levels use: They use the details of the story and prior knowledge to anticipate not only the pattern of the story but the meaning its circular structure conveys.

Why Are Engaging Language and Expression So Important?

It's worth revisiting the definition for high-quality language and expression in Chapter 5, focusing on how that quality functions in terms of meaning-making. Quite simply, the quality with which a story or thought is expressed has a strong impact on how willing others are to attend to it. Music and poetry have always had enormous power to enlighten and to console as well as to *soothe the savage beast within*. It is no accident that great orators tend to end up in positions of power.

On a practical level, making sure that young children's receptive experiences of reading and writing involve high-quality language has a significant impact on literacy development. The use of what are referred to as "robust words and expressions" and of strong imagery build vocabulary and comprehension more effectively than drills or quizzes ever could. Fostering phonemic awareness from infancy makes a huge difference in language as well as literacy development. Rhyme, alliteration, and other forms of language play are fun for the tongue; they build fluency in the ability to distinguish and produce the individual sounds that make up words and build understanding of *word families* that use the same initial or final sounds—all important parts of alphabet knowledge. So, too, chants and refrains put the structure and rhythm of the language into listeners' ears, mouth, and body in a most satisfactory way. Vivid word choice, strong imagery, and pleasing rhythms offer the same kind of benefits to English language learners.

As is true for early childhood classics such as *Goldilocks* or the *Three Little Pigs*, children are developing their own expressive reading skills as they enthusiastically join in refrains such as the plaintive appeal from the rock chopper, "Genie, I made a mistake . . ." or the way Genie crosses his arms and demands, "Are you sure?" before doing another *Piffle, Paffle, Poof!* transformation. They also are building awareness of how tone of voice can convey meaning; Once they are able to read aloud, they instinctively understand that fluency and expression do make a difference.

When the language and expression are as delightful as in this case, hearing or reading the story again and yet again is natural. In fact, the attraction of language is so great that after a single hearing, children may be able to repeat the lyrics of a song or tell an appealing story with engaging language play. This kind of repetition is very different from rote memorization. The old-fashioned term "knowing something by heart" is wonderfully apt—it communicates how the words and message are remembered because the individual considers them worth remembering and worth saying in a way that expresses their deep meaning. At the end of a story-telling, I often ask, "Did you like that story?" and when the children respond with a resounding "Yes!" I make a sweeping motion and say, "Then take the story, it's yours now. You can tell it in your own words, in your own way." I've often heard from parents that many took me at my word as they repeated each week's story at home.

In whatever way it happens, each time a good story is revisited, the way it is understood shifts or deepens. The movement from engagement to a deeper exploration of meaning is even more compelling when the imagery as well as the language is strong.

WHAT DOES IT MEAN TO EXPLORE USING A DISCIPLINED INQUIRY?

Just as there are many different ways to be strong, there are many ways to explore, construct, and represent understanding; so, too, it is always possible to dig deeper as we wonder and wander through the landscape of learning.

How Can We Play with a Rich Story to Explore Its Meaning?

The many different strategies that have been described all are ways to take a story out of the book and literally to put it into the children's minds and bodies; they also are meant to suggest how important it is that the meaning of the story come to life in some form of representation. This emphasis on meaning-making needs to begin and to become a habit of mind long before the mechanics of reading and writing; our goal is for it to last for a lifetime. Limiting children to a ping-pong match of comprehension questions or worksheet drills restricts the way they process texts; even worse, children may conclude that in the context of school, books are only about right answers and not about anything interesting. Particularly for those for whom the mechanics of literacy are challenging and those whose primary exposure to texts is in school, their future academic success is deeply compromised.

In contrast, the depth and the staying power of all that can be learned from a story are maximized when a text is explored through multiple modes, including dramatization, music, movement, drawing, or constructive activities. Each of these modes gives learners an intriguing problem to solve that naturally engages them in constructing the *meaning the story has for them,* taking into account *what happens* in the story.

In the family literacy workshop as well as in professional development sessions, adults are often amazed by how much more they have to think when they are asked to play with a story using different modes, especially when they have to work with others. Inevitably there is a buzz of talk, bursts of laughter, and serious problem solving. In the Case in Point above the young man doing the rap and the puppet group both insisted on having a little more time to prepare their segments—once they figured out what they wanted to do, they were determined to do it well.

One factor in creating a high degree of engagement is that the invitation to come up with a creative expression must be framed in a way that is open-ended, yet provides some structure. It turns out that giving no directions is as counterproductive as prescribing exactly what the outcome should be. The trick to empowerment is to set a goal to keep in mind as choices are made. For example, the drawing group for *Who's the Strongest* debated about doing a single picture showing the rock chopper as the sun or a series of three pictures; they decided on the series since that would make it easier for the seven group members to all contribute. An 8-year-old in the group was delighted to be able to concentrate on doing a magnificent genie, while his 3-year-old sibling busily filled in the sun's shape with an orange crayon.

So, too, having goals for an activity impacts decisions about what materials to provide. In workshops that involve adults, I always favor musical "instruments" made from household objects, as I did in the family literacy workshop. It is important for parents and teachers to realize that the impulse to make music is natural; one does not need fine instruments or training in their use to tap into this impulse.

As far as the making or building activities go, the collection of materials offered to adults can be almost random. Participants in the StoryBus workshops laughingly say that they thought it was impossible to make a strong house out of the heap of pipe cleaners, bits of cardboard and paper, tongue depressors, ribbon, glue, and other odds and ends they had to work with; they end up feeling very proud of the ingenious and remarkably sturdy structures they come up with. With young children, it's important to include materials that might suggest a use, such as paper plates and paper bags for puppets or masks. However, the children should be free to carry out their own ideas; preschoolers may not be interested or capable of producing something that an adult thinks looks good enough to post on a bulletin board or the home fridge. The youngest children who spend all their time squishing clay instead of making a pig are appropriately engaged in functional play. In any case, the elegance of the final product is not important: it is the conversation that grows out of their work that fuels the teaching/learning.

Once again, the image of a ladder is telling. Children need to move back and forth between the concrete, pictorial, and symbolic levels of understanding and thinking. Third graders who are asked, "How does the rock chopper change in the course of the story?" might be able to circle the correct answer in a multiple-choice test, but making real meaning about what it means to be your best self is not so easy; they need a well-facilitated conversation that allows them to make a connection to the comments or examples of others as well as to wander a bit off in one direction and use a clarifying question to send them off on a more promising path.

However, the same question can be meaningfully explored using multiple modes of representation. One group might create illustrations for the story, while another group works at presenting it as a pantomime. Both will have to solve the problem of how to show the difference between the unhappy rock chopper at work at the beginning of the story and the way he is contentedly working hard at the end. Each group has to translate their response into drawings or into movements that involves them in literally experiencing the understanding that changes in feeling are communicated by nonverbal cues such as facial expression and bearing. Doing so is likely to get them thinking and conversing as they work about what happened to make the rock chopper go from unhappily wishing he was strong to being pleased to be his strongest best self

While exploring a story's meaning through multiple representations accesses the multiple intelligences (MI), that is not the same as creating activities that are designed for particular styles of learners, such as visual or kinesthetic learners. Using different modalities is more directly related to perspectivism; it reflects the strong belief of Gardner and other MI proponents that the intelligences reflect the different ways things can be known and that knowledge can be represented (Chen et al., 2009; Gardner, 1993, 2006). Multimodal activities such as the one used at the family literacy workshop allowed each individual to play in more depth with the way music, movement, or the visual arts might deepen understanding of the story; becoming a member of the audience exposed them to another perspective; everyone went away seeing that each mode of representation had its own delights—and experiencing all of them enriched the meaning.

How Can Exploring Rich Stories Support Perspectivism?

Among the many benefits of play, one of the most important is the way it supports *perspectivism*. The ability to see different points of view and to negotiate a common ground that allows an activity to move forward is as vital for social-emotional development as it is for higher-order thinking. This is a developmental issue—under 5, young children work hard at establishing their place in the physical and social world as they begin to move about and do things on their own. They find it very hard to differentiate between their own preferences, emotions, and needs and those of others. However, as they settle into the 5–7 shift, they develop a whole new capacity to generalize and differentiate the uses and meanings associated with one thing or experience. They recognize, for example, that if you are engaged in solitary play with your blocks, you can do what you please; if you and a friend decide to make a castle, you may have to give up some of your plans to include hers. The payoff may well be that discussing alternatives means the final outcome is better and, in fact, you both had much more fun.

The older we get, the more important it is to be able to shift the lens from which we view things and to take the viewpoint of others into consideration. Working as a learning community helps with that process as authentic conversations and joint problem solving create many opportunities to clarify our thoughts. In the same way, we benefit from insights and needs of others (Bergen, 2002).

Who's the Strongest is virtually a compendium of perspectivism. The story literally revolves around the point that abstract qualities are *relative*; as the rock chopper learns that as *strong* as the sun, the cloud, the wind, and the mountain are, circumstances can make something else *stronger*; in the end, it isn't possible to be the *strongest* in an absolute sense—we can only get better, incrementally doing our personal best. Creating more opportunities to interact with and revisit the parable deepens our understanding that what it means to be strong, or brave, or important can change radically, depending on circumstances and personal values.

There is a natural progression from extending understanding of the rock chopper to deepening self-understanding. Using pictures and words, children might develop a poster or book on the theme "This is what I'm good at . . . ." or "I know I am strong because . . . ." Of course, the younger children are, the more likely they are to understand abstract qualities in quite concrete ways. A 5-year-old once explained to me that it was better to be a kid than a grown-up because kids were more *flexible*. I was quite impressed by the child's understanding of the importance of not being set in one's ways—until he demonstrated what he meant by doing a split. The 9-year-old chatting with us tried a backward handstand and said another way that she was flexible was that she knew a few different ways to solve tricky math problems.

By primary school—and on into adulthood—this tale offers powerful ways to support social-emotional learning as well as to increase self-understanding. The parable invites being explored in a variety of ways:

- Before the story, ask, "What do you mean when you say someone is strong?" Afterward, explore how the story might have changed or affected their understanding of what it means to be strong.

- Combine the idea of strong with specific roles: How would you describe a *strong person? strong teacher? strong student?* Are there different ways to be strong in those roles?
- Read and compare other stories about who is the strongest such as *The Mouse Bride* by Cowley (1995), *The Moles and the Mireuk* by Kwon (1993), or *Tales of Tricksters* by DeSpain (2001), Aesop's fable about the sun and wind, or the legend of St. Christopher (Hodges, 2009). Challenge the students to come up with a tale of their own using the pattern of describing a sequence of four things or forces that go from seeming strong to being less strong as circumstances change.

Along with all its richness as a literary text and potential for social-emotional learning, *Who's the Strongest* also can launch a variety of science investigations. Younger children can do this at the concrete level by exploring how the ways that the rock chopper behaves as the sun, cloud, rain, and mountain reflect the ways that these natural phenomena work. Five- and 6-year-olds might be interested in consulting informational books or other resource materials to come up with more examples of how natural features or forces like the sun, clouds, wind, or a mountain are strong.

In primary school, the task might be to explore how natural forces such as sun, clouds (rain), wind, and geological forces can be "strong" factors for the good of growing things, but tornados, hurricanes, volcanoes, and earthquakes also can be destructive. A classroom might choose to explore only one of these forces, or children could be broken up into working groups. There are many wonderful works of children's literature that feature one or another of these forces of nature, including pourquoi tales, Aardemma's *Bringing the Rain to Kapiti Plain* (1992), a cumulative tale about the weather cycle in the African Savannah, or the informational book *This Pebble in My Pocket* by Hooper (1996). By second grade, many children are happy to do research about natural disasters.

What Does It Mean to Use Stories Intentionally in a Disciplined Inquiry?

No matter how many potential texts or approaches there might be to carry out an effective inquiry, in the end only one of them can be used. Teachers must make highly intentional instructional decisions about which text and which coherent sequence of activities will be the most strategic to use in light of the specific learning goals and needs and interests of this particular community of learners.

- The decision to use a particular text might begin either because a certain story seems especially compelling to explore or because after research into the possibilities the text seemed particularly promising to use in exploring a theme or topic targeted for inquiry by local or state standards.
- However the text or story is chosen, it is essential to think through what is the most strategic way to incorporate it into the inquiry:
  * Does it make sense to launch the inquiry with the story or might it offer some kind of model or vehicle for a culminating event?
  * What other texts can this one be used with?
  * Which of the many strategies that have been discussed is best to use with this text in this particular community of learners engaged in this specific inquiry?

HOW DOES EVALUATION ENTER INTO THE USE OF RICH TEXTS FOR INQUIRY?

One of the core conditions for quality intellectual work is that it is intrinsically rewarding—preferably as the result of an inquiry that the learner was intrinsically motivated to engage in exploring.

What Kind of Evaluation Do Learners Engage in?

Young learners need to be scaffolded and supported in the evaluation process. Developmentally, they are just beginning to develop the ability to generalize criteria or do the analysis involved in applying them. Younger children focus heavily on the concrete. While they might have an intuitive sense of metaphorical meaning, they usually have difficulty in expressing it. When asked whether they would like to be the sun, cloud, wind, or mountain in the story of *Who's the Strongest* preschoolers and kindergarteners are likely to make a choice that reflects their feelings or experiences. Thus one might say, "I live on a mountain so that's what I would be"; another might declare, "I get really scared in rainstorms so I'm not choosing the cloud." Well into primary school, children are likely to have a preference for a character that has the same gender.

Children should also realize that often enough the evaluation process results in a measured or ambivalent conclusion rather a decisive judgment that labels elements of the inquiry as good/bad or right/wrong. It is perfectly fine to find one text or activity more engaging or meaningful

FIGURE 9.1. The Dynamics of Quality Intellectual Work

THE DYNAMICS OF QUALITY INTELLECTUAL WORK

ENGAGEMENT
Inquiry to Self: Addresses
personal affective dimension
SATISFYING

Engage, Explore, Evaluate
Play/Quality Intellectual Work
Satisfying, Intentional Problem Solving

EXPLORATION
Inquiry to Inquiry/text: Calls on
prior knowledge to develop and
implement exploration process
INTENTIONAL

EVALUATION
Inquiry to World: Assesses
results of problem solving
PROBLEM SOLVING

than another. It is even possible not to have particularly enjoyed some aspect of the exploration but, nonetheless, to see that in the end it did contribute to the final understanding or outcome.

Children need a great deal of support in recognizing that it is all right to make mistakes—that error is a gift that often leads to greater learning. To deliver that message convincingly, parents and teachers should be comfortable explaining that they don't know an answer—and then talk about what they might do to find out what they want to know; they should be equally quick to acknowledge making a mistake, in a matter-of-fact manner—and follow up by sharing how it might be corrected, or what they have learned from it.

If a child's response suggests a confusion or misconception, instead of labeling the answer as "wrong," or correcting it, teachers should use non-judgmental questions and conversation that will push the child's thinking; if the important habit of rich conversations has been well established, other members of the learning community will play an important part in clarifying and extending everyone's understanding.[1]

Finally, it is important to explicitly bring closure to individual learning activities and major inquiries by having the group discuss how things went, beginning with the positives and moving onto what might be done differently another time. The teacher/facilitator plays an active role in highlighting the ways different members of the learning community might have gone about exploring the problem, although each arrived at a different but satisfactory conclusion. However, closure does not necessarily mean consensus. There can be a range of legitimate opinions about many issues, especially those arising from the social sciences or those in the social-emotional domain. The emphasis should be on how well supported different positions are, as well as some indication of the spectrum they cover. In this discussion, teacher/facilitators need to make it very clear that they are also members of the learning community and share ways in which their own understanding has deepened.

What Kind of Evaluation Should Teachers/Facilitators Engage In?

Teachers who are committed to quality intellectual work make formative assessment a habit of mind and of practice. To use the lovely phrase of my colleague Donna Johnson, the best teachers are always working at "becoming better students of their students." They are engaged in that study at all phases, from planning to implementation to reflection.

- When *planning*, the teacher evaluates what kind of specific learning goals are appropriate for the children with whom they are working. They are keen observers of the strengths, challenges, interests, and quirks of each learner in the community and take into consideration how each new inquiry or learning phase can build on prior knowledge and be explicitly linked to recently completed inquiries or other areas of the curriculum. They work at identifying aspects of the new material that are likely to pose conceptual or linguistic challenges to their learners and reflect on how to tailor the way an activity is carried out or on prompts and questions that might be used. In some cases, the challenge will reflect points that can lead to misconceptions or confusion at the developmental stage of the learners. Other times, individual needs and challenges are involved. Finally, at this point, teachers think through the step-by-step logistics of the activity, including preparing any necessary materials.
- In the *implementation* stage all the intentional planning they have done allows effective teachers to concentrate on monitoring the learners' responses so that they can adjust, tweak, or change the activity as necessary. Teachers know their role is to coach or facilitate learning by providing effective guidance and feedback: It is not to impose knowledge or to hold the learners at fault if

they don't understand. When errors, misconceptions, or unex-
pected wonderings and wanderings arise, they use questions
and conversations involving the whole learning community to
clarify and build understanding.

- Finally, at the end of the day good teachers *reflect* on their practice. The reflection might include journaling, watching a video,
consulting with a colleague or coach—or it might be no more
than replaying the day as one drives home. In all cases, productive reflection is focused on analyzing learning activities in light
of the established goals. Furthermore, it should always begin
positively by identifying what went well or at least saved things
from complete disaster. It is important to tease out what factors
contributed to the productive aspects: Was it the advance planning? The nature of the text or the activity? The level of engagement? Don't forget to also take into account the disposition of
the class as well as one's own level of interest and enthusiasm.

These same factors should be considered as teachers think about what
they might do differently another time. Best practice means understanding that error is a gift. In her study of mindsets, Dweck (2007) notes
that the most salient feature of those with a growth mindset is that they
see mistakes or miscalculations as opportunities to learn; instead of be-
moaning problems, they focus on *problem solving*. However well a lesson
might have gone, this mindset is always ready to reflect and discover how
changing the materials used or structuring the activity somewhat differently might facilitate more learning another time.

Perhaps the most important evaluation a teacher engages in is looking rigorously for evidence of student learning in both the implementation and reflection phases. It is not enough for children to have had
fun—as the examples show again and again, play is serious business and
when it goes well, there should be an observable benefit or gain. By the
same token, indications that individuals or the whole group really did not
develop the understanding that the inquiry was designed to further are
important data. Analyzing it includes factoring in what one knows about
the learners, as well as considering what developmental or linguistic challenges might have been involved.

WHAT MAKES TEACHING/LEARNING DYNAMIC?

This final chapter has looked at how the parable *Who's the Strongest* can
serve as an example of a *praxis*—a set of pedagogical practices that re-

flect the deeply held beliefs about teaching and learning that have been explored throughout the book. Figure 9.1 is meant to represent how focusing on quality intellectual work as a serious form of play and on using rich texts as highly effective tools for applying the 3 Es and the SIP principle come together in a dynamic that lifelong learners continuously spiral through.

I must note that the examples given throughout this book reflect the particularities and peculiarities of my personal experience, including the good fortune to have stumbled into ways to be an oral storyteller as well as to have fallen into many different wonderful communities of learners. So this book is by no means the last word on using the teaching/learning dynamic to promote quality intellectual work on the part of the youngest learners all the way to the oldest. If you like this praxis, do take it—it is yours to do in your own way with your own communities of learning.

TRY AND APPLY

1. Choose a fable or parable such as *Who's the Strongest* and develop a rich inquiry question that would engage learners in exploring text-to-self, text-to-text, and text-to-world connections through a series of activities. If possible, carry out the inquiry with a community of learners (children or colleagues) and write up a reflection on what happened and what you learned—from and about the learners as well as about your own practice.
2. Develop a position paper in which you explore how you see the praxis described in this book as having application to you and your practice. Are there aspects of it you find particularly compelling? In what ways do you see yourself modifying or changing it?

The Essential ABCs

Always **B**e **C**onversing
Always **B**e **C**onnecting
Always **B**uild **C**ompetence

LETTER-BY-LETTER LEARNING POINTS

A is for *Asking:* Good questions lead to more learning than correct answers.

B is for *Benefit:* The intrinsic rewards of learning outshine gold stars and high grades.

C is for the *C-P-S Trajectory*: Learning begins with the Concrete, moves to Pictorial and only then to the Symbolic.

D is for *D & D*: Positive *Disposition* leads to *D*eepening understanding; it is equally valid to say *D*elight in learning leads to a positive *D*isposition.

E is for the 3 *E's—Engage, Explore, Evaluate*: Along with the fourth E of *E*rror, the E's are more efficacious than the 3 R's—'Reading, 'Riting, 'Rithmetic, aka Rote Right Responses.

F is for *Focus:* Focusing in on specific learning goals that will develop and foster conceptual understanding is more efficacious than flinging out a flurry of loosely related factoids.

G is for GI to GRR Principle: Guided Inquiry leads to Gradual Release of Responsibility—learners who are given increasing responsibility for constructing their understanding take ownership of the knowledge they have acquired.

H is for *Habits of Mind:* Lifelong learners are always *curious*; they know that *digging deeper* and *persisting* through the inevitable glitches that come with *problem solving* results in a heightened sense of *confidence* and *competence*.

I is for *Inquiry:* It acts as a ladder that allows learning to move up, down, and around different levels of thinking/understanding.

J is for the *Joy of Learning:* If the seed is planted and nurtured in early childhood, it will bear fruit for a lifetime.

K is for *Keen Observation:* Keeping our eyes open to the nuances is an essential factor in the teaching/learning dynamic.

L is for *Learning Communities:* Functioning as a learning community leads to more learning than fighting for top grades—that goes for everyone, including the teacher/facilitator.

M is for *Multiple* Intelligences: Everyone's profile is unique and always open to change.

N is for *No Naked* Numbers: *N*aked *n*umbers—like naked facts—don't make sense; clothing problem situations in their stories leads to effective problem solving.

O is for *Open* Questions create *Ownership*: Posing open questions and opening the discussion to questions owned by the learning community is the best way to develop deep understanding.

P is for *Problem* Solving is a *Process*: The first step is to identify an authentic problem situation; to choose strategically among possible ways to resolve it; to try it out and evaluate the results; in all likelihood, the process will cycle around again.

Q is for *Quality* Intellectual Work: Learners are actively involved in a disciplined inquiry that leads to a performance, product, or discussion that has meaning beyond the classroom.

R is for the *RPP* Principle: *R*eceptive *P*recedes *P*roductive Understanding.

S is for *SIP*: Play and learning are both characterized by *S*atisfying, *I*ntentional, *P*roblem Solving

T is for *Thoughtful Talk*: Consistently asking "Why do you think that?" builds the habit of inquiry and nurtures higher-order thinking.

U is for *Understanding*: Digging deeper is more productive than knowing a little about lots of things.

V is for *Visual* as well as *Verbal Validation*: Evidence of learning should not be limited to *V*erbal statements; *V*isual (and kinesthetic) representations of knowledge are equally *V*alid.

W is for *Wondering* and *Wandering*: Lifelong learners find their own way through the landscape of learning .

X is for *'Xploring*: While the "big idea" questions of science are different from those of the humanities or social sciences, they all need exploring through a disciplined inquiry.

Y is for *Yet* . . . : However strong understanding might be, there is always a "Yet . . .", another perspective or possible way to proceed that makes learning an ever spiraling process.

Z is for *ZPD*: Vygotsky's Zone of Proximal Development recognizes that learning is a continuous process that respects the GQ (Goldilocks's Quotient)—an effective learning task is neither too easy nor too hard but just right for challenging the learner to stretch to a new level of understanding.

Notes

Chapter 1

1. One of the best known versions of this old tale is the Caldecott Award–winning one by Marcia Brown. However, she has several soldiers trick one old woman. I feel contemporary versions by Heather Forest and John Muth do a much better job of conveying how cooperation and sharing are rewarding for everyone. Both are wonderfully illustrated to convey the multicultural dimension of the story.

2. Arleen McCarty Hynes was the Patients' Librarian at St. Elizabeth's Hospital in Washington, D. C., from 1970 to 1981. With Dr. Ken Gorelick, she established the first training course and certification program in the field of biblio-poetry therapy. For more details about this creative arts therapy, see Hynes and Hynes-Berry (1984/2011).

3. In the early 1990s several dedicated early childhood specialists in Chicago formed Hug-a-Book, a 501(c)(3) not-for-profit, to address the fact that many Head Start and other early childhood classrooms did not even come close to meeting the standard of having two books per child in the classroom library. As important as the others' contributions were, no one would deny that most of the credit goes to Sue, who literally turned her family's front room into a depository where participating teachers could come to choose books that would best meet the needs and interests of their classrooms.

4. In effect, the Latin origins of the verb *educate* are constructivist: the prefix *e-* stands for *ex* meaning "out"; the root word is *ducare* meaning "to lead." The word *instruction* also promotes this approach: *instructus*, from *in-* meaning "on" plus *struere* meaning "to pile, build." *Achievement*, on the other hand, signals a finality instead of an ongoing process; it derives from *ad caput venire* meaning "to come to a head."

5. Wenger (2006) defines a *community of practice* as a "group of people who share a concern or passion for something they do and learn how to do it better as they interact regularly." In early childhood education, professional organizations such as the National Association for the Education of Young Children (NAEYC) comprise such communities, but so do teacher study groups.

6. "Pedagogical content knowledge . . . represents the blending of content and pedagogy into an understanding of how particular topics, problems, or issues are organized, represented, and adapted to the diverse interests and abilities of learners, and presented for instruction. Pedagogical content knowledge is the category most likely to distinguish the understanding of the content specialist from that of the pedagogue" (Shulman, 1987, p. 4).

Chapter 2

1. For research on the positive effects of engaging students and thus increasing their intrinsic motivation to learn, see Bowen's literature review, "Student Engagement and Its

Relation to Quality Work Design." The issue of intentionally designing rich engaging activities is related to the complex issue of the influence a positive child/teacher relationship has to school success (Bowen, 2006; Hughes et al., 2008; Pianta, 2007). Research establishing the power of positive praise goes back at least to the 1980s (Brophy, 1988).

2. Ironically, China's educational reform movement in the first decade of the twenty-first century is driven by the concern that even though their students score high in international standardized mathematics and science tests, the Chinese educational system has produced virtually no important innovative thinkers or innovations—only imitations (Zhao, 2009). For an amusing comment on the difference in how the two systems treat stories, see "Teaching the Cinderella Fairytale: China vs. America" (Tingting, 2009).

3. The Annenberg Report used the definition developed by Newman, King, and Secada at the University of Wisconsin as part of a 5-year, federally funded study looking at the connection between school restructuring and student achievement (Newman,1996). Sadly, the conclusion they reached for the first year of the Chicago Schools Project was that activities meeting the standards for quality intellectual work were few and far between. Philip Schlechty (2001) has identified 10 critical qualities for intellectual work that correlate well to the three criteria used here. Schlechty includes: *product focus, clear and compelling standards, protection from adverse consequences for initial failure, significance of performance, affiliation, novelty and variety, choice, authenticity, organization of knowledge*, and *content and substance*.

4. This same principle of giving children a voice applies to portfolio documentation and assessment. If children are engaged and invested in a project or performance, it is important to do their best, just as athletes will set "personal best" goals.

5. For a more extended discussion of the history of American schooling and the implications of a system driven by the 3 Rs see Ravitch (2000), especially Chapter 1. She cautions that even the Progressive movement tended to sacrifice academic learning as the primary goal of schooling.

6. The vision statement on the Education Development Center website is representative of the current broad understanding of literacy: "To make meaning and build understanding, students need both general literacy skills and content-specific literacy skills" (www.EDC.org).

7. See Willingham (2008/2009). Also, Joan Almon of the Alliance for Childhood talks with Daniel Willingham and Justin Snider about the proper role of rote memorization in learning in a podcast from Jackstreet.com (jackstreet.com/jackstreet/ WMBK.RTRoteMemorization.cfm).

8. The Biological Science Curriculum Study (BSCS), under leadership of its Principal Investigator, Roger Bybee, developed an instructional model for constructivism, called the "Five Es", which include *Engage, Explore, Explain, Extend* and *Evaluate*. They continue to associate the model with science education (Bybee, 2006). Many years before I knew about this model, Dr Thomas Romberg, from the University of Wisconsin, Madison had discussed the 3 Es as a constructivist approach. In effect, *Explore, Explain* and *Extend* are collapsed into a single E, which Romberg designated as *Explore*. I have been using the idea of the 3 Es ever since, for a variety of reasons. On one hand, replacing the 3Rs with 3Es is a nice counterpoint; triads are more elegant than quintets; when *exploration* is seen as a disciplined inquiry, *explaining* and *extending* are part of the process. As the discussion indicates, I see the model extending across the curriculum

9. Much of the material issued by such educational think tanks as the Association for Supervison and Curriculum Development (ASCD) either provides further evidence of the efficacy of focusing on meaningful work (e.g., Grennan, 2002) or lays out strategies that can be used in the secondary and presecondary classrooms to call for this kind of work; this is the focus of Marzano's approach, for example (Marzano,1992, 2007).

10. Very important work is being done on the creation and efficacy of learning communities by the Developmental Studies Center in San Franciso (http://www.devstu.org; see Schaps, et al., 2004) and by the Responsive Classroom program of the Northeast Foundation for Children, Inc. (http://www.responsiveclassroom.org).

11. Newman et al.'s (1998) position paper came out after the Sharing Session in which Heidi presented her activity. Stone Soup had not been made cognizant of what the study was looking for and our network was not included in either the study or control groups.

12. These activities are representative of what I have done or seen done in classrooms, before and after the Stone Soup project. It isn't really possible to credit the originators because these ideas evolved in collegial discussions, were adaptations of other activities, or emerged from the interests of a particular class.

Chapter 3

1. Virtually every culture where tales have been collected include at least one that folklorists would classify as a "Cinderella" type—to be exact, one that conforms to Aarne and Thompson types 510A, 510B, or 511 (Sierra, 1992, p. 162). Disney's passive heroine is now often assumed to be the "true" Cinderella; however, in most of the 500 variants of the tale, it is the heroine herself, not the prince, who acts in a way that brings a happily ever after. The glass slipper motif is a confusion between the old French *vair,* meaning *deerskin,* and *verre,* which means *glass.*

2. *Children's Questions: A Mechanism for Cognitive Development* by M. Chouinard (2009) is an excellent study of how important it is for children to be able to ask questions and engage in conversations about the answers. See also Small (2010), who discusses how important it is to go beyond one right answer.

3. While it may be a myth that states use third-grade reading scores to predict how many prison beds they will need, there is no question that prison inmates do show a disproportionately high number of illiterates or those with low literacy skills.

4. Reyhner (2008) provides a full review of the conflict between the behaviorist approach of those who emphasize direct instruction phonics in reading instruction and the more constructivist approach of the Whole Language movement. The actual strategies and philosophy advocated by the Whole Language gurus, such as Goodman (1987), are very compatible with the Balanced Literacy approach.

5. From *Crisis in the Kindergarten* by Miller and Almon (2009, p. 45). Indications are that the research supporting phonics instruction reflects the demands of high-stakes testing. It should be noted that isolated decoding skills are easier to drill and to measure than are more complex, holistic features of literacy such as comprehension (Gamse, Bloom, Kemple, & Jacob, 2008, p. 72; Manzo, 2008). These findings validate criticisms raised by Goodman (2006) about the usefulness of the DIBELS test that was mandated to be the primary assessment for NCLB standards, as well as the reliability of the research on which it is based.

6. Opponents of the Whole Language movement accuse this approach of using such an "anything goes" attitude that it results in no standards being applied and, they say, little student achievement.

7. As a team member of Erikson's New Schools Project from 2005 to 2009, I worked with pre-K–3 classrooms in selected Chicago Public Schools. The project shared beliefs and incorporated strategies highly compatible with the Responsive Classroom (Northeast Foundation for Children), the Developmental Studies Center, and others who endorse functioning as a learning community and emphasis on a positive climate as critical factors in achievement.

8. Bloom's taxonomy identifies six levels of thinking, ranging from the lowest one of recall information to the highest level of evaluative thinking, while Gallagher and Ascher (1963) identify 4 corresponding levels of questions. Vogler (2008) provides an excellent

discussion of Bloom and Gallagher and Ascher in his study of the kind of questions used by teachers. I have combined several categories, resulting in three levels of inquiry. My modification of Bloom and the discussion compatible with the beliefs about teaching/learning found in Marzano & Kendall, *The New Taxonomy of Educational Objectives* (2006).

9. It is important to recognize that many 5- and 6-year-olds are still very concrete in their understanding; developmentally, they have trouble distinguishing between fantasy and everyday reality; furthermore, they are not bothered by contradictions between them. They will quickly agree that in our everyday world, fairy godmothers don't produce fancy dresses with a flick of the wand. However, in their minds, they may well believe that in the world of the story this kind of magic is commonplace—that what happened in the story truly happened.

10. I remember a fifth grader who angrily demanded to know why the father in *The Korean Cinderella* didn't do something to protect his daughter from the stepmother. She got more and more incensed, insisting, "It's not right that you ignore your own flesh and blood for someone you picked up on the street!" Clearly, her anger was rooted in the painful realities of her own life. Classmates tried to calm her down, reminding her that we were talking about the father in the story, not her father. She grew less angry as she conceded that point. Her response is a good example of how stories can have a biblio-therapeutic dimension, without crossing the boundaries into therapy.

11. The shift in the balance of learning was first formulated by Pearson and Gallagher (1983). Since then, as each of these exponents have shared their valuable practices, they have offered their own representations of how the shift works; see Fisher and Frey (2008); Routman (1999), Harvey and Goudvis (2007), Miller (2002), and Boushey and Moser (2006).

Chapter 4

1. This description reflects Polya's (2009) definition of the problem-solving cycle in mathematics; however, the heuristic works across all disciplines.

2. Csikszentmihalyi associates "flow" with what he calls "good work," that is, work that is well done and that is satisfying because the worker sees what is being done as meaningful and important. Ackerman also uses terms such as *rapture* when describing personally meaningful activities that can range from taking long bike trips to studying penguins.

3. These categories of play were first formulated by Smilansky (1968), building on the thinking of Piaget (1945). The essay by Fleer and the one by Johns in Dau's collection on play (2001) draw attention to the importance of recognizing how cultures outside the middle class, Euro-American mainstream may see play as having a different function, including a survival mechanism or a form of Rogoff's "guided participation."

4. The Alliance for Childhood (Miller & Almon, 2009) and the Albert Shanker Institute (2009) have both issued reports that argue effectively and passionately for the importance of play in early childhood classrooms.

5. This kind of imaginative "as if" play may or may not be universal. As Fleer (2001, p. 70) points out, the play of Aboriginal children in Australia may be governed somewhat differently as the children begin to lay the groundwork for skillful performance of the gender-driven expectations about the roles and responsibilities of the adult. Rogoff's (2003) discussion of *guided participation* in indigenous Latin American cultures makes a similar point.

6. Cooper, Capo, Mathes, and Gray (2007) found significant improvement using three different standardized measures in classrooms that used Paley's techniques, when compared to control classrooms. See also Bergen (2002) for further discussion of the ways dramatic play supports cognition.

7. While everyone's learning calls for this coordination, specialists are seeing that those with learning disabilities can be helped by doing carefully designed kinesthetic exercises; Hannaford's system is called *Brain Gym*; Davis and Braun (2010) takes a strengths approach to dyslexia that involves visual and kinesthetic exercises. See also Hansen, Bernstorf, and Stuber (2007), Haraksin-Probst (2008), and Jensen (2000). Harman (n.d.) succinctly reviews the music/movement/cognition connection.

8. Ely (2005) showed that young children have a strong propensity to play with phonological features of language. He points to a study that showed a good 25% of what children uttered had some form of language play including rhyme, alliteration, repetition, nonsense words, and innovation on a statement. Bergen and Maurer (2000) provide further support for the important interplay between symbolic play, phonological awareness, and literacy skills.

9. For example, children are invited to come up with movements and improvise sound effects to bring to life metaphors about how other members of their family see them. One group joined in humming while the narrator recited, "My grandmother sees me as a blanket waiting to be cuddled every weekend"; someone stepped on a soda can to go with, "My grandpa sees me as a toy crusher" (Katz & Thomas, 2003, pp. 129–152).

10. Details about the program, including the research, can be found online at the *Reading in Motion* website (http://www.readinginmotion.org).

11. McCaslin (2006), Spolin (1986), and Freeman (2007) are excellent resources; Chicago's *Reading in Motion* began as a theater program for schools. The *Reading in Motion* website (http://www.readinginmotion.org) includes videos.

12. Dorothy Heathcote developed a very powerful form of creative dramatics that brings social studies to life by taking middle and upper elementary age students through a progressively complex series of activities that becomes a real "simulation" of a historical event or condition. See Wagner (1999) for descriptions of Heathcote's work and suggestions for implementing this strategy.

13. Googling the term *reader's theater* yields many helpful online resources about how to implement reader's theater. *Reading in Motion* tends to emphasize reader's theater strategies, precisely because they are promoting reading skills. However, the lower- and higher-level comprehension dynamic is similar for reenactment and for reader's theater (Worthy, 2005).

14. Well-meaning but untrained individuals can do more harm than good by dabbling in therapeutic interventions, especially in the context of a full group (see Hynes & Hynes-Berry, 1984/2011). At the same time, classroom teachers need to be very mindful of not forcing devastating historical situations on children too early, as Schweber (2008) points out in her discussion of a third-grade unit on the Holocaust.

Chapter 5

1. Selecting high-quality children's literature for distribution and use in classroom libraries has long been a delightful feature of my professional activities. In turn, I have had many opportunities to explain and explore the criteria in workshops for Hug-a-Book; currently I evaluate books as part of the professional development curriculum offered by the Erikson Institute in conjunction with StoryBus, a project of the Dolores Kohl Education Foundation. I also do reviews for the Children's Literature Comprehensive DataBase (http://clcd-literatureforchildrenandya.blogspot.com).

2. For convenience this discussion will use the more inclusive term *text* since it concerns a wide variety of formats, including oral storytelling, picture books, or excerpts from longer works.

3. The criteria for informational texts nominated for the NCTE Orbis award set a useful standard (NCTE, 2011).

4. Nodelman's opening chapter examines how complex "picture reading" is, and the significant role the cultural assumptions and knowledge one brings to the book art affects the meaning that we take from it.

5. African Americans in projects such as Stone Soup, StoryBus, and the Erikson Math Project report that Leola's grandmother echoes very strong messages they were given as to what kind of behavior was expected of a "well brought up" child. As was true for Victorians, failure to conform to these norms was not acceptable because it reflected badly on the family.

6. In 1989 Jon Scieszka's *The True Story of A Wolf* did much to call on all of these new capabilities; in effect, he initiated the genre of "fractured fairy tales." There is no question that these ironic and amusing versions of the childhood classics delight adults and are equally popular with children from about age 7 and up. Preschoolers tend to be confused by them. They prefer stories told with little elaboration, just as older children find those versions "babyish."

7. Paul Galdone, Valeri Gorbachev, and Jan Brett should be included in this category—all of which stay close to the charming prose of Robert Southey's original version (available in Opie & Opie, 1980; or online in *Wikipedia*). In the board books by dePaola and Barton the text is even more spare—the story is reduced to bare bones, making these versions an excellent introduction to the wonders of the tale for those who might be approaching it for the first time and need support in establishing Inquiry Level 1 understanding for linguistic or developmental reasons—very young children and English language learners.

8. *Somebody and the Three Blairs* (Tolhurst,1990) creates a delightful dissonance between the story created by words and that suggested by illustrations which features a human family who go to the park with their toddler, only to have their house invaded by "somebody" who looks just like an overgrown cuddly teddy bear and acts very much like the Blair toddler.

Chapter 6

1. The National Council of Teachers of Mathematics (NCTM) has recognized measurement as one of the five major content areas of school mathematics. The others are algebraic thinking, number sense and operations, geometry, and data and possibility. Measurement is also recognized as the intersection of mathematics and science.

2. Ginsberg (2006, p. 151) discusses children's inherent interest in the everyday math issues of *How many? How many more?*

3. In the 1930s in New Hampshire a remarkably forward-looking school superintendent introduced a very successful program that asked teachers to stop all formal arithmetic instruction below grade 6 and to stress language development, algebraic reasoning, and problem-solving instead. His original report is available at http://www.inference.phy.cam.ac.uk/sanjoy/benezet/.

4. Consider what happens when you line preschoolers up by pointing and giving them number names: "You're 1, you're 2, you're 3." A child who has just had a fourth birthday may well have a fit and refuse to get into line asserting, "I'm NOT 3!" That child is one of many who equate the first few number names with age (and take it as incontrovertible truth that any kind of *bigger* is equivalent to *better* (Hynes-Berry & Itzkowich, 2009).

5. There is a very strong developmental element to young children's number sense; brain research indicates that the intuitive understanding of numerosity for quantities from 1-5 in very young children corresponds approximately to their chronological age (Sousa, 2008). At about 5, they enter what is conmmonly called the "5–7" shift, which signals a significant increase in the cognitive ability to abstract and generalize. By the end of this period, strong number sense is typically established, including the ability to make sense of place

value and multi-digit numbers. The many children who have not been supported in establishing a strong foundation in concrete and pictorial understanding of number sense tend to get lost as increasing emphasis is placed on doing number operations on a symbolic level.

6. A disheartening body of evidence indicates that the reason many women choose early childhood classrooms is that they see it as a way to avoid teaching mathematics. In consequence, they tend to communicate their math phobia to their young charges (Sian Beilock, 2010).

7. The study done by Duncan et al. (2007) drew this conclusion based on a large sample of children. NCTM's position paper on early math in September 2007 endorsed the importance of strong early mathematics for long-term performance. See *Preschool Matters*, Jan/Feb 2010, vol 8, no 1 at http://nieer.org/psm/?article=298; see also Camilli et al (2010).

8. The International Academy of Education's report cites research that shows "an emphasis on teaching for meaning has positive effects on student learning, including better initial learning, greater retention, and an increased likelihood that the ideas will be used in new situations. These results have also been found in studies conducted in high-poverty areas." At the same time, the report calls for creating a "classroom learning context in which students can construct meanings" (Grouws & Cebulla, 2000, p. 13).

9. Again, emerging research on the brain has established what has been long known intuitively: New learning doesn't have the staying power of what we recognize or have experienced again and again; the more we reinforce this experience, the more staying power it has. Indications are that at best we can hold 6–8 things in short-term memory but can instantly access what is well established in long-term memory (Sliva, 2003, pp. 36–37).

10. At both the initial and intermediate stages of mathematizing, manipulatives such as counting cubes, base ten materials, and the like, as well as schematic drawings, offer a powerful way to transition from the concrete to a pictorial stage that moves toward the symbolic. For example, the name towers allow focusing on the comparison of length without reference to individual names—you cannot tell which of the 10 cube towers refers to Savannah and which is Mireille's.

11. The Fibonnaci sequence also represents the "golden rectangle" that is an important aesthetic feature of many paintings, sculptures, and works of architecture.

12. McDonald (2007) gives an excellent discussion of how to analyze counting books. See also Carlson (n.d.) and Wilburne et al. (2007).

13. Erikson Institute's very successful Early Mathemathics Project, with which I am involved, puts a book at the center of all of its professional development workshops. In the early 1990s, I retold 30 folktales to begin each unit of the Britannica math program I project-directed. Each story had a mathematical problem situation embedded in it that illustrated the mathematical concept that was being explored in the unit. Thus *The Knee-High Man* introduced measurement as comparison to kindergarteners, while a story about the Chinese Zodiac challenged second graders to see the importance of identifying "Which kind of bigger" is being considered.

14. See Whitin and Piwko (2008), "Mathematics and Poetry: The Right Connection." Piwko's rubric takes into account mathematical accuracy as well as setting a standard for the writing process.

Chapter 7

1. Trickster tales are universal. While origin tales almost always feature animals such as Anansi the Spider or Coyote, the trickster has human form as well, such as High John the Conqueror in African American tradition, the Jack tales popular in England and Appalachia (Chase, 2003), Juan Bobo in Latin countries, and Hodja in Turkey. Many folk tra-

ditions include clever women who use riddles or tricks to establish their superiority. MacDonald's *Storytellers Sourcebook: A Subject, Title, and Motif Index to Folklore Collections for Children* (1982/1999) and Krauss (1998) are invaluable resources for individual picture books and collections of myths and legends told for children.

2. Gardner argues that standard IQ tests only evaluate verbal and mathematical intelligences, ignoring the complex array of other capacities or intelligences that humans can excel in, including musical, kinesthetic, visual-spatial, naturalistic, interpersonal, and intrapersonal. In addition to Gardner, Thomas Armstrong (2009) provides helpful discussions of the implications for classrooms. Chen et al. (2009) look at the implications of this approach, which celebrates a diversity of strengths for learners in different kinds of classrooms and cultures.

3. Logs or lab books are close to being the most valuable piece of intellectual property that real scientists possess. They include all kinds of details that might seem irrelevant but in retrospect might provide an invaluable insight about a variable or factor that would explain the results.

4. For examples of using this strategy before introducing a text, see Chapter 8.

5. For specifics about FOSS (Full Option Science System) see http://www.fossweb.com/

6. Songs that convey accurate scientific information can be effective memory aids but composing such a song takes fairly deep understanding. YouTube includes many examples of how complex the learning/teaching potential is, for example, in the Volcano song (http://www.youtube.com/watch?v=BcFtpWjZwlE); even high-energy physics can make some sense (http://www.youtube.com/watch?v=j50ZssEojtM).

7. Buhrow and Garcia (2006) and Guccione (2011) persuasively argue that using visuals and informational books allow English language learners develop their conceptual understanding of ideas without limiting them to their proficiency in English. As they carefully "read" the pictures about phenomena, they can use whichever laguage they like to process the information, instead of having to deal simultaneously with conceptual and linguistic challenges. Duron-Flores and Maciel (2006) offer excellent suggestions about strategies appropriate for each level of English language learning.

8. I was introduced to this remarkably effective strategy many years ago in a workshop—regretfully I do not remember the presenter.

9. One of the best guides for how to systematically do this kind of formative assessment that takes into account the whole child, and his/her individual profile is Bridging (Chen & McNamee, 2007).

10. The tale was first collected in 1912 by Henriette Rothschild Kroeber for *The Journal of American Folklore*.

11. For information about these projects, go to the ESIP website (http://www.esiponline.org). Among other projects, ESIP sponsors Search It! Science, a specialized web-based search engine and database that allows readers, teachers, and librarians to search for appropriate science-related titles by combining their concerns: topics, genre, grade level, length, and so on (http://searchit.heinemann.com).

Chapter 8

1. I was introduced to this powerful approach to classroom management by Laurie Sharapan Sahn of Sears School in Winnetka, Illinois, in personal communication. See also Sahn (2008).

2. The strategy of "Reading an Object" is a formal strategy in bibliotherapy groups where *realia* can be used with clinical mental health patients to encourage responses to a poem (Hynes & Hynes-Berry, 2011). Alvarado and Herr (2006) offer a valuable resource outlining hands-on investigations using a related process.

3. Shoe Sort has been used in Erikson's Early Mathematics Project to illustrate the "big idea" in algebraic thinking that a collection can be sorted in many different ways, depending on the attribute(s) chosen for the sort.

4. The sad fact is that by third grade it is possible to predict which children are likely to end up as dropouts. Even more chilling is the way that many states, including California and Texas, factor in third-grade failure rates in reading and mathematics on state tests when forecasting their future prison needs.

5. Stroud's picture book identifies 10 block patterns that were said to be part of an established quilt code (Burns & Bouchard, 2003; Tobin & Dobard, 1999). While indications are that the code was not nearly as strictly established as Tobin claims, there is very good reason to believe that quilts, like the spirituals, were important signals for those making their way along the Underground Railroad (Brackman, 2006).

6. Great care should be taken about introducing the evils that result from man's inhumanity to man to young children, given how difficult it is to gain perspective on these issues as adults. See Schweber (2008) for a discussion of doing a unit on the Holocaust with third graders.

Chapter 9

1. The English educator Paul Swan (2001) argues that teachers should see children's misconceptions as helpful and even necessary for developing mathematical understanding. In the same way, working scientists often find that a null or negative result can lead to a highly productive way to solve the problem.

Bibliography of Children's Literature

This listing includes works that are referenced in the text, including those listed in Try and Apply sections in each chapter. Listings of multiple versions of the classic tales or stories related to quilts are by no means exhaustive; many new entries are being published regularly. Stone Soup variants are listed in Other Works, although they are featured in the Case in Point. Versions of *Who's the Strongest* are in Pourquoi Tales.

VERSIONS OF CLASSIC TALES

Three Little Pigs

Artell, M. (2006). *Three little Cajun pigs*. New York: Dial.
Davis, D. (2007). *The pig who went home on Sunday: An Appalachian folktale*. Little Rock: August House.
Galdone, J. C., & Galdone, P. (1979). *The three little pigs*. New York: Clarion Books.
Gay, M. (2004). *The three little pigs*. New York: Groundwood Books.
Hooks, W. H. (1997). *The three little pigs and the fox*. New York: Aladdin.
King-Smith, D. (2008). *All pigs are beautiful*. Cambridge, MA: Candlewick..
Knight, B. T. (1998). *From mud to house*. Danbury, CT: Children's Press.
Laird, D. (1990). *Three little Hawaiian pigs and the magic shark*. Honolulu: Barnaby Books.
London, J. (2004). *The eyes of gray wolf*. San Francisco: Chronicle Books.
Lowell, S. (1992). *The three little javelinas*. Flagstaff. AZ: Northland.
Scieszka, J. (1996). *The true story of the three little pigs*. New York: Puffin Books.
Trivizas, E. (1997). *The three little wolves and the big bad pig*. New York: McElderry.
Walton, R. (2003). *Pig, pigger, piggest*. Salt Lake City, UT: Gibbs Smith.
Whatley, B. (2005). *Wait! No paint*. New York: HarperCollins.
Wiesner, D. (2001). *The three pigs*. New York: Clarion Books.
Zemach, M. (1991). *The three little pigs: An old story*. New York: Farrar, Straus, & Giroux.

Cinderella

Climo, S. (1990). *The Irish Cinderlad*. New York: HarperCollins.
Climo, S. (1991). *The Egyptian Cinderella*. New York: HarperCollins.
Climo, S. (1996). *The Korean Cinderella*. New York: HarperCollins.

Coburn, J. R. (2000). *Domitila: A Cinderella tale from the Mexican tradition*. Walnut Creek, CA: Shen's Books.

Craft, K. Y. (2000). *Cinderella*. San Francisco: Chronicle Books.

Fleischman, P. (2007). *Glass slipper, gold sandal: A worldwide Cinderella*. New York: Henry Holt.

Greaves, M., & Chamberlain, M. (2000). *Tattercoats*. London: Frances Lincoln.

Huck, M. (1994). *Princess Furball*. New York: Greenwillow Books.

Martin, R. (1998). *The rough-face girl*. New York: Putnam Juvenile.

Louie, A. (1996). *Yeh-Shen: A Cinderella story from China*. New York: Putnam Juvenile.

Perrault, C., & Koopmans, L. (2002). *Cinderella*. New York: North-South Books.

Pollock, P., & Young, E. (1996). *The turkey girl: A Zuni Cinderella story*. Boston: Little, Brown.

Schroeder, A., & Sneed, B. (2000). *Smoky Mountain Rose: An Appalachian Cinderella*. New York: Puffin Books.

Sierra, J. (1992). *Cinderella*. Phoenix, AZ: Oryx Press.

Souci, R. D. S. (1989). *The talking eggs*. New York: Dial.

Souci, R. D. S. (2002). *Cendrillon: A Caribbean Cinderella*. New York: Aladdin.

Steptoe, J. (1993). *Mufaro's beautiful daughters* (Big Book ed.). New York: HarperCollins Festival.

Tomlinson, H. (2010). *Toads and diamonds*. New York: Henry Holt.

Goldilocks

Arnosky, J. (1996). *Every autumn comes the bear*. New York: Putnam Juvenile.

Aylesworth, J. (2003). *Goldilocks and the three bears*. New York: Scholastic. Press.

Barton, B. (1999). *The three bears*. New York: HarperCollins Festival.

Brett, J. (1987). *Goldilocks and the three bears*. New York: Putnam.

Buehner, C. (2009). *Goldilocks and the three bears* (Reprint ed.). New York: Puffin Books.

dePaola, T. (2004). *Tomie's three bears and other tales*. New York: Putnam Juvenile.

Ernst, L. C. (2003). *Goldilocks returns*. New York: Simon & Schuster.

Fearnley, J. (2002). *Mr. Wolf and the three bears*. New York: Harcourt Children's Books.

Galdone, P. (1985). *The three bears*. New York: Sandpiper.

George, J. C. (1998). *Look to the North: A wolf pup diary*. New York: HarperCollins.

Gorbachev, V. (2003). *Goldilocks and the three bears*. New York: North-South Books.

Greenaway, T. (1992). *Amazing bears: Eyewitness junior*. New York: Knopf.

Hopkins, J. M. (2007). *Goldie Socks and the three libearians*. New York: Upstart Books.

London, J. (1998). *Honey Paw and Lightfoot*. San Francisco: Chronicle Books.

Lowell, S. (2004). *Dusty Locks and the three bears*. New York: Owlet Paperbacks.

Opie, I., & Opie, T. L. P. (1980). *The classic fairy tales*. New York: Oxford University Press.

Ransom, C. (2005). *Goldilocks and the three bears/Ricitos de oro y los tres osos*. Greensboro, NC: Carson-Dellosa.

Rosales, M. (1999). *Leola and The Honeybears: An African-American retelling of Goldilocks*. New York: Scholastic.

Sander, S. (2009). *Goldilocks and the three bears*. New York: Grosset & Dunlap.

Simon, S. (2002). *Wild Bears: Level 1*. San Francisco, CA: Chronicle.

Stanley, D. (2007). *Goldie and the three bears*. New York: HarperCollins.

Tolhurst, M. (1990). *Somebody and the three bears*. New York: Orchard Books.

Wiley, M. (2008). *The 3 bears and Goldilocks*. New York: Atheneum.

POURQUOI TALES

Aardema, V. (1992). *Bringing the rain to Kapiti Plain.* New York: Puffin Books.

Aardema, V. (1994). *Misoso: Once upon a time tales from Africa* (Illus. ed.). New York: Knopf Books for Young Readers.

Aardema, V. (1998). *Borreguita and the coyote.* New York: Dragonfly Books.

Aardema, V. (2000). *Anansi does the impossible!: An Ashanti tale.* New York: Aladdin.

Aardema, V. (2008). *Why mosquitoes buzz in people's ears.* New York: Dial

Arkhurst, J. C. (1992). *The adventures of spider: West African folktales.* Boston: Little, Brown

Badoe, A. (2008). *The pot of wisdom: Ananse stories.* New York: Groundwood Books.

Bryan, A. (1987). *Beat the story-drum, pum-pum.* New York: Atheneum.

Bryan, A. (1999). *The story of lightning and thunder.* New York: Aladdin.

Bryan, A. (2003). *Beautiful blackbird.* New York: Atheneum.

Caduto, M. J. (1997). *Earth tales from around the world.* Golden, CO: Fulcrum Publishing.

Chase, R. (2003). *The Jack tales.* New York: Sandpiper.

Courlander, H. (1996). *A treasury of Afro-American folklore: The oral literature, traditions, recollections, legends, tales, songs, religious beliefs, customs, sayings and humor of peoples of African descent in the Americas* (2nd ed.). New York: Marlowe.

Courlander, H., & Herzog, G. (2008). *The cow-tail switch: And other West African stories.* New York: Square Fish.

Cowley, J. (1995). *The mouse bride.* New York: Scholastic..

Daly, N. (1995). *Why the sun & moon live in the sky.* New York: HarperCollins.

Dayrell, E. (1990). *Why the sun and the moon live in the sky.* New York: Sandpiper.

DeSpain, P. (2001). *Tales of tricksters.* Little Rock: August House.

Diakite, B. W. (2000). *The hunterman and the crocodiles.* New York: Scholastic.

Forest, H. (1996). *Wisdom tales from around the world.* Little Rock: August House.

Hamilton, M. (2005). *How & why stories.* Little Rock: August House.

Kimmel, E. (2000). *The two mountains: An Aztec legend.* San Francisco: Shen's Books.

Krauss, A. (1998). *Folktale themes and activities for children. Vol. 1: Pourquoi tales.* Englewood, CO: Libraries Unlimited.

Kwon, H. H. (1993). *The moles and the mireuk.* New York: Houghton Mifflin.

Lester, J. (1992). *The knee-high man and other tales.* New York: Puffin Books.

MacDonald, M. (2005). *Earth care.* Little Rock: August House.

McDermott, G. (1977). *Arrow to the sun: A Pueblo Indian tale.* New York: Puffin Books.

McDermott, G. (1987). *Anansi the spider: A tale from the Ashanti* (1st ed.). New York: Henry Holt.

McDermott, G. (1996). *Zomo the rabbit: A trickster tale from West Africa.* New York: Sandpiper.

McDermott, G. (2001). *Raven: A trickster tale from the Pacific Northwest.* New York: Sandpiper.

Oughton, J. (1996). *How the stars fell into the sky: A Navajo legend.* New York: Sandpiper.

Pinkney, J. (2009). *The lion & the mouse.* Boston: Little, Brown .

Sherlock, P. M. (1988). *West Indian folk-tales.* New York: Oxford University Press.

Wisniewski. D. (1995). *The rain player.* New York: Sandpiper.

Whitmal, E. (2006, May 1). *Knee high man wants to be sizable.* http://www.footstepsmagazine.com

Woerksom, D. V., & Cain, E. L. (1976). *The rat, the ox, and the zodiac: A Chinese legend.* New York: Crown.

Wolfman, J. (2004). *How and why stories for readers theatre.* Portsmouth, NH: Teacher Ideas Press.

QUILT STORIES

Bourgeois, P. (2003). *Oma's quilt.* Tonawanda, NY: Kid's Can Press.
Coerr, E. (1986). *The Josefina story quilt.* New York: Harper and Row
Crane, C. (2010). *The handkerchief quilt.* New York: Sleeping Bear Press.
Flournoy, V. (1985). *The patchwork quilt.* New York: Dial
Guback, G. (1994). *Luka's quilt.* New York: Greenwillow Books.
Hopkinson, D. (1995). *Sweet Clara and the freedom quilt.* New York: Dragonfly Books.
Hopkinson, D. (2005). *Under the quilt of night.* New York:Dragonfly Books.
Johnston, T., & dePaola, T. (1996). *The quilt story.* New York: Penguin.
Jonas, A. (1994). *The quilt.* New York: Puffin Books.
Lowell, S. (2008). *The elephant stitch quilt: Stitch by stitch to California.* New York: Farrar,
    Strauss & Giroux.
McKissack, P. C. (2008). *Stitchin' and pullin'.* New York: Random House.
Paul, A. P. (1995). *Eight hands round: A patchwork alphabet.* New York: HarperCollins.
Polacco, P. (2010). *The keeping quilt* (Rev. ed.). New York: Simon & Schuster Children's.
Ransome, C. (2002). *The promise quilt.* New York: Walker Books.
Ringgold. F. (1995). *Aunt Harriet's Underground Railroad in the sky.* New York: Dragonfly
    Books.
Ringgold. F. (1996). *Cassie's word quilt.* New York: Dragonfly Books.
Root, P. (2003). *The name quilt.* Boston, MA: Farrar, Strauss & Giroux.
Stroud, B. (2007). *The patchwork path: A quilt map to freedom.* Cambridge, MA: Candlewick.
Van Leeuwen, J. (2007). *Papa and the pioneer quilt.* New York: Dial.
Vaughan, M. (2001). *Secret to freedom.* New York:Lee & Low.
Wolff, F., & Savitz H. M. (2008). *The story blanket.* Atlanta: Peachtree.
Woodson, J. (2005). *Show way.* New York: Putnam.

OTHER WORKS OF CHILDREN'S LITERATURE

Allen, P. (1996). *Who sank the boat?* New York: Putnam Juvenile.
Anno, M. (1992). *Anno's counting book.* New York: Scholastic..
Aliki. (1971). *The Story of Johnny Appleseed.* New York: Aladdin.
Aylesworth, J. (2009). *The Mitten.* New York: Scholastic.
Bancroft, H. (1996). *Animals in winter: Let's read and find out.* New York: Collins.
Brett, J. (1989). *The mitten.* New York: Putnam.
Balliett, B. (2004). *Chasing Vermeer.* New York: Scholastic Press.
Boelts, M. (2007). *Those shoes.* Cambridge, MA: Candlewick Press.
Brown, M. (1997) *Stone soup.* New York: Aladdin.
Bunting, E. (1998). *Going home.* New York: HarperCollins
Christiansen, C. (2009). *The mitten tree.* New York: Fulcrum.
Choi, Y. (2003). *The name jar.* New York: Dragonfly.
Compestine, Y. C. (2007). *The real story of Stone Soup.* New York: Dutton.
Clements, A. (1988). *Big Al.* New York: Simon & Schuster.
Connor, L. (2004). *Miss Bridie chose a shovel.* New York:Houghton Mifflin Books for
    Children.
Crews, D. (1995). *Ten black dots.* New York: Greenwillow Books.
D'Agnese, J. (2010). *Blockhead: The life of Fibonnaci.* New York: Henry Holt
Dee, R. (1990). *Two ways to count to ten.* New York: Henry Holt.

DeSpain, P., & Lyttle, K. (1994). *Twenty-two splendid tales to tell from around the world.* Little Rock, AR: August House.

Diakite, B. W. (2003). *The magic gourd.* New York: Scholastic. Press.

Eglieski, R. (2000). *The gingerbread boy.* New York: HarperCollins .

Ehrlert, L. (1991). *Growing vegetable soup.* New York: Sandpiper.

Emberley, R. (1995). *Three cool kids.* Boston, MA: Little Brown.

Forest, H. (2005). *Stone Soup.* Little Rock, AR: August House.

Fox, M. (1994). *Tough Boris.* San Diego: Harcourt Brace.

Frasier, D. (1991). *On the day you were born.* San Diego: Harcourt Brace Jovanovich.

Frasier, D. (1990). *Miss Alianeus: A vocabulary Disaster.* New York: Sandpiper.

Fraser, M. (1996). *The ten mile day: The building of the transcontinental railroad* (Owlet ed.). New York: H. Holt.

Garland, S. (1997). *The lotus seed.* New York: Sandpiper.

Gerstein, M. (2003). *The man who walked between the towers.* New Milford, CT: Roaring Brook Press.

Giganti, P. (1998). *Each orange had 8 slices.* New York: Greenwillow Books.

Giganti, P. (1999). *How many snails?* New York: Greenwillow Books.

Gourley, R (2010). *Bring me some apples and I'll make you a pie.* New York: Clarion.

Hall, Z. (1996). *The apple pie tree.* New York: Scholastic.

Henkes, K. (1996). *Chrysanthemum.* New York: HarperTrophy.

Hodges, M. (2009). *The legend of St Christopher.* Grand Rapids, MI: Eerdmans.

Hong, L. T. (1993). *Two of everything.* Morris Grove, IL: Whitman.

Hooper, M. (1996). *This pebble in my pocket: A history of our earth.* New York: Viking.

Hurst, C. O. (2001). *Rocks in his head.* New York: Greenwillow.

Hulme, J. (2005). *Wild Fibonnaci: Nature's secret code revealed.* San Francisco: Tricycle Press.

Hutchins, P. (1994). *The doorbell rang.* New York:Greenwillow Books.

Johnson, D.B. (2000). *Henry hikes to Fitchburg.* Boston, MA: Houghton Mifflin

Kellog, S S. (2000) *The missing mitten mystery.* New York: Dial Press.

Kimmel, E. (2011) *Cactus soup.* New York: Marshall Cavendish.

Krauss, R. (2007). *The growing story.* New York: HarperCollins.

Krauss, R. (2004) *The carrot seed: 60th anniversary edition.* New York: HarperCollins.

London, P. (1998). *Honey paw and lightfoot.* New York: Chronicle Books.

MacDonald, M. R. (2004). *Three-minute tales.* Little Rock: August House.

Martin, J. B. (2009). *Snowflake Bentley* (Reprint). New York: Sandpiper.

McCully, E. A. (2006). *Marvelous Mattie: How Margaret E. Knight became an inventor .* Boston, MA: Farrar, Straus & Giroux

Merriam, E. (1996). *12 ways to get to 11.* New York: Aladdin.

Morris, A. (1998). *Shoes, shoes, shoes.*New York: HarperCollins

Mosel, A. (2007). *Tikki Tikki Tembo.* New York: Square Fish.

Muth, J. (2003). *Stone soup.* New York: Scholastic.

Nelson, R. (2004). *Float and sink* (First Step Non Fiction). New York: Lerner.

Niz, E. S. (2006). *Floating and sinking.* Mankato, MN: Capstone Press.

Pak, S. (2001). *Dear Juno.* New York: Puffin Books.

Raines, S., & Canaday, R. (1989). *Story stretchers: Activities to expand children's favorite books (Pre-K and K).* Silver Spring, MD: Gryphon House.

Raines, S., & Isbell, R. (1999). *Tell it again: Easy to tell stories with activities for young children.* Silver Spring, MD: Gryphon House.

Raines, S., & Isbell, R. (2000). *Tell it again 2: Easy to tell stories with activities for young children.* Silver Spring, MD: Gryphon House.

Recovits, H. (2004). *My name is Yoon.* New York: Farrar, Strauss & Giroux.

Say, A. (2009). *Tea with milk* (Reprint). New York: Sandpiper.

Schertle, A. (2000). *Down the road*. New York: Sandpiper.

Scieszka, J., & Smith, L. (1995). *Math curse*. New York: Viking Juvenile.

Seeger, P. (1986). *Abiyoyo*. New York: Aladdin.

Seeger, P., & Jacobs, P. D. (2004). *Abiyoyo returns*. New York: Aladdin.

Sendak, M. (1988). *Where the wild things are*. New York: HarperCollins.

Seuss, Dr. (1957) *The cat in the hat*. New York: Random House.

Shannon, D. (1998). *No David!* New York: Blue Sky Press

Shaw, C. G. (1993). *It looked like spilt milk* (Board book). New York: HarperCollins Festival.

Sis, P. (2000). *Starry messenger: Galileo Galilei*. New York: Farrar, Straus & Giroux.

Stewart, M. (2006). *Will it float or sink?* Danbury, CT: Children's Press.

Slobodkina, E. (1996). *Caps for sale*. New York: HarperFestival.

Thompson L (2007). *The apple pie that Papa baked*. New York: Simon & Schuster.

Tompert, A. (1997). *Grandfather Tang's story*. New York: Dragonfly Books.

Tresselt, A. (1989). *The mitten*. New York: HarperCollins.

Viorst, J. (2009). *Alexander, who used to be rich last Sunday*. New York: Atheneum.

White, E. B. (2001). *Charlotte's web*. New York: HarperCollins

Williams, K. L. (2005). *Circles of hope*. Grand Rapids, MI: Eerdmans Books for Young Readers.

Williams, K. L. (2010). *My Name is Sangoel*. Grand Rapids, MI: Eerdmans Books for Young Readers.

Willis, K. (2000). *Mister and me*. New York: Putnam Juvenile.

Wilson, K. (2002). *Bear snores on*. New York: Scholastic.

Zipes, J., Paul, L., Vallone, L., Hunt, P., & Avery, G. (2005). *The Norton anthology of children's literature: The traditions in English* (Illus. ed.). New York: W. W. Norton.

References

Ackerman, D. (2000). *Deep play*. New York: Vintage.

Albert Shanker Institute. (2009). *Preschool curriculum: What's in it for children and teachers*. Retrieved from http://www.shankerinstitute.org/Downloads/Early%20 Childhood%2012-11-08.pdf

Almon, J. (2008). *The vital role of play in early childhood education*. Waldorf Research Institute. Retrieved August 1, 2009 http://www.waldorfresearchinstitute.org/pdf/ BAPlayAlmon.pdf

Alvarado, A.E. & Herr P.R. (2003) Inquiry-based learning using everyday objects: Hands-on instructional strategies that promote active learning in grades 3–8 New York: Corwin Press.

Armstrong, T. (2009). *Multiple intelligences in the classroom* (3rd ed.). Alexandria, VA: ASCD.

Bandura, A. (1997). *Self-efficacy: The exercise of control*. New York: Worth.

Barone, D. M., & Xu, S. H. (2007). *Literacy instruction for English language learners pre-K–2*. New York: Guilford Press.

Beilock, S. L., Gunderson, L. A., Ramirez, G., & Levine, S. C. (2011). *Female teachers' math anxiety impacts girls' math achievement*. Proceedings of the National Academy of Sciences, USA. www.pnas.org/cgi/doi/10.1073/pnas.0910967107

Bergen, D. (2002), The role of pretend play in children's cognitive development. *ECRP* 4(1), http://ecrp.uiuc.edu/v4n1/bergen.html

Bergen, D., & Maurer, D. (2000). Symbolic play, phonological awareness, and literacy skills at three age levels. In J. F. Christie (Ed.), *Play and literacy in early childhood: Research from multiple perspectives* (pp. 45–62). Mahwah. NJ: Erlbaum.

Bernstorf, E. (2004). *The music and literacy connection*. Lanham, MD: Rowman & Littlefield Education.

Bloom, B. S. (1956). *Taxonomy of educational objectives, Handbook 1: Cognitive domain* (2nd ed.). Addison Wesley.

Boushey, G., & Moser, J. (2006). *The daily five*. Portland, ME: Stenhouse.

Bowen, E. (2006.). *Student engagement and its relation to quality work design: A review of the literature*. Retrieved from http://chiron.valdosta.edu/are/ebowenLitReview.pdf

Brackman, B. (2006). *Facts and fabrications: Unraveling the history of quilts and slavery: 8 projects, 20 blocks, first-person accounts*. Concord, CA: C&T Publishing.

Brophy, J. (1988). Research linking teacher behavior to student achievement: Potential implications for instruction of Chapter 1 students. *Educational Psychologist, 23*(3), 235–286.

Brown, S., & Vaughan, C. (2009). *Play: How it shapes the brain, opens the imagination, and invigorates the soul*. New York: Avery.

Bruner, J. (1987). *Actual minds, possible worlds*. Cambridge, MA: Harvard University Press.

Bruner, J. (1992). *Acts of meaning: Four lectures on mind and culture*. Cambridge, MA: Harvard University Press.

Buhrow, B., & Garcia, A. U. (2006). *Ladybugs, tornadoes, and swirling galaxies* (illus. ed.). Portland, ME: Stenhouse.

Burns, E., & Bouchard, S. (2003). *Underground railroad sampler.* Paducah, KY: Quilt In A Day.

Burns, M. M., & Flowers, A. A. (1999, September/October). Whatever happened to . . . ? A list of recovered favorites and what makes a book memorable after all. *The Horn Book Magazine, 75,* 574–586.

Burns, M. (2004) *Math and literature, grades K–1.* Sausolito, CA: Math Solutions.

Burns, M., Sheffield, S. (2004). *Math and literature, grades 2–3.* Sausalito, CA: Math Solutions

Bybee, R. (2006, August 13–15). *Enhancing science teaching and student learning: A BSCS perspective.* Paper presented at the 2006 ACER Research Conference, Canberra, Australia.

Camilli, G., Vargas, S., Ryan, S., & Barnett, W. S. (2010,). Meta-analysis of the effects of early education interventions on cognitive and social development. *Teachers College Record, 112* (3), 579–620. Retrieved from http://www.tcrecord.org/Content. asp?ContentID=15440

Carlson, A. (n.d.). Concept books and young children. Retrieved from http://comminfo.rutgers. edu/professional-development/childlit/books/CARLSON.pdf

Celic, C. (2009). *English language learners day by day.* Portsmouth, NH: Heinemann.

Chen, J., & Chang, C. (2006). A comprehensive approach to technology training for early childhood teachers. *Early Education and Development, 17*(3), 443–465.

Chen, J., & McNamee, G. (2007). *Bridging: Assessment for teaching and learning in early childhood classrooms.* Thousand Oaks CA: Corwin Press.

Chen, J., Moran, S., & Gardener G. (Eds). (2009). *Multiple intelligences around the world.* San Francisco, CA: Jossey-Bass.

Chouinard, M.M. (2009). *Children's questions: A mechanism for cognitive development* (Monographs of the Society for Research in Child Development) Boston, MA: Blackwell Publishing.

Clements, D. H., & Sarama, J. A. (2009). *Learning and teaching early math: The learning trajectories approach.* New York: Routledge.

Cooper, P. J., & Allen, N. B. (1999). *The quilters: Women and domestic art: An oral history.* Lubbock: Texas Tech University Press.

Cooper, P. M. (1993). *When stories come to school: Telling, writing, & performing stories in the early childhood classroom.* New York: Teachers & Writers Collaborative.

Cooper, P. M. (2009). *The classrooms all young children need: Lessons in teaching from Vivian Paley.* Chicago: University of Chicago Press.

Cooper, P. M., Capo, K., Mathes, B., & Gray, L. (2007). One authentic early literacy practice and three standardized tests: Can a storytelling curriculum measure up? *Journal of Early Childhood Teacher Education, 28*(3), 251–275.

Cross, C. T., Woods, T. A., & Schweingruber, H. (Eds.); Committee on Early Childhood Mathematics; National Research Council. (2009). *Mathematics learning in early childhood: Paths toward excellence and equity.* Washington, DC: National Academies Press.

Csikszentmihalyi, M. (1997). *Creativity: Flow and the psychology of discovery and invention* (4th ed.). New York: HarperCollins.

Csikszentmihalyi, M. (1998). *Finding flow: The psychology of engagement with everyday life.* New York: Basic Books.

Dau, E. (Ed.). (2001). *Child's play.* Baltimore, MD: Brookes.

Davis, R. D., & Braun, E. M. (2010). *The gift of dyslexia: Why some of the smartest people can't read . . . and how they can learn* (Rev. ed.). New York: Perigee Trade.

Developmental Studies Center. *Making meaning: Being a writer.* Oakland, CA: Developmental Studies Center.

Dockett, S. (2001). Thinking about play, playing about thinking. In E. Dau (Ed.), *Child's Play* (pp. 28–46). Baltimore: Brookes.

Douglas, R., Klentschy, M. P., Worth, K., & Binder, W. (Eds.). (2006). *Linking science and literacy in the K–8 classrom*. National Science Teachers Association Press.

Duckworth, E. (2001). *Tell me more: Listening to learners explain*. New York: Teachers College Press.

Duckworth, E. (2006). *The having of wonderful ideas: And other essays on teaching and learning* (3rd ed.). New York: Teachers College Press.

Duke, N. K., & Kays, J. (1998). "Can I say 'Once upon a time'?": Kindergarten children developing knowledge of information book language. *Early Childhood Research Quarterly, 13*(2), 295–318.

Duncan, G. J., Dowsett, C. J., Claessens, A., Magnuson, K., Huston, A. C., Klebanov, P., et al. (2007). School readiness and later achievement. *Developmental Psychology, 43*(6), 1428–1446.

Duron-Flores, M., & Maciel, E. (2006). English language development and the science-literacy connection. In R. Douglas, M. P. Klentschy, K.Worth, & W. Binder (Eds.), *Linking science and literacy in the K–8 classrom* (pp. 321–336). Washington, DC: NSTA Press.

Duschl, R. A., Schweingruber, H. A., & Shouse, A. W. (Eds.). (2007). *Taking science to school: Learning and teaching science in grades K–8*. Washington, DC: National Academies Press.

Dweck, C. S. (2007). *Mindset: The new psychology of success*. New York: Ballantine Books.

Dweck, C. S., & Bempechat, J. (1983). Children's theories of intelligence: Implications for learning. In S. Paris, G. Olson, & H. Stevenson (Eds.), *Learning and motivation in children*. Hillsdale. NJ: Erlbaum.

Edwards, C., Gandini, L., & Forman, G. (1998). *The hundred languages of children: The Reggio Emilia approach—advanced reflections* (2nd ed.). Elsevier Science.

Elkind, D. (2007). *The power of play: Learning what comes naturally*. Philadelphia, PA: Da Capo Press.

Ely, R. (2005). Language and literacy in the school years. In J. B. Gleason (Ed.), *The development of language* (6th ed., pp. 395–443). Boston: Allyn & Bacon.

Epstein, A. S. (2007). *Intentional teacher: Choosing the best strategies for young children's learning*. Washington, DC: National Association for the Education of Young Children.

Erikson, E. H. (1998). *The life cycle completed: Extended version with new chapters on the ninth stage of development by Joan M. Erikson*. New York: W. W. Norton.

Fisher, D., & Frey, N. (2008). *Better learning through structured teaching: A framework for the gradual release of responsibility*. Alexandria, VA: ASCD.

Fleer, M. (2001). Universal fantasy: The domination of Western theories of play. In E. Dau (Ed.), *Child's Play* (pp. 67–80). Baltimore: Brookes.

Fosnot, C. T., & Dolk, M. (2001). *Young mathematicians at work: Constructing number sense*. Portsmouth, NH: Heinemann.

Freeman, J. (2007). *Once upon a time: Using storytelling, creative drama, and reader's theater with children in grades pre-K–6* (annot. ed.). Westport, CT: Libraries Unlimited.

Galinsky, E. (2010). *Minds in the making: The seven essential life skills every child needs*. New York: HarperCollins .

Gallagher, J. J., & Ascher, M. J. (1963). A preliminary report on analyses of classroom interaction. *Merrill-Palmer Quarterly, 9*(1), 183–194.

Gallas, K. (1995). *Talking their way into science: Hearing children's questions and theories, responding with curricula*. New York: Teachers College Press.

Gamse, B. C., Bloom, H. S., Kemple, J. J., & Jacob, R. T. (2008). *Reading First impact study: Interim report* (NCEE 2008-4016). Washington, DC: National Center for Education Evaluation and Regional Assistance, Institute of Education Sciences, U.S. Department of Education. Retrieved from http://www.eric.ed.gov/ERICWebPortal/contentdelivery/servlet/ERICServlet?accno=ED501218

Gardner, H. E. (1993). *The unschooled mind: How children think and how schools should teach.* New York: Basic Books.

Gardner, H. E. (2006). *Multiple intelligences: New horizons in theory and practice.* New York: Basic Books.

Gartrell, D. (2003). *The power of guidance: Teaching social-emotional skills in early childhood classrooms.* Florence, KY: Wadsworth.

Genishi, C., & Dyson, A. H. (2009). *Children, language, and literacy: Diverse learners in diverse times.* New York: Teachers College Press.

Ginsburg, H. P. (2006). Mathematical play and playful mathematics. In D. G. Singer, R. M. Golinkoff, & K Hirsch-Pasek (Eds.), *Play-learning: How play motivates and enhances children's cognitive and social-emotional growth* (pp. 145–168). New York: Oxford University Press

Goodman, K. S., (1987). *Language and thinking in school: A whole-language curriculum.* Somers, NY: Richard C. Owen.

Goodman, K. S. (2006). *The truth about DIBELS: What it is, what it does.* Portsmouth, NH: Heinemann

Gopnik, A. (2009). *The philosophical baby: What children's minds tell us about truth, love, and the meaning of life.* Farrar, Straus & Giroux.

Grennan, K., & Jablonski, M. (2002) Collaboration between student affairs and faculty on student-related research. *New Directions For Student Services, 1999*(85), 73–81.

Grouws, Douglas A., & Cebulla, K. (2000). Elementary and middle school mathematics at the crossroads. In T. L. Good (Ed.), *American education: Yesterday, today, and tomorrow* (pp. 209–255). Chicago: University of Chicago Press.

Guccione, L. (2011). Integrating literacy and inquiry for English learners. *The Reading Teacher 64*(8), pp 567–577.

Hall, C., & Coles, M. (1997). Gendered readings: Helping boys develop as critical readers. *Gender and Education, 9*(1), 61–68.

Halpern, R. (2008). *The means to grow up: Reinventing apprenticeship as a developmental support in adolescence.* New York: Routledge.

Hamilton, M., & Weiss, M. (2005). *Children tell stories: Teaching and using storytelling in the classroom* (2nd ed.). Somers, NY: Richard C. Owen.

Hannaford, C. (2005). *Smart moves: Why learning is not all in your head* (2nd ed). Arlington, VA: Great River Books.

Hansen, D., & Bernstorf, E. (2002). Linking music learning to reading instruction. *Music Educators Journal, 88*(5), 17–21.

Hansen, D. Bernstorf, E., & Stuber, G. M. (2004). *The music and literacy connection.* (ERIC document reproduction service No. ED488727)

Haraksin-Probst, L. (2008). *Making connections: Movement, music & literacy.* High/Scope Press.

Harman, M. (n.d.). Music and movement—instrumental in language development. *Early Childhood News.* Retrieved June 7, 2010, from http://www.earlychildhoodnews.com/earlychildhood/article_view.aspx?ArticleID=601

Haroutunian-Gordon, P. S. (2009). *Learning to teach through discussion: The art of turning the soul.* New Haven, CT: Yale University Press.

Hart, B., & Risley, T. R. (2003). The early catastrophe: 30 million word gap by age 3. *American Educator, 27*(1), 95–118. Retrieved from http://www.aft.org/pdfs/americaneducator/spring2003/TheEarlyCatastrophe.pdf

Hartman, D. (2002). *Using informational books in the classroom. Letting the facts (and research) speak for themselves.* Red Brick Learning. Retrieved from http://www.capstonepub.com/CAP/downloads/misc/LNCB_HartmanPaper.pdf

Harvey, S., & Goudvis, A. (2007). *Strategies that work: Teaching comprehension for understanding and engagement* (2nd ed.). Portland, ME: Stenhouse. (Original work published 2000)

Helm, J. H. & Benneke, S. (2003). *The power of projects: Meeting contemporary challenges in early childhood classrooms—strategies and solutions.* New York: Teachers College Press.

Helm, J. H., & Katz, L. (2001). *Young investigators: The project approach in the early years.* New York: Teachers College Press.

Hirsh-Pasek, K., Golinkoff, R. M., Berk, L. E., & Singer, D.G. (2009). *A mandate for playful learning in preschool.* New York, NY: Oxford University Press.

Hughes, J. N., Luo, W., Kwok, O-M., & Loyd, L. K. (2008). Teacher-student support, effortful engagement, and achievement: A 3-year longitudinal study. *Journal of Educational Psychology, 100*(1), 1–14.

Hyde, A. (2006). *Comprehending math: Adapting reading strategies to teach mathematics, K–6.* Portsmouth, NH: Heinemann.

Hynes, A., & Hynes-Berry, M. (2011). *Bibliopoetry therapy: The interactive process, a handbook* (2nd ed.). St. Cloud, MN: North Star Press.

Hynes-Berry, M., & Itzkowich, R. (2009). The gift of error. In A. Gibbons & C. Gibbs (Eds.), *Conversations on early childhood teacher education* (pp. 104–112). Redmond, WA: Teaching Strategies.

Immordino-Yang, M. H. (2008). The smoke around mirror neurons: Goals as sociocultural and emotional organizers of perception and action in learning. *Mind, Brain, and Education, 2*(2), 67–73.

Immordino-Yang, M. H., & Damasio, A. R. (2007). We feel, therefore we learn: The relevance of affective and social neuroscience to education. *Mind, Brain, and Education, 1*(1), 3–10.

Jalongo, M. R. (2004). *Young children and picture books.* Washington, DC: National Association for the Education of Young Children.

Jensen, E. (2000). *Music with the brain in mind.* Thousand Oaks, CA: Corwin. Press.

Johns, V. (2001). Embarking on a journey: Aboriginal children and games. In E. Dau (Ed.), *Child's play* (pp. 60–66). Baltimore: Brookes.

Johnson, A. P. (1998). How to use creative dramatics in the classroom. *Childhood Education, 75*(1), 2–6. Retrieved from http://findarticles.com/p/articles/mi_qa3614/is_199810/ai_n8822428/

Karasel, N., Ayda, O., & Tezer, M. (2010). The relationship between mathematics anxiety and mathematical problem solving skills among primary school students. *Procedia–Social and Behavioral Sciences, 2*(2), 5804–5807. doi:10.1016/j.sbspro.2010.03.946

Karelitz, E. B. (1993). *The author's chair and beyond: Language and literacy in a primary classroom.* Portsmouth, NH: Heinemann.

Katz, L. G. (1998). What can we learn from Reggio Emilia? In C. Edwards, L. Gandini, & G. Forman (Eds.), *The hundred languages of children: The Reggio Emilia approach—advanced reflections* (2nd ed.). San Francisco: Elsevier Science.

Katz, L.G., & Chard, S. (2000). *Engaging children's minds: The project approach.* Denver, CO: Praeger.

Katz, L. G. (2010). Knowledge, understanding, and the disposition to seek both. *Exchange, 32*(6), 46–47.

Katz, S. A., & Thomas, J. A. (2003). *The word in play: Language, music and movement in the classroom* (2nd ed.). Baltimore: Brookes.

Keene, E. O., & Zimmermann, S. (2007). *Mosaic of thought: The power of comprehension strategy instruction* (2nd ed.). Portsmouth, NH: Heinemann. (Original work published 1987)

Kohn, A. (1999). *Punished by rewards: The trouble with gold stars, incentive plans, A's, praise, and other bribes* (2nd ed.). New York: Mariner Books.

Kohn, A. (2000). *The schools our children deserve: Moving beyond traditional classrooms and "tougher standards."* New York: Mariner Books.

Kohn, A. (2006). *Beyond discipline: From compliance to community* (10th ed.). Alexandria, VA: Association for Supervision & Curriculum Development.

Kraus, A. (1998). *Folktale themes and activities for children: Vol. 1. Pourquoi tales* (annot. ed.). Santa Barbara, CA: Libraries Unlimited.

Kuhlthau, C. C., Maniotes, L. K., & Caspari, A. K. (2007). *Guided inquiry: Learning in the 21st century.* Santa Barbara, CA: Libraries Unlimited.

Logue, M.E., & Detour, A. (2011). You be the bad guy: a new role for teachers in supporting children's dramatic play. *Early Childhood Research and Practice, 13*(1). Retreived from http://ecrp.uiuc.edu/v13n1/logue.html

MacDonald, M. R. (1982). *The storyteller's sourcebook: A subject, title, and motif index to folklore collections for children.* Florence, KY: Gale.

MacDonald, M. R. & Sturm, B. (1999). *The storyteller's sourcebook: A subject, title, and motif index to folklore collections for children.* Florence, KY: Gale.

MacDonald, M. R. (2005). *Three minute tales.* Little Rock: August House.

Manzo, K. K. (2008). Reading First doesn't help pupils "get it." *Education Week, 27*(36), 1, 14.

Martinez, M. (1998). What is problem-solving? *Phi Delta Kappan, 79*(8), 605–609.

Marzano, R. J. (1992). *A different kind of classroom: Teaching with dimensions of learning.* Alexandria, VA: Association for Supervision & Curriculum Development.

Marzano, R. J. (2007). *The art and science of teaching: A comprehensive framework for effective instruction.* Alexandria, VA: Association for Supervision & Curriculum Development.

Marzano, R. J., & Kendall, J. S. (2006). *The new taxonomy of educational objectives* (2nd ed.). Thousand Oaks CA: Corwin Press.

McCaslin, N. (2006). *Creative drama in the classroom and beyond* (8th ed.). Boston: Allyn & Bacon.

McDonald, J. (2007). Selecting counting books: Mathematical perspectives. *Young Children, 62*(3), 38–42.

Mendoza, J., & Reese, D. (2001). Examining multicultural picture books for the early childhood classroom: Possibilities and pitfalls. *Early Childhood Research and Practice, 3*(2), 1–27.

Michaels, S., Shouse, A., & Schweingruber, H. (2007). *Ready, set, science!: Putting research to work in K–8 science classrooms.* Washington, DC: National Academies Press.

Miller, D. (2002). *Reading with meaning.* Portland, ME: Stenhouse.

Miller, D. (2008). *Teaching with intention.* Portland, ME: Stenhouse.

Miller, E., & Almon, J. (2009). *Crisis in the kindergarten: Why children need to play in school.* New York: Alliance for Childhood.

Mooney, M. E. (2004). *A book is a present: Selecting text for intentional teaching.* Somers, NY: Richard C. Owen.

Mullis, I. V. S., Jenkins, F., & Johnson, E. G. (1994). *Effective schools in mathematics: Perspectives from the NAEP 1992 assessment.* Research and Development Report. (Report No. NAEP-23-RR-01). Princeton, NJ: National Assessment of Educational Progress. (ERIC Document Reproduction Service No. ED377059)

National Council of Teachers of English (NCTE). (2011). *NCTE Orbis Pictus Award for Outstanding Nonfiction for Children.* NCTE website. Retrieved from http://www.ncte.org/awards/orbispictus

Newmann, F. M. (1996). *Authentic achievement: Restructuring schools for intellectual quality.* Jossey-Bass.

Newmann, F. M., Lopez, G., & Bryk, A. S. (1998). *The quality of intellectual work in Chicago schools: A baseline report.* Chicago: Consortium on Chicago School Research.

Noddings, N. (2005). *The challenge to care in schools: An alternative approach to education* (2nd ed.). New York: Teachers College Press.

Noddings, N. (2008, February). All our students thinking: Teaching students to think [Special issue]. *Educational Leadership, 65*(5), 8–13. Retrieved from http://www.ascd.org/publications/educational_leadership/feb08/vol65/num05/All_Our_Students_Thinking.aspx

Nodelman, P. (1990). *Words about pictures: The narrative art of children's picture books.* Athens: University of Georgia Press.

Nodelman, P., & Reimer, M. (2002). *The pleasures of children's literature* (3rd ed.). Boston: Allyn & Bacon.

Olness, R. (2004). *Using literature to enhance content area instruction: A guide for K–5 teachers.* Newark, DE: International Reading Association.

Opitz, M., & Guccione, L. (2009) *Comprehension and English language learners: 25 oral reading strategies that cross proficiency levels.* Portsmouth, NH: Heinemann.

Paley, V. G. (1993). *You can't say you can't play.* Cambridge, MA: Harvard University Press.

Paley, V. G. (2005). *A child's work: The importance of fantasy play.* Chicago: University of Chicago Press.

Paley, V. G., & Coles, R. (1991). *The boy who would be a helicopter.* Cambridge, MA: Harvard University Press.

Paradise, R., & Rogoff, B. (2009). Side by side: Learning by observing and pitching in. *Ethos, 37*(1), 102–138. doi:10.1111/j.1548-1352.2009.01033.x

Pearson, P. D., & Gallagher, M. C. (1983). The instruction of reading comprehension. *Contemporary Educational Psychology, 8,* 317–344.

Piaget, J. (1970). Piaget's theory. in P. Mussen (Ed.), *Carmichael's manual of child psychology* (Vol. 1). New York: John Wiley & Sons

Piaget, J (1972). *Play, dreams and imitation in childhood.* New York: Norton.

Piaget, J., & Inhelder, B. (2000). *The psychology of the child* (2nd ed.). New York: Basic Books.

Pianta, R. C., La Paro, K. M., & Hamre, B. K. (2007). *Classroom assessment scoring system (CLASS) manual, pre-K.* Baltimore: Brookes.

Polya, G. (2009*). How to solve it: A new aspect of mathematical method.* Princeton, NJ: Princeton University Press.

Ravitch, D. (2000). *Left back: A century of battles over school reform.* New York: Simon & Schuster.

Ravitch, D. (2010). *The death and life of the great American school system.* New York: Basic Books.

Rea, D., & Mercuri, S. (2006). *Research-based strategies for English language learners: How to reach goals and meet standards, K–8.* New York: Heinemann.

Reyhner, J. (2008). *The reading wars: Phonics versus whole language.* http://jan.ucc.nau.edu/~jar/Reading_Wars.html

Risley, T. R., & Hart, B. (1995). *Meaningful differences in the everyday experience of young American children.* Baltimore: Brookes.

Rogoff, B. (1991). *Apprenticeship in thinking: Cognitive development in social context.* New York: Oxford University Press.

Rogoff, B. (2003). *The cultural nature of human development.* New York: Oxford University Press.

Rojas, J. (2006). Una jornada de aprendizaje valiosa para compartir (A learning journey worth sharing out). In R. Douglas, M. P. Klentschy, & K. Worth (Eds.), *Linking science and literacy in the K–8 classroom* (pp. 285–295). Alexandria, VA: NSTA Press.

Roseberry, A. S., & Hudicourt-Barnes, J. (2006). Using diversity as a strength in the science classroom. In R. Douglas, M. P. Klentschy, K. Worth (Eds.), *Linking science and literacy in the K–8 classroom* (pp. 305–320). Alexandria VA: NSTA Press.

Routman, R. (1999). *Conversations: Strategies for teaching, learning, and evaluating* (annot. ed.). Portsmouth, NH: Heinemann.

Sahn, L.S., & Reichel, A.G. (2008). Read all about it: A classroom newspaper integrates the curriculum. *Young Children 63*(2), 12–18.

Saul, W., Reardon, J., & Pearce, C. (2002). *Science workshop: Reading, writing, and thinking like a scientist* (2nd ed.). Portsmouth, NH: Heinemann.

Schaps, E., Battistich, V., & Solomon, D. (1997). School as a caring community: A key to character. In A. Molnar (Ed.), *The construction of children's character*. Ninety-sixth yearbook of the National Society for the Study of Education (pp. 127–139). Chicago: National Society for the Study of Education.

Schlechty, P. C. (2001). *Inventing better schools: An action plan for educational reform*. San Francisco, CA: Jossey-Bass.

Schlechty, P. C. (2002). *Working on the work: An action plan for teachers, principals, and superintendents*. San Francisco, CA: Jossey-Bass.

Schulman, L. S. (1987). Knowledge and teaching: Foundations of the new reform. *Harvard Educational Review, 57*(1), 1–22.

Schweber, S. (2008, October). "What happened to their pets?": Third graders encounter the Holocaust. *Teachers College Record, 110*(10), 2073–2115.

Shatzer, J. (2008, May). Picture book power: Connecting children's literature and mathematics. *Reading Teacher*. Available at http://www.readwritethink.org/resources/resource-print.html?id=20948&tab=1

Siena, M. (2009). *From reading to math: How best practices in literacy can make you a better math teacher, grades K–5*. Sausalito, CA: Math Solutions.

Singer, D., Golinkoff, R, M., & Hirsch-Pasek, K. (Eds). (2009). *Play = learning: How play motivates and enhances children's cognitive and social-emotional growth*. New York: Oxford University Press.

Sierra, J. (1992). *Cinderella*. Westport, CT: Oryx Press.

Sipe, L. R. (2007). *Storytime: Young children's literary understanding in the classroom*. New York: Teachers College Press.

Sliva, J. (2003). *Teaching inclusive mathematics to special learners K–6*. Thousand Oaks, CA: Corwin.

Small, M. (2010). Beyond one right answer. *Educational Leadership, 68*(1), 29–32.

Smilansky, S. (1968). *The effects of sociodramatic play on disadvantaged preschool children*. New York: John Wiley.

Sousa, D. (2005). *How the brain learns*. Thousand Oaks, CA: Corwin Press.

Sousa, D. (2006). *How the special needs brain learns*. Thousand Oaks CA: Corwin Press.

Sousa, D. (2009, June). Brain-friendly learning for teachers. Revisiting teacher learning [Special issue]. *Educational Leadership, 66*. Retrieved from http://www.ascd.org/publications/educational_leadership/summer09/vol66/num09/Brain-Friendly_Learning_for_Teachers.aspx

Spolin, V. (1986). *Theater games for the classroom: A teacher's handbook*. Evanston, IL: Northwestern University Press.

Sullivan, M. (2009). *Connecting boys with books 2: Closing the reading gap*. Chicago, IL: American Library Association.

Swan, M. (2001). Dealing with misconceptions in mathematics. In P. Gates (Ed.), *Issues in mathematics teaching* (pp. 147–165). London: Routledge Falmer.

Sweeney, L. B. (2001). *When a butterfly sneezes: A guide for helping kids explore interconnections in our world through favorite stories*. Denver, CO: Pegasus Press.

Stone Soup Network. (1999). *Annual report to the Annenberg Schools Challenge*. Unpublished document.

Tingting. (2009, November 11). Teaching the Cinderella fairytale: China vs. America. *ChinaSmack*. Retrieved from http://www.chinasmack.com/2009/stories/teaching-cinderella-fairytale-china-vs-america-differences.html

Tobin, J. L., & Dobard, R. G. (1999). *Hidden in plain view: A secret story of quilts and the underground railroad*. New York: Anchor Books.

Tomlinson, C. A., & McTighe, J. (2006). *Integrating differentiated instruction & understanding by design: Connecting content and kids*. Alexandria, VA: ASCD.

Turkle, S. (2008). *Falling for science: Objects in mind.* Cambridge, MA: MIT Press.

Van den Heuvel-Panhuizen, M. (2000). Mathematics in the Netherlands, a guided tour. *Freudenthal Institute CD-Rom for ICME9.* Utrecht: Utrecht University. Available at http://www.fi.uu.nl/en/rme/TOURdef+ref.pdf

Van den Heuvel-Panhuizen, M., & Buys, K. (2008). *Young children learn measurement and geometry: A learning-teaching trajectory with intermediate attainment targets for the lower grades in primary school.* Rotterdam: Sense.

Van Hoorn, J., Nourot, P. M., Scales, B., & Alward, K. (2006*). Play at the center of the curriculum* (4th ed.). Upper Saddle River, NJ: Prentice-Hall.

Vogler, K. (2008, Summer). Asking good questions. Thinking skills now [Special issue]. *Educational Leadership, 65(Online).* Retrieved from http://www.ascd.org/publications/educational_leadership/summer08/vol65/num09/Asking_Good_Questions.aspx

Vygotsky, L. S. (1978). *Mind in society: Development of higher psychological processes* (14th ed.). Cambridge, MA: Harvard University Press.

Wagner, B. J. (1999). *Dorothy Heathcote: Drama as a learning medium* (Rev. ed.). Portsmouth, NH: Heinemann.

Washburn, K. (2010). Guest blog: Report from the learning and the brain conference. *Blogs: Betty Ray.* Retrieved from http://www.edutopia.org /kevin-washburn-learning -brain-intelligence-factors

Wenger, E. (2006). *Communities of practice: A brief introduction.* Retrieved from http://www.ewenger.com/theory/

Weinbaum, A., Allen, D., Blythe, T., Simon, K. Siedel, S., & Rubin, C. (2004). *Teaching as inquiry.* New York: Teachers College Press.

Whitin, D. J., & Piwko, M. (2008, March). Mathematics and poetry: The right connections. *Beyond the Journal: Young Children on the Web.* Retrieved from http://www.naeyc.org/files/yc/file/200803/BTJ_Whitin.pdf

Whitin, D., & Wilde, S. (1995a). *It's the story that counts.* Portsmouth NH: Heinemann

Whitin D. & Wilde, S. (1995b). *Read any good math lately?: Children's books for mathematical learning.* Portsmouth NH: Heinemann.

Wiggins, G., & McTighe, J. (2005). *Understanding by design* (2nd ed.). Upper Saddle River, NJ: Prentice-Hall.

Wilburne, J. M., Napoli, M., Keat, J. B., Dile, K., Trout, M., & Decker, S. (2007). Journeying into mathematics through storybooks: A kindergarten story. *Teaching Children Mathematics, 14*(4), 232–237.

Williams, M., Cross, D., Hong, J., Aultman, L., Osborn, J., & Schultz, P. (2008). "There are no emotions in math": How teachers approach emotions in the classroom. *Teachers College Record, 110*(8), 1574–1610.

Willingham, D. (2008/2009, Winter). Ask the cognitive scientist: What will improve a student's memory? *American Educator,32,* 17–25, 44. Retrieved from http://www.aft.org/pdfs/americaneducator/winter0809/willingham.pdf

Worthy, J. (2005). *Readers theater for building fluency: Strategies and scripts for making the most of this highly effective, motivating, and research-based approach to oral reading.* Teaching Strategies.

Zambo, D. (2008). Mathematics thinkers and doers: Everyone needs a positive story. *Teaching Children Mathematics, 15*(4), 226-234.

Zhao, Y. (2009*). Catching up or leading the way: American education in the age of globalization.* Association for Supervision & Curriculum Development.

Zins, J. E., Weissberg, R. P., Wang, M. C., & Walberg, H. J. (2004). *Building academic success on social and emotional learning: What does the research say?* New York: Teachers College Press.

Index

NAMES

Aardema, Verna, 123, 162
Ackerman, Diane, 65, 173 n. 2
Aliki, 99
Allen, N. B., 57
Allen, Pamela, 131
Almon, Joan, 44, 65, 171 n. 7, 172 n. 5, 173 n. 4
Alward, K., 69–71
Anno, M., 112
Armstrong, Thomas, 177 n. 2
Arnosky, Jim, 90–91
Ascher, M. J., 172–173 n. 8
Aultman, L., 25
Aylesworth, Jim, 81, 95, 97, 99

Bancroft, H., 99
Bandura, A., 24
Barnett, W. S., 176 n. 7
Barone, D. M., 92
Battistich, V., 172 n. 10
Baylor, Byrd, 129
Beilock, Sian, 176 n. 6
Benneke, S., 124
Bergen, D., 161, 173 n. 6, 174 n. 8
Berk, L. E., 63, 65
Bernstorf, E., 70, 71, 173 n. 7
Binder, W., 135
Bloom, B. S., 49, 50, 172 n. 5, 172–173 n. 8
Bobo, Juan, 176–177 n. 1
Boelts, M., 117
Bouchard, S., 178 n. 5
Boushey, G., 45, 173 n. 11
Bowen, E., 24, 25, 170–171 n. 1
Brackman, B., 178 n. 5
Braun, E. M., 44, 174 n. 7
Brett, Jan, 99, 175 n. 7

Bridges, Ruby, 46
Brophy, J., 170–171 n. 1
Brown, Marcia, 99, 170 n. 1
Brown, Margaret Wise, 118
Brown, S., 65
Bruner, J., 27, 63
Bryan, Ashley, 123
Bryk, A. S., 25–26, 29, 172 n. 11
Buehner, Caralyn, 82, 95–97
Buehner, Mark, 95–96
Buhrow, B., 45, 85, 91, 177 n. 7
Bunting, Eve, 141
Burningham, John, 18
Burns, E., 178 n. 5
Burns, M. M., 84, 117
Buys, K., 113
Bybee, Roger, 171 n. 8

Camilli, G., 176 n. 7
Canaday, R., 117
Capo, K., 173 n. 6
Carlson, A., 176 n. 12
Caspari, A. K., 124
Caulkins, Lucy, 134
Celic, C., 85
Chang, C., 16
Chard, S., 124
Chase, R., 176–177 n. 1
Chen, J., 16, 126, 160, 177 n. 2, 177 n. 9
Choi, Y., 99
Chouinard, M. M., 172 n. 2
Christiansen, Candace, 99
Claessens, A., 176 n. 7
Coles, M., 84
Compestine, Y. C., 99
Connor, L., 140–141
Cooper, P. J., 57
Cooper, Patsy M., 69, 173 n. 6

Cowley, J., 162
Crews, Donald, 77, 112
Cross, C. T., 113, 116
Cross, D., 25
Csikszentmihalyi, M., 65, 173 n. 2

D'Agnese, J., 116
Dau, E., 173 n. 3
Davis, R. D., 44, 174 n. 7
Dayrell, E., 121
Decker, S., 176 n. 12
Dee, R., 117
dePaola, T., 148, 150, 175 n. 7
DeSpain, P., 162
Detour, A., 68
Dobard, R. G., 178 n. 5
Dockett, S., 68
Dolk, M., 50
Douglas, R., 135
Dowsett, C. J., 176 n. 7
Duckworth, E., 27
Duke, N. K., 84
Duncan, G. J., 176 n. 7
Duron-Flores, M., 84–85, 124, 177 n. 7
Duschl, R. A., 127, 128
Dweck, C. S., 24, 32, 42, 44, 48, 166

Edwards, C., 126
Eglieski, R., 76
Ehlert, Lois, 99
Eile, K., 176 n. 12
Elkind, D., 65
Ely, R., 174 n. 8
Emberley, R., 76
Epstein, A. S., 63
Ernst, L. C., 97

Fearnley, J., 77

Fisher, D., 173 n. 11
Fleer, M., 173 n. 3, 173 n. 5
Flournoy, Valerie, 92, 137, 139, 148, 150
Flowers, A. A., 84
Forest, Heather, 99, 170 n. 1
Forman, G., 126
Fosnot, Cathy T., 50, 115
Fraser, M., 119
Frasier, Debra, 86, 96, 99
Freeman, J., 174 n. 11
Frey, N., 173 n. 11

Galdone, Paul, 175 n. 7
Galinsky, E., 31, 66
Gallagher, J. J., 172–173 n. 8
Gallas, K., 124
Gamse, B. C., 172 n. 5
Gandini, L., 126
Garcia, A. U., 45, 85, 91, 177 n. 7
Gardener, G., 126, 160, 177 n. 2
Gardner, Howard E., 126, 160, 177 n. 2
Garland, A., 141
Gartrell, D., 24
Gerstein, M., 132
Giganti, Paul, 112
Golinkoff, R. M., 63, 65
Goodman, K. S., 172 n. 4, 172 n. 5
Gopnik, A., 68
Gorbachev, Valeri, 175 n. 7
Gorelick, Ken, 170 n. 2
Gottschall, Sue, 3, 13–14
Goudvis, A., 45, 47, 173 n. 11
Gourley, R., 99
Gray, L., 173 n. 6
Grennan, K., 171 n. 9
Guback, G., 148
Guccione, L., 91, 177 n. 7

Hall, C., 84
Hall, Zoe, 99
Halpern, R., 55
Hamilton, M., 75
Hamre, B. K., 25, 48
Hannaford, C., 70
Hansen, D., 70, 174 n. 7
Haraksin-Probst, L., 174 n. 7
Harman, M., 174 n. 7
Hart, B., 44
Hartman, D., 85
Harvey, S., 45, 47, 173 n. 11

Heathcote, Dorothy, 174 n. 12
Helm, J. H., 33, 124
Henkes, Kevin, 87, 94, 99
Hirsch-Pasek, K., 63, 65
Hodges, M., 162
Hong, J., 25
Hong, Lily T., 117, 119
Hooper, M., 162
Horsch, Patty, 5
Hudicourt-Barnes, J., 124
Hughes, J. N., 25, 170–171 n. 2
Hulme, J., 116
Hurst, C. O., 132
Huston, A. C., 176 n. 7
Hutchins, Pat, 118, 119
Hyde, A., 114
Hynes, Arlene McCarty, 4, 13, 170 n. 2, 174 n. 14, 177 n. 2
Hynes-Berry, M., 4, 13, 17, 170 n. 2, 174 n. 14, 175 n. 4, 177 n. 2

Immordino-Yang, M. H., 32
Isbell, R., 117
Itzkowich, R., 17, 175 n. 4

Jacob, R. T., 172 n. 5
Jalongo, M. R., 82, 84, 90
Jensen, E., 174 n. 7
Johnson, A. P., 75
Johnson, D. B., 119
Johnson, Donna, 165
Johnston, Tony, 148, 150

Karelitz, E. B., 75
Katz, Lillian G., 23, 27, 33, 63, 124
Katz, S. A., 27, 63, 71, 75, 174 n. 9
Kays, J., 84
Keat, J. B., 176 n. 12
Keene, E. O., 45, 47
Kellog, Steven, 99
Kemple, J. J., 172 n. 5
Kendall, J. S., 172–173 n. 8
Kimmel, Eric, 99
King, Martin Luther, 46
Klebanov, P., 176 n. 7
Klentschy, M. P., 135
Knight, B. T., 37
Kohn, Alfie, 24
Krauss, A., 176–177 n. 1
Krauss, Ruth, 119, 132

Kroeber, Henriette Rothschild, 177 n. 10
Kuhlthau, C. C., 124
Kwok, O-M., 25, 170–171 n. 2
Kwon, H. H., 162

La Paro, K. M., 25, 48
Lester, J., 117
Levine, Ellen, 99
Logue, M. E., 68
London, Jonathan, 90–91
Lopez, G., 25–26, 29, 172 n. 11
Lowell, Susan, 20, 37
Loyd, L. K., 25
Luo, W., 25

MacDonald, M. R., 2, 75, 176–177 n. 1
Maciel, E., 84–85, 124, 177 n. 7
Magnuson, K., 176 n. 7
Maniotes, L. K., 124
Manzo, K. K., 172 n. 5
Martin, J. B., 132
Martinez, M., 32–33
Marzano, R. J., 171 n. 9, 172–173 n. 8
Mathes, B., 173 n. 6
Maurer, D., 174 n. 8
McCaslin, N., 174 n. 11
McClintock, Barbara, 95
McCully, E. A., 132
McDermott, Gerald, 123
McDonald, J., 119, 176 n. 12
McNamee, G., 177 n. 9
McTighe, J., 143
Mendoza, J., 93
Merriam, Eve, 77, 112
Michaels, S., 124
Mies Van Der Rohe, Ludwig, 151
Miller, D., 45, 47, 63, 173 n. 11
Miller, E., 44, 65, 172 n. 5, 173 n. 4
Mooney, M. E., 63
Moran, S., 126, 160, 177 n. 2
Morris, Ann, 140
Mosel, Arlene, 99
Moser, J., 45, 173 n. 11
Muth, John, 99, 170 n. 1

Napoli, M., 176 n. 12

Nelson, R., 132
Newmann, F. M., 25–26, 28, 29, 34, 171 n. 3, 172 n. 11
Niz, E. S., 132
Nodelman, Perry, 82, 90, 97, 175 n. 4
Nourot, P. M., 69–71

Opie, I., 175 n. 7
Opie, T. L. P., 175 n. 7
Opitz, M., 91
Osborn, J., 25

Pak, S., 129
Paley, Vivian G., 63, 68–69, 173 n. 6
Parks, Rosa, 74
Pearce, C., 134
Persephone, 138–139
Piaget, J., 27, 34, 49, 63, 65, 173 n. 3
Pianta, R. C., 25, 48, 170–171 n. 1
Piwko, M., 118, 176 n. 14
Polacco, Patricia, 149, 150
Polya, G., 173 n. 1

Raines, Shirley, 117
Ransom, C., 96, 97
Ravitch, Diane, 25, 171 n. 5
Reardon, J., 134
Recovits, H., 99
Reese, D., 93
Reimer, M., 90
Reyhner, J., 44, 172 n. 4
Risley, T. R., 44
Rogoff, Barbara, 55, 56, 69, 173 n. 3, 173 n. 5
Rojas, J., 84–85
Romberg, Thomas, 171 n. 8
Root, Phyllis, 148, 150
Rosales, Melodye, 93
Roseberry, A. S., 124
Routman, R., 45, 173 n. 11
Ryan, S., 176 n. 7

Sahn, Laurie Sharapan, 177 n. 1
Saul, Wendy, 134
Savitz, H. M., 148
Say, A., 141
Scales, B., 69–71
Schaps, E., 172 n. 10
Schertle, Alice, 18, 99, 140

Schlechty, Philip C., 33, 34, 171 n. 3
Schulman, L. S., 15, 170 n. 6
Schulz, P., 25
Schweber, S., 174 n. 14, 178 n. 6
Schweingruber, H. A., 113, 116, 124, 128
Scieszka, Jon, 20, 76, 108, 175 n. 6
Seeger, Pete, 18, 59–79, 97
Sendak, M., 96
Seuss, Dr., 70, 96
Shannon, David, 18, 77
Shatzer, J., 119
Shaw, C. G., 77
Sheffield, S., 117
Shouse, A. W., 124, 128
Siena, M., 114
Sierra, J., 172 n. 1
Simon, Seymour, 91
Singer, D. G., 63, 65
Sipe, L. R., 47–48, 82, 87–89, 90
Sis, P., 132
Sliva, J., 125, 176 n. 9
Slobodkina, E., 119
Small, M., 172 n. 2
Smilansky, S., 173 n. 3
Smith, L., 108
Snider, Justin, 171 n. 7
Solomon, D., 172 n. 10
Sousa, D., 24, 32, 44, 70, 125, 175–176 n. 5
Spolin, V., 71, 174 n. 11
Stroud, Betty, 137, 144, 151, 178 n. 5
Stuber, G. M., 174 n. 7, 177–178 n. 5
Stuve-Bodeen, Stephanie, 129
Sullivan, M., 84
Swan, Paul, 178 n. 1
Sweeney, Linda B., 131

Thomas, J. A., 27, 63, 71, 75, 174 n. 9
Thompson, L., 99
Tingting, 171 n. 2
Tobin, J. L., 178 n. 5
Tolhurst, M., 175 n. 8
Tomlinson, C. A., 143
Tompert, Ann, 117, 119
Tresselt, Alvin, 99
Trivizas, E., 76

Trout, M., 176 n. 12
Tubman, Harriet, 147

Van den Heuvel-Panhuizen, M., 113
Van Hoorn, J., 69–71
Vargas, S., 176 n. 7
Vaughan, C., 65
Vogler, K., 172–173 n. 8
Vygotsky, L. S., 27, 34, 49

Wagner, B. J., 174 n. 12
Walberg, H. J., 25
Walton, R., 37
Wang, M. C., 25
Washburn, K., 24, 44
Weiss, M., 75
Weissberg, R. P., 25
Wells, Rosemary, 87, 94
Wenger, E., 170 n. 5
Whatley, B., 37
White, E. B., 77–78
Whitin, D. J., 117, 118, 176 n. 14
Wiesner, D., 37
Wiggins, G., 143
Wilburne, J. M., 176 n. 12
Wilde, S., 117
Wiley, Margaret, 94–95
Willems, Mo, 94
Williams, K. L., 99, 132
Williams, M., 25
Willingham, D., 65, 110, 125, 171 n. 7
Willis, K. W., 18
Wolff, F., 148
Woods, T. A., 113, 116
Woodson, Jacqueline, 144
Worth, K., 135
Worthy, J., 174 n. 13

Xu, S. H., 92

Zhao, Y., 171 n. 2
Zimmermann, S., 45, 47
Zins, J. E., 25

SUBJECTS

Abiyoyo (Seeger), 18, 59–79, 97
Achievement, teaching for, 6, 42, 44, 156
Adjectives, as naked numbers, 110–112
Albert Shanker Institute, 173 n. 4
All Aboard Reading Series, 96
Alliance for Childhood, 171 n. 7, 173 n. 4
Alphabet books, 85–86
Amazing Bears: Eyewitness Junior, 91
Amazing Facts strategy, 130–131, 141
Ancona (Montessori-based school), 1–4
Animal characters, 86–87
Animals in Winter (Bancroft), 99
Annenberg Foundation Schools Initiative, 3–4,
    13–14
Annenberg Schools Challenge Grant project,
    25, 171 n. 3
Anno's Counting Book (Anno), 112
Apple Pie That Papa Baked, The (Thompson), 99
Apple Pie Tree, The (Hall), 99
Apples and Pie, 99
Arithmetic
    in 3Rs, 30–32, 171 n. 5, 171 n. 8
    as dinosaur of academic vocabulary, 31
    mathematics versus, 30–32, 109–112,
        113–114
"As if" thinking, 68, 173 n. 5
ASK principle, 137–138, 144, 146–148
ASLC (Association for Library Service to
    Children), 84, 85
Association for Supervision and Curriculum
    Development (ASCD), 171 n. 9
Authentic intellectual work, 25–26, 29

Backwards Planning, 143
Balanced Literacy approach, 45, 47–48, 61,
    84, 123, 172 n. 4
Basic Skills approach, 43–44, 45
Being a Writer (Developmental Studies
    Center), 79
Beowulf, 2
Biblio-poetry therapy, 4, 13, 170 n. 2
Biblio-poetry Therapy (Hynes & Hynes-Berry), 4
Big ideas, 22, 35, 79, 118, 143
Biological Science Curriculum (BSCS), 171
    n. 8
Blockhead (D'Agnese), 116
Boy Who Would be a Helicopter (Paley & Coles),
    69
Brain research, 23–25, 32, 44, 70, 125, 176
    n. 9
Brer Fox tales, 86
Bringing the Rain to Kapiti Plain (Aardemma),
    162

Bring Me Some Apples and I'll Make You a Pie
    (Gourley), 99

Cactus Soup (Kimmel), 99
Caldecott award, 170 n. 1
Caps for Sale (Slobodkina), 119
Carrot Seed, The (Krauss), 132
Cat in the Hat, The (Dr. Seuss), 96
Charlotte's Web (White), 46, 77–78
Chicago Schools Project, 171 n. 3
Children's Literature Comprehensive
    Database, 174 n. 1
Child's Work, A (Paley), 69
Chrysanthemum (Henke), 99
Cinderella, 2, 18, 39–58, 78, 80, 86, 179–180
Circles of Hope (Williams), 132
CLASS: Classroom Assessment Scoring
    System, 48
Classic tales, 76–77, 86, 179–180. *See also*
    Cinderella; Goldilocks; Three Little Pigs
Classroom climate, 48–49
Closed questions, 41, 48, 49, 128
Cognition theory, 23–25, 27, 63
Cognitive dissonance, 17, 32–33
Communities of practice, 14, 170 n. 5
Competence, in quality intellectual work,
    24–25
Comprehension, as basic skill, 45
Concept books, 85–86, 117
Conceptual framework, in Guided Inquiry,
    124
Connections
    between classroom climate and thinking,
        48–49
    importance of, 45–47
    kinds of, 46–47
    between literacy and literary
        understanding, 47–48
Construction of knowledge, 26–27, 65, 71,
    113, 126–127
Constructive play, 67
Content area learning, 71
Conversation, 49–50, 56–57
Counting books, 85–86
C-P-S principle, 139
Creative Dramatics, 72–76
    enactment of set text, 73–75
    learning dynamic, 72–73
    narrative pantomime, 72
    Reader's Theater, 75–76, 174 n. 13
Creativity, play and, 65
Critical thinking, 49–54

Daily Five approach, 45–46
David Goes to School (Shannon), 18
Dear Juno (Pak), 129
Deep play (Ackerman), 65
Developmentally appropriate practice
  evaluation of rich texts, 163–165
  inquiry across the curriculum and, 138, 139
  picture books and, 94–95, 98
Developmental Studies Center (San Francisco), 79, 172 n. 7, 172 n. 10
Disciplined inquiry, 27–29, 158–166
  evaluation in, 163–166
  exploring meaning in, 158–160
  inquiry across the curriculum, 136–152
  intentional use of stories in, 162–163
  perspectivism in, 160–162
  teaching/learning dynamic in, 166–167
  in Three Es, 32
Disney, 39–41, 172 n. 1
Disposition toward inquiry, 23
Dolores Kuhl Education Foundation, 174 n. 1
Doorbell Rang, The (Hutchins), 118, 119
Down the Road (Schertle), 18, 99, 140
Dramatic play, 59–60, 66–69, 72–76

Each Orange Had 8 Slices (Giganti), 112
Early Math Project, 175 n. 5, 176 n. 13, 178 n. 3
Education Development Center, 171 n. 6
Edwardo, The Horriblist Boy in the Whole Wide World (Burningham), 18
Elizabeth's Doll (Stuve-Bodeen), 129
Enactment of set text, 73–75
Encyclopedia Britannica Educational Corporation, 4–5
Engagement
  in developing questions, 143
  of learners in satisfying inquiry, 155–158
  quality of work and, 62
  in Three Es, 32, 36, 132–134, 171 n. 8
English language learners, informational text structure and, 84–85
Equity, in choosing books, 91–94, 98
Erikson Institute (Chicago), 174 n. 1
  Early Mathematics Project, 175 n. 5, 176 n. 13, 178 n. 3
  New Schools Project, 5, 48, 172 n. 7
  Teacher Education Department, 5
Error/mistakes
  as a gift, 164–166
  in science, 32–33, 131
  scientific method and, 33–34, 127, 131
  in Three Es, 32–33
Essential ABCs, 168–169
Evaluation

  by learners, 163–165
  in science, 132–134
  by teachers/facilitators, 165–166
  in Three Es, 32, 33, 36, 133, 171 n. 8
  in use of rich texts, 163–166
Every Autumn Comes the Bear (Arnosky), 90–91
Everybody Needs a Rock (Baylor), 129
Executive function, 24
Explicit instruction, 45
Exploration, in Three Es, 32, 36, 132–134

Fairy tales, 2, 76–79, 86
Fantasies, 86
Flow (Czikszentmihalyi), 173 n. 2
Folk tales, 2, 79
FOSS (Full Option Science System), 129, 177 n. 5
Freudenthal Institute, 113–114
From Mud to House (Knight), 37
Functional/sensory play, 67, 70–71

Games with rules, 66, 67
Gender
  informational text structure and, 84
  math phobia, 176 n. 6
Gift of Dyslexia (Davis & Braun), 44
Gilgamesh, 2
Gingerbread Man, 76
Going Home (Bunting), 141
Goldilocks, 18, 80–99, 119, 157, 180
Goldilocks Returns (Ernst), 94–95
Gradual Release of Responsibility (GRR) model, 55
Grandfather Tang's Story (Tompert), 117, 119
Graphic organizers, 91
Graphics
  in informational texts, 91
  text-to-graphics connections, 46–47
Growing Story, The (Krauss), 119, 132
Growing Vegetable Soup (Ehlert), 99
Guided Inquiry
  learning communities and, 33
  in science, 123–125
Guided participation (Rogoff), 56, 173 n. 5

Habit of curiosity, 23
Habits of mind, 31
Henry Hikes to Fitchberg (Johnson), 119
Higher order thinking, 18, 65, 68, 90, 115–116, 123, 160–162
Historical fiction, 87
History of science, 132–134
Honey Paw and Lightfoot (London), 90–91
Hotline 21 (TV program), 3–4
How Big Is a Foot?, 117

How Many Snails (Giganti), 112
Hug-a-Book Foundation, 3–4, 5, 80, 120, 122, 123, 170 n. 3, 174 n. 1

If Your Name Was Changed At Ellis Island (Levine), 99
Iliad, 2
Important Book, The (Brown), 118
Informational books, 84, 117, 177 n. 7
Informational text structure, 84–85, 90–91, 94
Inquiry across the curriculum, 136–152
　book matrix for, 148–149
　developmental appropriateness, 138, 139
　mapping out learner understanding, 148–149
　mapping out project, 146–148
　in mathematics, 138, 140, 141–142, 149–151
　patchwork quilt as integrated curriculum inquiry, 141–148
　questions in, 142–145
　Reading an Object in, 138–141
　in science, 138, 142, 149–151
　in social studies, 137–138, 142, 146–148, 149–151
Inquiry Ladder, 50–54, 61, 65, 70, 97, 127
Institute of Education Sciences (IES), 44
Intellectual curiosity, 22–23
Intentional
　in mathematics, 117
　in SIP Principle, 63–64, 69–76, 117
　use of stories in disciplined inquiry, 162–163
International Academy of Education, 176 n. 8
It Looked Like Spilt Milk (Shaw), 77

Keeping Quilt, The (Polacco), 149
Knee-High Man, The (Lester), 117, 176 n. 13
K-W-C strategy, 114–115
K-W-L strategy, 114–115, 133

Ladder of Inquiry, 50–54, 61, 65, 70, 97, 127
Landscape of learning (Fosnot), 50
Language development
　importance of engaging language and expression, 157–158
　picture books and, 84–85, 89–90
　sensory involvement in play and, 70–71
Leading questions, 41, 49
Learning
　play and, 65
　teaching for, 42, 45–49
Learning communities, 6, 11–19, 172 n. 10
　guided inquiry and, 33
　parallel processing in, 16–19
　pedagogical content knowledge in, 15–19

as professional communities of practice, 14
projects and, 33
stone in the soup for, 12–14
stories good to play with in, 78–79
texts as catalysts in, 12–14
in *Three Little Pigs* project, 33–38
Leola and the Honeybears (Rosales), 93
Lifelong learning, 6, 15, 24–25, 132, 163–166
Linking Science and Literacy in the K-8 Classroom (Douglas et al.), 135
Literacy development, 47–48
　Balanced Literacy approach to, 45, 47–48, 61, 84, 123, 172 n. 4
　connection between literary understanding and, 47–48
　defining literacy, 84
　learning from patchwork quilts, 149–151
　stories as tools for, 68–69
　in 3Rs, 31
Literary quality, 87–91
　components of, 87–90
　developmentally appropriate practice and, 94–95
　features of specific books, 95–98
　in informational texts, 90–91
　workmanship and tools in, 98
Literary text structure, 86–91, 94, 95–98
Literary understanding, 47–48
Little Red Riding Hood, 21, 38
Lotus Seed, The (Garland), 141
Luka's Quilt (Guback), 148, 149

Making Meaning (Developmental Studies Center), 79
Man Who Walked Between the Towers, The (Gerstein), 132
Marvelous Mattie (McCully), 132
Mastery, teaching for, 42
Math Curse (Scieszka & Smith), 108
Mathematics, 103–119
　arithmetic versus, 30–32, 109–112, 113–114
　higher order thinking in, 115–116
　inquiry across the curriculum and, 138, 140, 141–142, 149–151
　as language of science, 127
　learning from patchwork quilts, 149–151
　mathematizing, 113–114, 117–119, 176 n. 10
　measuring without numbers, 106
　naked numbers, 108–112
　SIP of play and, 112–116
　story in, 4–5, 104–109, 112–119
　in 3R's, 30–32, 171 n. 5, 171 n. 8
Tikki Tikki Tembo (Mosel), 99, 103–119
　units, 106–108

Mathematics in the City project (Fosnot et al.), 50, 118
Mathematization, 113–114, 117–119, 176 n. 10
McArthur Genius Award, 68–69
McCool, Finn, 2
Meaning-making,
literacy and, 31
picture books and, 83–87, 90
in quality intellectual work, 5–6, 29–30, 46–47
Measurement, 104–109, 110
Metacognition, 132–133
Miss Alianeus (Frasier), 99
Miss Bridie Chose a Shovel (Connor), 140–141
Missing Mitten Mystery, The (Kellog), 99
Mr. and Me (Willis), 18
Mr. Wolf and the Three Bears (Fearnley), 77
Mitten, The, 99
Mitten Tree, The (Christiansen), 99
Moles and the Mireuk, The (Kwon), 162
Mosaic of Thought (Keene & Zimmerman), 45
Motivation to learn
intrinsic, 170–171 n. 1
need to know in, 21–23, 27, 32–33, 36, 128, 155
Mouse Bride, The (Cowley), 162
Mufaro's Beautiful Daughters, 53
Multiple intelligences (Gardner), 126–128, 160, 177 n. 2
My Name is Sangoel (Williams), 99
My Name is Yoon (Recovits), 99
Myths, 2, 86

Naked numbers, 108–112
as adjectives, 110–112
arithmetic versus mathematics and, 109–112, 113–114
problem with, 109–110, 126
units and, 108–109, 110
Name Jar, The (Choi), 99
Name Quilt, The (Root), 148, 149
Narrative story structure, 85, 86, 89
National Association for the Education of Young Children (NAEYC), 170 n. 5
National Council of Teachers of English (NCTE), 84, 174 n. 3
National Council of Teachers of Mathematics (NCTM), 31, 175 n. 1, 176 n. 7
National Research Council, 113, 127–128
National Science Foundation Elementary Science Integration Projects (ESIP), 134, 177 n. 11
Need to know, 21–23, 27, 32–33, 36, 128, 155
New Schools Project, 5, 48, 172 n. 7
No, David! (Shannon), 77

No Child Left Behind (NCLB), 44, 66, 172 n. 5
Northeast Foundation for Children, 172 n. 7, 172 n. 10
Number sense, 77, 110–112
Nursery rhymes, 70

Odyssey, 2
"100 Languages of Children" (Reggio Emilia), 126
On the Day Your Were Born (Frasier), 86
Ontogeny recapitulates phylogeny, 22, 49
Open-and-shut closed questions, 41, 48
Open Court, 44
Open questions, 41–42, 45, 48, 49, 54, 114, 143, 159
Orbis Pictus Award for Outstanding Nonfiction for Children, 84, 174 n. 3

Parallel processing, 16–19
in introducing preservice and inservice teachers, 17–18
nature of, 16
in problem solving done by learners and teachers, 18–19
in promoting pedagogical content knowledge (PCK), 16–19
starting with story in, 17–18
Patchwork Path, The (Stroud), 137, 144, 151
Patchwork Quilt, The (Flournoy), 92, 137, 139, 146, 148, 149
Pedagogical content knowledge (PCK), 15–19
defined, 15, 170 n. 6
nature of, 15–16
parallel-processing in promoting, 16–19
Perspectivism, 160–162
Phonics instruction, 172 n. 5
Picture books, 80–99
developmentally appropriate, 94–95, 98
equity in choosing books, 91–94, 98
as good tools for learning, 81–82
illustrations and graphics in, 90, 91
informational text structures, 84–85, 90–91, 94
literary text structures, 86–91, 94, 95–98
quality intellectual work and, 87–91, 95–98
reading for meaning and, 83–87, 90
Pig, Pigger, Piggest (Walton), 37
Play, 59–79
"as if" thinking in, 68, 173 n. 5
dramatic play, 59–60, 66–69, 72–76
in improving classroom experience, 61–62
intentional ways of playing with stories to learn, 69–76
mathematics and, 112–116
picture books and, 96–98

as quality intellectual work, 63–66
science and, 127
SIP Principle in, 63–66, 71–72, 74–76,
    112–119, 158–163
turning readers into writers, 76–78
types of, 65–66, 67
Pourquoi tales, 120–135, 181–182
    Guided Inquiry and, 123–125
    nature of, 122
    in science class, 120–135
    subjects of, 123
    Sun and Moon story, 120–122, 132
    Who's the Strongest? parable, 153–163,
        166–167
Praxis
    assessing quality of picture books, 80–99
    defined, 14, 166–167
    learning communities in, 6, 11–19
    nature of, 6
    practice becoming, 34–36
    quality intellectual work in, 6, 20–79
Preschool Matters, 176 n. 7
Problem solving
    engaging learners in satisfying inquiry,
        156–157
    in mathematics, 113, 117–118
    parallel processing in, 18–19
    in SIP Principle, 64, 117–118
Project-based learning, 33, 124
Public Education and Business Coalition
    (PEBC), 45–47

Quality intellectual work, 6, 20–79
    as authentic intellectual work, 25–26, 29
    big ideas and, 22, 35, 79, 118, 143
    competence in, 24–25
    construction of knowledge in, 26–27, 65,
        71, 113, 126–127
    disciplined inquiry in, 27–29, 158–166
    dynamics of, 164, 166–167
    engaging learners in satisfying inquiry,
        155–158
    higher order thinking and, 18, 65, 68, 90,
        115–116, 123, 160–162
    intellectual curiosity in, 22–23
    learning communities and, 33–38
    meaning beyond the classroom and, 5–6,
        29–30, 46–47
    motivation to learn in, 21–22
    nature of, 25–26
    nature of quality learning in, 21–23
    ontogeny recapitulates phylogeny in, 22,
        49
    ownership of learning, 23–24
    picture books and, 87–91, 95–98
    play in. *See* Play

practice becoming praxis in, 34–36
    in pre-K to grade 3 classrooms, 34, 81–82
    questions in. *See* Questions
    stories in, 153–167
    three Es and, 32–33, 36, 132–134, 171 n. 8
    three Rs and, 30–32, 171 n. 5, 171 n. 8
Questions, 39–58
    activating schema, 46–47, 61
    in Basic Skills approach, 43–44, 45
    characteristics of good, 142–143
    connection between learning to read and
        learning to think, 45–49
    importance of, 49–54, 56–57
    influence on answers, 41–44
    inquiry across the curriculum and,
        142–145
    Inquiry Ladder and, 50–54, 61, 65, 70,
        97, 127
    and play in picture books, 96–98
    teachers giving up control of, 55–57
    types of, 41–42, 45, 48, 49, 54, 114, 143,
        159
Quilters, The (Cooper & Allen), 57
Quilt stories, 57–58, 136–152, 182
Quilt Story, The (Johnston & dePaola), 148, 149

Ramayana, 2
Read-alouds, 46–47
Reader's Theater, 75–76, 174 n. 13
Reading
    play in turning readers into writers, 76–78
    teaching with focus on answers, 42–44
    in 3 R's, 30–32, 171 n. 5, 171 n. 8
Reading an Object
    examples of, 140–141
    to launch inquiry, 141, 148
    in making sense of stories, 138–141
    rules for, 139–141
    in science, 128–129
    strategy of, 177 n. 2
Reading First program, 44
Reading in Motion, 71, 174 nn. 11–13
Realistic fiction, 86–87
Real Story of Stone Soup, The (Compestine), 99
Reggio Emilia approach, 124, 126, 129–130
Responsive Classroom program, 172 n. 7, 172
    n. 10
Rich texts
    evaluation in use of, 163–166
    exploring meaning of, 158–160
    perspectivism and, 160–162
'Rithmatic. *See* Arithmetic
'Riting. *See* Writing
Robert F. Sibert Medal, 84
Rocks in His Head (Hurst), 132
Rote answers, in 3R's, 30, 31

Rough-Faced Girl (Algonquin version of
  Cinderella), 53

Schemas, 46–47, 61, 86
Science
  constructing and representing
    understanding in, 126–127
  developing and supporting proficiency in,
    128–135
  evidence and explanations in, 131–134
  explanations of natural world in, 128–131
  Guided Inquiry and, 123–125
  inquiry across the curriculum and, 138,
    142, 149–151
  learning from patchwork quilts, 149–151
  nature and development of scientific
    knowledge, 132–134
  outside of school, 126
  pourquoi tales and, 120–135
  scientific method in, 20–21, 28, 131–132,
    142
  scientific practices and discourses, 134–135
  state standards for, 27–29, 125
  story in, 4–5, 20–38, 120–135
  teaching and learning in, 127–128
  Three Little Pigs and, 20–38, 131
Science Workshop (Saul et al.), 134
Self-efficacy, 24–25
Sensory play, 67, 70–71
Setting, 76
Shoes, Shoes, Shoes (Morris), 140
Show Way (Woodson), 144
SIP Principle, 63–66, 71–72, 74–76, 112–119,
  158–163
Snowflake Bentley (Martin), 132
Social-emotional learning, 66–68
Social studies
  inquiry across the curriculum and, 137–
    138, 142, 146–148, 149–151
  learning from patchwork quilts, 149–151
Sociodramatic/imaginative play, 67, 68
Somebody and the Three Blairs (Tolhurst), 175
  n. 8
Song of Roland, 2
Songs, 70, 177 n. 6
Sputnik, 49
Standardized tests, 25, 125
Standards, for science, 27–29, 125
Starry Messenger (Sis), 132
Stearns County Bookmobile, 1
Stith-Thompson Index, 2
Stone Soup, 11–14, 99
Stone Soup Network, 3–4, 13–14, 21, 33–34,
  120, 122, 123, 172 n. 12, 175 n. 5
Stone Soup Partnership, 27–28
Story Blanket, The (Wolff & Savitz), 148

StoryBus project, 5, 80, 159, 174 n. 1, 175 n. 5
Story cousins, 53
Story cycles, 2
Story dictation and dramatization, 69
Story of Johnny Appleseed, The (Aliki), 99
Storytelling
  mathematics and, 4–5, 104–109, 112–119
  meaning emerging from teaching and
    learning, 5–6
  in parallel processing, 17–18
  in quality intellectual work, 153–167
  reading an object and, 138–141
  science and, 4–5, 20–38, 120–135
  Stone Soup Network, 3–4, 13–14, 21, 33–
    34, 120, 122, 123, 172 n. 12, 175 n. 5
  story/text as catalyst in, 12–14
  transparency in, 2–3
Storytime (Sipe), 47–48
Strategic thinking, 64
Sundiata, 2

Taking Science to School (Duschl), 127–128
Tales of Tricksters (DeSpain), 162
Talking Eggs, The (Cajun version of *Cinderella*),
  53
Taxonomy of Educational Objectives (Bloom),
  49–50
Teacher action research, 3
Teaching for achievement/mastery, 6, 42, 44,
  156
Teaching for understanding/learning, 6, 42,
  44, 156
Teaching/learning dynamic
  in disciplined inquiry, 166–167
  errors in, 32–33
  ownership of learning, 23–24
  strategies in, 3–4
  texts as catalysts in, 13–14
Tea with Milk (Say), 141
Ten Black Dots (Crews), 77, 112
Ten Mile Day, The (Fraser), 119
Text structure
  informational, 84–85, 90–91, 94
  literary, 86–91, 94, 95–98
  reading for meaning and, 83–87
Text-to-graphics connections, 46–47
Text-to-self connections, 46, 54, 55, 62, 74
Text-to-text connections, 46
Text-to-world connections, 46, 53, 74
Think-alouds, 55
This Pebble in My Pocket (Hooper), 162
Those Shoes (Boelts), 117
3Rs, 30–32, 171 n. 5, 171 n. 8
Three Billy Goats Gruff, 76
Three Es, 32–33, 36, 132–134, 171 n. 8
Three Little Javelinas, The (Lowell), 20, 37

Three Little Pigs, 20–38, 78, 80, 86, 119, 131, 157, 179
Three Little Wolves and the Big Bad Pig, The (Trivizas), 76
Three Pigs, The (Wiesner), 37
Tikki Tikki Tembo (Mosel), 99, 103–119
Transparency, in storytelling, 2–3
Trickster tales, 176–177 n. 1
True Story of a Wolf, The (Scieszka), 175 n. 6
True Story of the Three Little Pigs, The (Scieszka), 20, 76
12 Ways to Get to 11 (Merriam), 77, 112
Two of Everything (Hong), 117, 119
Two Ways to Count to Ten (Dee), 117

Underground Railroad, 137–138, 144, 146–148, 151
Understanding, teaching for, 6, 42, 44, 156
Understanding by Design (UbD), 143
U.S. Department of Education, 44
University of Wisconsin, 171 n. 3
"Unlocked" closed questions, 41, 128

Visual representations, 129–130

Wait No Paint (Whatley), 37
When a Butterfly Sneezes (Sweeney), 131

Where the Wild Things Are (Sendak), 96
Whole language movement, 172 n. 4, 172 n. 6
Who Sank the Boat? (Allen), 131
Who's the Strongest? parable, 153–163, 166–167
Why the Sun and Moon Live in the Sky (Dayrell), 121
Wild Bears (Simon), 91
Wild Fibonacci (Hulme), 116
Word families, 157
Words About Pictures (Nodelman), 90
Word study
    constructive play in content area learning, 71
    sensory involvement in play and, 70–71
Word walls, 43, 124
WOW (Working on the Work) factor, 33–34
Writer's workshops, 134–135
Writing
    constructive play in content area learning, 71
    play in turning readers into writers, 76–78
    in 3Rs, 30–32, 171 n. 5, 171 n. 8
    writer's workshops in science, 134–135

Yeh-Shen (Chinese version of *Cinderella*), 39–42, 50, 53, 55
You Can't Say You Can't Play (Paley), 69

About the Author

For **Mary Hynes-Berry,** stories are like chicken soup—they are bound to make things better. She can't say enough about all she has gained from listening to and telling stories in the context of her family. In the same way, the three-plus decades she has spent doing oral storytelling in classrooms taught her so much about what a powerful tool stories can be to spark learning across the curriculum. Stories have proved an equally important tool for the work she does in professional development and with preservice teachers as a faculty member at Erikson Institute, a graduate school in child development.